ENTERTAINMENT LAW & PRACTICE

2007 Supplement

Jon M. Garon

Carolina Academic Press

ISBN: 978-1-59460-469-0

ISBN: 978-1-59460-469-0

Carolina Academic Press
700 Kent Street
Durham, NC 27701
Telephone (919) 489-7486
Fax (919) 493-5668
www.cap-press.com

ENTERTAINMENT LAW & PRACTICE

2007 SUPPLEMENT

TABLE OF CONTENTS

PREFACE

The changes to the legal regimes and business models that impact entertainment law continue to evolve at a tremendous pace. Most of the materials added in the 2005 supplement remain in this supplement as well, including the critical decision of *MGM Studios, Inc., v. Grokster*, which has substantially revised secondary liability doctrine for copyright.

This edition of the supplement adds a new Chapter 17, Visual Arts and Cultural Artifacts. As globalization has taken root in every area of practice, the traditions surrounding artifacts have undergone a revolution in the legal and business practices surrounding museums and their collections. Suddenly, the impact of moribund treaties is making headlines around the world.

Based on faculty requests, I have included a small portion of the material that I originally made available in the Teacher's Manual in this supplement, so that is available for all students. Other material from the Teacher's Manual may also be appropriate for such distribution, so I encourage the classroom reproduction of the Teacher's Manual materials whenever you feel they are appropriate.

All questions, comments, and inquiries should be directed to me, Jon M. Garon, Hamline University School of Law, 1536 Hewitt Avenue, St. Paul, Minnesota, 55104, telephone (651) 523-2968, telecopier (651) 523-2435, e-mail jgaron@hamline.edu.

CHAPTER I: THE NATURE OF ENTERTAINMENT LAW

A.   Overview

Please add the following to Notes and Questions at page 13:

f. In a new twist on the impact of cyberspace on First Amendment interests, the New Orleans municipal ordinance that licenses street artists in the French Quarter limited the licenses to "to manually paint, sketch or draw on plain surfaces only...." Artist Marc Trebert retouches digital photographs with pastels, in violation of the ordinance. With some incredulity, the court explains the New Orleans position. "The City argues that Trebert's digital photographs are not entitled to First Amendment protection because they are not "art." ... The question is not whether plaintiff's work is art, but whether it is "speech" within the protection of the First Amendment." Ignoring the "art" question, the court found the photographs to be speech and the ordinance as inconsistent with the First Amendment. *Trebert v. City of New Orleans*, No. 04-1349, 2005 U.S. Dist. LEXIS 1560 (E.D. La. 2005) (featured opinion in *infra* Chapter XVII).

B.   Transactions in Ideas

Please add the following to Notes and Questions at page 27:

d. Was the idea behind *American Idol* stolen? *Star Search* did not sue, and a short court opinion dismissed other claims. See *Keane v. Fox Television Stations, Inc.*, 2005 WL 627973 (5th Cir. 2005).

C.   Written Submission Agreements

Please add the following sample agreement after *FASA Corp. v. Playmates Toys, Inc.* at page 36:

Entertainment industries must greatly control the access to potential projects in order to avoid claims of access to copyrighted material. Unsolicited materials are returned unread. Only agents or lawyers are permitted to submit materials. Contracts explicitly waiving the right for compensation are sometimes required. These steps are necessary to protect the creators of copyrighted works from claims of copyright infringement, breach of contract, and theft of ideas.

Sample Nondisclosure Submission Agreement

The written submission agreement can take two forms. The first requires the submitting party to waive any rights to the ideas or contract. The submitting party must rely exclusively on copyright protections, as applicable. In the context of unsolicited material, this should be the expectation of both parties.

The second form may be used in the context of solicited material, through adoption of a nondisclosure agreement. Heavily utilized in some entertainment industries such as software and videogames, these are far less common in the film, television, and publishing industries. Nonetheless, the purposes and effectiveness are the same.

The following is a sample of such an agreement that adopts this approach:

NONDISCLOSURE AGREEMENT

This Agreement ("Agreement") is entered into as of the date written below, by and between _____ a(n) individual/corporation with offices located at _____ _____ ("Creator") and _____ a(n) individual/corporation with offices located at _____ _____ ("Recipient") with reference to the following facts:

Creator has developed specifications for a certain entertainment property ("Property") which Creator wishes to provide to Recipient for the purpose of developing a business relationship for the participation in the development or production of the Property.

Recipient has skills and experience relevant to the development of the Property and desires to engage in discussions which may lead to the participation in the creation or production of the Property.

In the course of discussions regarding the development of such Property information and specifications related to the Property shall be given to Recipient by Creator, and the parties wish to protect the proprietary nature of such information and recognize that no disclosure can be made without this Agreement.

NOW, THEREFORE, in consideration of the mutual covenants and agreements contained herein, Recipient and Creator agree as follows:

1.   Confidentiality. Recipient shall not directly or indirectly disclose, disseminate, publish, or use for its business advantage or for any other purpose, at any time during or after the term of this Agreement, any information received from Creator deemed confidential by the other party ("Confidential Information") without the express written permission of Creator for a period of five (5) years following the date of receipt of the Confidential Information.

    a.   Definitions. For purposes of this Agreement, Confidential Information shall be defined as any information not generally known in the industry about Creator's ideas, concepts, products, designs, intellectual property, trade secrets, services, or any combination thereof, whether or not such information would be recognized as proprietary absent this Agreement, including but not limited to information related to the Property developed by Creator.

    b.   Limitations. Notwithstanding any other provision of this Agreement, Recipient shall not be liable for disclosing, disseminating, publishing or using information which (i) was already known prior to the receipt of the Confidential Information; (ii) is now or becomes public information through no wrongful act of the Recipient; (iii) is independently developed or acquired by Recipient without any use of the Confidential Information in such development; or (iv) is required to be disclosed by law.

2.   Documents and Materials. The documents and materials of Creator (including but not limited to all scripts, scenarios, treatments, data, reports, projections, records, notes, lists, specifications and designs) are furnished in

accordance of this Agreement and shall remain the sole property of Creator. This information (collectively know as "Evaluation Material") shall upon the termination of this Agreement be promptly returned to Creator, including all copies thereof, which are in the possession or control of Recipient, its agents, and its representatives.

3.   Term and Renewal. The term of this Agreement shall be one (1) year commencing as of the date hereof; provided however, that Paragraph 1 of this Agreement shall survive termination of this Agreement and shall remain in full force and effect for a period of five (5) years.

4.   Miscellaneous.

a.   Further Documents. Each of the parties agrees to execute, acknowledge and deliver any and all further documents which may be required to carry into effect this Agreement and its respective obligations hereunder, all of which further documents shall be in accordance with and consistent with the terms of this Agreement

b.   Resolution of Disputes; Attorneys' Fees. The parties recognize that irreparable injury, as well as monetary damages may result from a material breach of this Agreement. In the event of a breach of this Agreement, the prevailing party may be entitled to injunctive relief in addition to any remedies available at law. Such prevailing party shall also be entitled to reasonable attorneys' fees and related expenses incurred as a result of such breach.

c.   Headings. Provision headings are solely for convenience and reference, and have no legal significance.

d.   Assignment. Neither party may assign this Agreement without the written consent of the other party.

e.   Notices. All notices, statements or other documents which either party shall desire to give to the other hereunder shall be in writing and shall be deemed given when delivered personally or by telecopier, or 48 hours after deposit in the U.S. mail, postage prepaid and addressed to the recipient party at the address set forth in the opening paragraph of this Agreement, or at such address as either party hereto may designate from time to time in accordance with this Paragraph.

f.   Amendments. This Agreement may be modified or amended only in a writing signed by both parties.

g.   Severability. If any provision of this Agreement shall be held to be invalid or unenforceable for any reason, the remaining provisions shall continue to be valid and enforceable. If a court finds that any provision of this Agreement is invalid or unenforceable, but that by limiting such provision it would become valid and enforceable, then such provision shall be deemed to be written, construed, and enforced as so limited.

h.   Entire Agreement. This Agreement contains the full and complete understanding between the parties hereto with reference to the within subject matter, supersedes all prior agreements and understandings, whether written or oral, pertaining thereto, and cannot be modified except by a written instrument signed by both of the parties hereto. Each of the parties acknowledges that no representation or promise not expressly contained in this Agreement has been made by the other or its agents or representatives.

        IN WITNESS WHEREOF, the undersigned have executed this Agreement the day and year written below.

Date: _____

        "Creator"

_____

By_____

Its_____

        "Recipient"

        (Company Name)

_____

By_____

Its_____

Please add the following to the Law Review Articles for Chapter I at page 38:

William O. Knox, *The Role of Novelty in a California Idea Submission Case*, 11 UCLA ENT. L. REV. 27 (2004)

Clay Calvert & Robert D. Richards, *Mediated Images of Violence and the First Amendment: From Video Games to the Evening News*, 57 ME. L. REV. 91 (2005).

Christine Haight Farley, *Judging Art*, 79 TUL. L. REV. 805 (2005).

David Nimmer, *The Moral Imperative Against Academic Plagiarism (Without a Moral Right Against Reverse Passing Off): 2003 Niro Scavonne Haller & Niro Distinguished Lecture*, 54 DEPAUL L. REV. 1 (2004).

CHAPTER II: INTERNATIONAL AND GLOBAL IMPLICATIONS OF ENTERTAINMENT LAW AND PRACTICE

B.   International Copyright

Please add the following section to International Copyright beginning at page 51:

"Making Available" or Communication Right[1]

[This overview of international copyright has been provided by the International Federation of the Phonographic Industry (IFPI).[2] The IFPI introductory materials on WIPO treaties, reproduction rights, technical measures, and rights management are reproduced in the Appendix.]

The WIPO Treaties: 'Making Available' Right (March 2003)

What Is The 'Making Available' Right?

The 'making available' right is an exclusive right for authors, performers and phonogram producers' to authorise or prohibit the dissemination of their works and other protected material through interactive networks such as the internet.

This exclusive right is one of the most important achievements of the WIPO Treaties and constitutes a basic requirement for the development of electronic commerce. The international community, in the 1996 Diplomatic Conference that adopted the treaties, unanimously acknowledged that record producers in particular needed this exclusive right to cover the use of their phonograms in the digital environment.

The reason was not only to fight piracy. The international community also recognised that the dissemination of phonograms in digital networks such as the internet constitutes a primary form of exploitation of music, and therefore should be subject to the control of the rights owner.

The making available right covers both the actual offering of the phonogram or other protected material and its subsequent transmission to members of the public. The exclusive right provides control over the act of 'making available' by all means of delivery—**by wire or wireless means**—and whenever **members of the public may access the work or phonogram from a place and at a time individually chosen by them**.

This broad formulation is capable of accommodating many different types of exploitation, from services allowing only the listening of music, to services allowing the download of permanent copies of music tracks, to exciting future uses of technology.

The key element is that the exclusive right covers all types of exploitation that allow the consumer to have a choice as to the time and the place to enjoy music. Therefore, not only 'music on demand' services but also all other services with a like effect (e.g. digital transmissions allowing for the identification and recording of specific music tracks) should be covered by this right.

---

[1] International Federation of the Photographic Industry, *The WIPO Treaties: 'Making Available' Right* (2003), http:// www.ifpi.org/content/library/wipo-treaties-making-available-right.pdf.

[2] Copyright International Federation of the Phonographic Industry (IFPI), London, www.ifpi.org. Reprinted with permission. Photographs, captions, and some inset text boxes have been removed.

The act of making available is subject to the control of the phonogram producer or other rights owner from the moment the work or phonogram is accessible to members of the public, regardless whether it has been accessed yet or not. It is the *accessibility* of the phonogram or work—the potential for it to be received or perceived by members of the public—that is the decisive factor. (WIPO Performances and Phonograms Treaty (WPPT), Articles 10, 14 and 16; WIPO Copyright Treaty (WCT), Article 8, 10 and Agreed Statement concerning Article 8.)

Executive Summary

The 'making available' right is one of the most important innovations of the WIPO Treaties. It is an 'exclusive right' that allows authors, phonogram producers, performers and other rights owners to fight piracy on the internet and offer new interactive uses of their works and recordings.

Implementing legislation should cover the initial act of putting a work or phonogram on an interactive network, as well as any subsequent transmissions. All services that have a degree of interactivity, target individual needs and/or have an impact on the primary market for a work or phonogram should be covered.

Why Is This Right Important?

This right is fundamental for the dissemination of music over digital networks and therefore for promoting the development of electronic commerce and of new business models by the recording industry. The development of such new business models is immensely attractive not only to copyright holders but also to consumers, who will be able to determine the content, timing and place of the transmissions they receive and therefore enjoy greater and easier access to music.

This right is also of the greatest importance, alongside the reproduction right, for phonogram producers to stop the unauthorised exploitation of their phonograms over the internet, for instance by pirates who upload and open to the public databases containing thousands of music tracks without the authorisation of the producer.

How Should This Be Implemented?

Existing or new exclusive right. The treaties leave open the possibility to implement this provision either on the basis of an existing exclusive right or through enactment of a new right. Different legal systems may justify different approaches. In principle, countries can include the 'making available' right within the sphere of the 'communication to the public' right—probably the preferred choice in most countries— or the distribution right.

Acts taking place by wire or wireless means. 'Making available' can happen either via physical networks such as a cable network or the internet, or via wireless means such as mobile phone networks or broadcasting signals. Implementing legislation therefore should make clear that this right applies notwithstanding the media or the transmission means by which music or other protected material is made available.

Broad definition of interactivity. The treaty defines the 'interactivity' criterion in a broad manner (*'from a place and at a time individually chosen'*). The right is thus designed to cover all forms of transmission that allow for a degree of interactivity. This should be measured by whether individual *members* of the public (not the public at large) can determine when and where they want to access a work or phonogram.

Not only should on-demand delivery of music over a network be covered, but also any service that allows the consumer a choice of content and of the moment of enjoyment of that content. This should include, for example, multichannel digital services (by online or wireless means) that play the same content several times a day and allow for the automatic identification and recording of all or part of the content. All new services that have a degree of interactivity, target individual needs and/or have an impact on the primary market should be covered.

Note that any implementation of this right must cover not only actual transmissions, but also the initial act of opening an interactive server to the public.

Protection of authors, phonogram producers and performers. The treaties require that authors (WCT Art. 8), phonogram producers (WPPT Art. 14) and performers whose performances are fixed in phonograms (WPPT Art. 10) benefit from the exclusive 'making available' right.

WIPO Treaty Text

WCT Art. 8. Without prejudice to the provisions of Articles 11(1) (ii), 11bis(1)(i) and (ii), 1ter(1) (ii), 14(1)(ii) and 14bis(1) of the Berne Convention, authors of literary and artistic works shall enjoy the exclusive right of authorising any communication to the public of their works, by wire or wireless means, including the making available to the public of their works in such a way that members of the public may access these works from a place and at a time individually chosen by them

WPPT Art. 10. Performers shall enjoy the exclusive right of authorising the making available to the public of their performances fixed in phonograms, by wire or wireless means, in such a way that members of the public may access them from a place and at a time individually chosen by them.

WPPT Art. 14. Producers of phonograms shall enjoy the exclusive right of authorising the making available to the public of their phonograms, by wire or wireless means, in such a way that members of the public may access them from a place and at a time individually chosen by them.

FREQUENTLY ASKED QUESTIONS (FAQS)

Are exceptions to the "making available" right allowed? In some cases. The new treaties allow limitations and exceptions to the 'making available' right that comply with the 'three- step-test' of Berne Article 9(2) (WCT Art. 10, WPPT Art. 16). These must be confined to certain special cases, must not conflict with a normal exploitation and must not prejudice the legitimate interest of the rights owner. Note that this approach is more rigorous than the Rome Convention, which vaguely allowed exceptions for 'private use'.

The three-part test highlights the need to take account of the economic effects of any exceptions. Many traditional exceptions are appropriate for the making-available right. For example, a library exception should not allow a library to 'make available' a phonogram to all 500 million internet users. A time-shifting exception would be inappropriate when works are made available interactively—the very nature of the exploitation is to allow the user to select the listening or viewing time.

Do the treaties require dealing with the issue of the liability of internet service providers?

No. Service-provider liability was not addressed in the treaties, and needs not be addressed in implementing legislation to comply with the treaties. The WCT contains an agreed statement to Art. 8: *'It is understood that the mere provision of physical facilities for enabling or making a communication does not in itself amount to a communication.'* This clarification is narrow and clear: merely providing wires and equipment does not itself amount to an act of communication. The treaty does not exclude, however, treating a *service* that transmits signals over any such 'physical facilities' as an act of communication to the public.

SAMPLE IMPLEMENTING LEGISLATION

IFPI Model Legislation: Authors, producers of phonograms and performers shall have the exclusive right to authorise or prohibit any communication to the public of their works, phonograms or performances fixed in phonograms, by wire or wireless means, including the making available to the public of their works, phonograms or performances fixed in phonograms in such a way that members of the public may access them from a place and at a time individually chosen by them.

EU Copyright Directive: Art. 3(2). Member States shall provide for the exclusive right to authorise or prohibit the making available to the public, by wire or wireless means, in such a way that members of the public may access them from a place and at a time individually chose by them:…(b) for phonogram producers, of their phonograms.

D.   Embargos and Domestic Trade Barriers

Please add the following to Notes and Questions at page 73:

f. In 1984, Alexey Pajitnov created *Tetris*, one of the world's most popular computer games. He transferred the rights to Computer Center of the Academy of Sciences of the U.S.S.R. since he was unable to exploit the rights himself. To what extent can the form Soviet computer scientist reclaim those rights? See *Blue Planet Software, Inc. v. Games Int'l, LLC*, 334 F. Supp. 2d 425 (S.D.N.Y. 2004).

g. Challenges to the legitimacy of § 104A of the Copyright Act continue, as companies find themselves barred from exploiting public domain works that have been reclaimed by foreign authors and owners. American publishers have challenged the constitutionality of the copyright restoration provisions. *Luck's Music Library, Inc. v. Gonzales*, 407 F.3d 1262 (D.C. Cir. 2005).

> Plaintiffs challenge the constitutionality of § 514 of the Uruguay Round Agreements Act ("URAA"), codified at 17 U.S.C. §§ 104A, 109, which implements Article 18 of the Berne Convention for the Protection of Literary and Artistic Works. … Section 514 of the URAA establishes copyrights of foreign holders whose works, though protected under the law where initially published, fell into the public domain in the United States for a variety of reasons — the U.S. failed to recognize copyrights of a particular nation, the copyright owner failed to comply with formalities of U.S. copyright law, or, in the case of sound recordings

"fixed" before February 15, 1972, federal copyright protection had been unavailable.

Id. at 1262-63.

The court rejected arguments that Congress lacked the power to pull these restored works from the public domain. Ironically, it used *Eldred v. Ashcroft*, 537 U.S. 186 (2003), to bolster the proposition that there needs to be a direct incentive or *quid pro quo* to the author.

> It is by no means clear that *Eldred* requires a direct incentive at all. The majority expressly relied on its understanding that adoption of the 20-year term extension enhanced the United States's position in negotiating with European Union countries for benefits for American authors. Here, similarly, the Senate argued in support of § 514 that its adoption helped secure better foreign protection for US intellectual property and was "a significant opportunity to reduce the impact of copyright piracy on our world trade position." S. Rep. No. 100-352, at 2 (1988).

Id. at 1264 (citation omitted).

E. Choice of Law

Please add the following to Notes and Questions at page 82:

d. The ownership of copyrights from the former Soviet Union and its state-owned entities continues to vex the licensees of those rights and the U.S. courts attempting to enforce the licensing agreements with those companies. In *Films by Jove, Inc. v. Berov*, 341 F. Supp. 2d 199 (E.D.N.Y. 2004), the U.S. licensee of 1500 animated films from the state-owned Soviet film studio Soyzmultfilm found itself fighting not just an infringement, but an attempt by the Russian Federation to negate the validity of the license. Through interpretations of governmental directives, the Russian Federation attempted to interpret the Russian Civil Code retroactively to include the intellectual property of the former Soyzmultfilm into a new state-owned company. The Eastern District of New York did not recognize this retroactive interpretation was an attempt to expropriate U.S. property and therefore against U.S. public policy.

e. Choice of law questions continue to challenge U.S. courts in both traditional copyright and in more modern Internet related cases. As an alternative view into the Casebook materials, the U.S. action related to the French ban on Yahoo!'s facilitation of the sale of Nazi paraphernalia provides a useful discussion of the First Amendment, comity, and the interplay between multiple courts.

Tensions between U.S. and foreign courts also highlight the differing national interests at stake involving the intersection of cyberspace on territorial law. See *Yahoo!, Inc. v. La Ligue Contre Le Racisme et L'Antisemitisme*, 169 F. Supp. 2d 1181 (N.D. Cal. 2001).

The French Court found that approximately 1,000 Nazi and Third Reich related objects, including Adolf Hitler's *Mein Kampf*, *The Protocol of the Elders of Zion* (an infamous anti-Semitic report produced by the Czarist secret police in the early 1900's), and purported "evidence" that the gas chambers of the Holocaust did not exist were being offered for sale on Yahoo.com's auction site. Because any French citizen is able to access these materials on Yahoo.com directly or through a link on Yahoo.fr, the French Court concluded that the Yahoo.com auction site violates

Section R645-1 of the French Criminal Code, which prohibits exhibition of Nazi propaganda and artifacts for sale. On May 20, 2000, the French Court entered an order requiring Yahoo! to (1) eliminate French citizens' access to any material on the Yahoo.com auction site that offers for sale any Nazi objects, relics, insignia, emblems, and flags; (2) eliminate French citizens' access to web pages on Yahoo.com displaying text, extracts, or quotations from *Mein Kampf* and *Protocol of the Elders of Zion*; (3) post a warning to French citizens on Yahoo.fr that any search through Yahoo.com may lead to sites containing material prohibited by Section R645-1 of the French Criminal Code, and that such viewing of the prohibited material may result in legal action against the Internet user; (4) remove from all browser directories accessible in the French Republic index headings entitled "negationists" and from all hypertext links the equation of "negationists" under the heading "Holocaust." The order subjects Yahoo! to a penalty of 100,000 Euros for each day that it fails to comply with the order. ...

[T]he purpose of the present action is to determine whether a United States court may enforce the French order without running afoul of the First Amendment. ...

Id. at 1184-85, 1191-92. The district court and subsequent Ninth Circuit opinions have each been reversed. In an en banc rehearing, the Ninth Circuit entered a judgment reversing and remanding the district court decision, with instructions to dismiss the action. *Yahoo! Inc. v. La Ligue Contre Le Racisme Et L'Antisemitisme*, 433 F.3d 1199 (9th Cir. 2006), *cert. denied*, __ U.S. __ 126 S. Ct. 2332 (2006).

Please add the following to Bibliography and Links at page 82:

William Gable, *Restoration of Copyrights: Dueling Trolls and Other Oddities Under Section 104A of the Copyright Act*, 29 COLUM. J.L. & ARTS 181 (2005)

Edward Lee, *The New Canon: Using or Misusing Foreign Law To Decide Domestic Intellectual Property Claims*, 46 HARV. INT'L L.J. 1 (2005).

Reto M. Hilty & Alexander Peukert, *"Equitable Remuneration" in Copyright Law: The Amended German Copyright Act as a Trap for the Entertainment Industry in the U.S.?*, 22 CARDOZO ARTS & ENT L.J. 401 (2004).

Jane C. Ginsburg, *The Concept of Authorship in Comparative Copyright Law*, 52 DEPAUL L. REV. 1063 (2003).

CHAPTER III: COPYRIGHT FOR ENTERTAINMENT LAW

B. Comparison between works – Ideas & Abstractions

Please add the following to Notes and Questions at page 109:

c. In *Metcalf v. Bochco*, 294 F.3d 1069 (9th Cir. 2002), the Ninth Circuit allowed the plaintiff's to avoid summary judgment by applying the sequence, order, and arrangement of *scenes a faire* and similarly unprotectable elements in an action where Jerome and Laurie Metcalf ("the Metcalfs") sued television producer Steven Bochco over the series, "City of Angels." Access was conceded because the Metcalfs had pitched the show three times to Bochco and other defendants. As a result, Judge Kozinski was reluctant to ignore the similarities:

> Bochco correctly argues that copyright law protects a writer's expression of ideas, but not the ideas themselves. General plot ideas are not protected by copyright law; they remain forever the common property of artistic mankind. Nor does copyright law protect "scenes a faire," or scenes that flow naturally from unprotectable basic plot premises. Instead, protectable expression includes the specific details of an author's rendering of ideas, or the actual concrete elements that make up the total sequence of events and the relationships between the major characters. Here, the similarities proffered by the Metcalfs are not protectable when considered individually; they are either too generic or constitute "scenes a faire." One cannot copyright the idea of an idealistic young professional choosing between financial and emotional reward, or of love triangles among young professionals that eventually become strained, or of political forces interfering with private action.
>
> However, the presence of so many generic similarities and the common patterns in which they arise do help the Metcalfs satisfy the extrinsic test. The particular sequence in which an author strings a significant number of unprotectable elements can itself be a protectable element. Each note in a scale, for example, is not protectable, but a pattern of notes in a tune may earn copyright protection. A common "pattern [that] is sufficiently concrete . . . warrants a finding of substantial similarity."

Id. at 1074 (citations omitted). Following *Metcalf v. Bochco*, the Ninth Circuit has continued to struggle with its own extrinsic text for copyright infringement. As it recently opined:

> We recognize the difficulties faced by the district court in this case. We have referred to "the turbid waters of the 'extrinsic test' for substantial similarity under the Copyright Act." The application of the extrinsic test, which assesses substantial similarity of ideas and expression, to musical compositions is a somewhat unnatural task, guided by relatively little precedent. ... The extrinsic test provides an awkward framework to apply to copyrighted works like music or art objects, which lack distinct elements of idea and expression. Nevertheless, the test is our law and we must apply it.

Swirsky v. Carey, 376 F.3d 841, 848 (9th Cir. 2004) (citations omitted).

Against this backdrop, the decision in *Murray Hill Publns, Inc. v. Twentieth Century Fox Film Corp.*, 361 F.3d 312 (6th Cir. 2003), providing for judgment as a matter of law, becomes more significant. Despite some surprise that a second person would claim authorship in the film *Jingle all the Way*, Fox was able to convince the appellate court that it was entitled to judgment as a matter of law denying any copyright infringement between its film and the screenplay entitled *Could This be Christmas*. Although Fox had the treatments to both films at the same time, the Jingle Treatment had been completed and submitted to Fox prior to its receiving the Christmas screenplay.

The Sixth Circuit reviewed the various abstraction-filtration-comparison schemes used by the Second, Ninth and D.C. Circuits to explain why even copyrightable elements may be filtered out for comparison between the works. The Court explained that "elements of a copyright defendant's work that were created prior to access to a plaintiff's work are to be filtered out at the first stage of substantial-similarity analysis," which eliminated all the common elements between *Jingle* and *Christmas*. *Id.* at 326.

The necessity of filtering out a defendant's own prior material appears self-evident. Access is irrelevant for portions of a plaintiff's work that could not have been drawn from the plaintiff. The interesting question is whether any such material had existed in *Metcalf v. Bochco*, or whether all the development had occurred by plaintiffs, rather than independently but at the same time as Bocho's own production activities. As a legal standard, the Sixth Circuit gloss that copyrightable elements of a defendant's work will be filtered out if it predates the plaintiff's work helps separate copying from common elements, and will likely seep into the jurisprudence of the other circuits.

D. Scope of Contractually Acquired Rights

Please add the following to Notes and Questions at page 131:

g. As the technology for publishing continues to change, the struggle to control reprints and print-on-demand continues. When publishing giant, Simon & Schuster attempted to sweep the board by retaining all rights in their published works regardless of level of prints sold, the Authors Guild stepped in to fight a public relations war so that authors could continue the practice of retaining their out-of-print or out-of-mind works. See Motoko Rich, *Publisher and Authors Parse a Term: Out of Print*, N.Y. TIMES, May 18, 2007 at C3.

h. In another interesting interpretative twist to publishing licenses, Northwestern University School of Law Professor Philip Postlewaite and his coauthor John Pennell sued for royalties they believed were due when publisher McGraw-Hill, Inc. sold the "Topical Line" imprint to Thomson Legal Publishing, Inc. What constitutes a sale of a work for purposes of royalties? See *Postlewaite v. McGraw-Hill, Inc.*, 411 F.3d 63 (2d Cir. 2005). Does the Second Circuit opinion make more sense than the district court opinion it chose not to follow?

Please add the following to Bibliography and Links at page 132:

David Nimmer, *Codifying Copyright Comprehensibly*, 51 UCLA L. REV. 1233 (2004).

William F. Patry & Richard A. Posner, *Fair Use and Statutory Reform in the Wake of Eldred*, 92 CAL. L. REV. 1639 (2004).

Gregory Duhl, *Old Lyrics, Knock-Offs Videos, and Copycat Comic Books: The Fourth Fair Use Factor in U.S. Copyright Law*, 54 SYRACUSE L. REV. 665 (2004).

CHAPTER IV: ETHICAL ISSUES

A.   Agent Regulation

Please insert following Waisbren v. Peppercorn Productions, Inc. at page 142:

Yoo v. Robi

126 Cal. App. 4th 1089, 24 Cal. Rptr. 3d 740 (Cal. Ct. App. 2005)

Howard Wolf brought this action to recover a commission allegedly due him under a personal management contract with Paul Robi, one of the original members of the legendary singing group The Platters. The trial court awarded judgment to Robi. Wolf and Robi both filed timely appeals. The principal issues in Wolf's appeal are whether Wolf violated the Talent Agencies Act (Cal. Lab. Code § 1700 *et seq.*) by procuring performance engagements for Robi without being licensed as a talent agency and, if so, whether such violation of the Act bars Wolf's recovery of a commission for procuring a recording engagement for Robi — an activity which the Act specifically exempts from the license requirement. …

We conclude substantial evidence supports the trial court's finding Wolf procured performance engagements for Robi in violation of the Act thus rendering his contracts with Robi void and barring his recovery of a commission for procuring a recording contract for Robi. We further conclude an appeal from a determination by the Labor Commissioner of a controversy arising under the Act may be filed either in a pending action between the parties to the controversy or in a separate, independent action.

In April 1986 Robi entered into a contract with Jango Records to record a Platters record album in exchange for consideration including royalties based on the number of albums sold. The Platters recorded the album in June and July of 1986 but Jango never released it.

At the time Robi and The Platters recorded the album for Jango, Robi also had a contract with Wolf under which Wolf was to perform certain services for Robi. This contract covered the period November 1985 to November 1986 and was one of a series of one-year contracts with identical terms spanning the period November 1983 to February 1988.

Under these contracts Wolf agreed to: "[A]dvise and counsel in the selection of literary and artistic material; advise and counsel in any and all matters pertaining to public relations; advise and counsel with relation to the adoption of proper formats for presentation of [Robi's] artistic talents [and] in the determination of proper style, mood, setting, business and characterization in keeping with [Robi's] talents; advise and counsel the selection of artistic talent to assist, accompany or embellish [Robi's] artistic presentation; and advise and counsel with regard to general practices in the entertainment industry and with respect to such matters of which [Wolf] may have knowledge concerning compensation and privileges extended for similar artistic values."

As compensation for his services Wolf was to receive "a sum equal to 10% of any and all gross monies or other considerations which [Robi] may receive as a result of [his] activities in and throughout the entertainment, amusement and publishing industries … ." Paragraph 8 of the contracts further provided Robi would pay Wolf "a similar sum following the expiration of the term [of the contract] upon and with respect to any and all engagements, contracts and agreements entered into or substantially negotiated during the term hereof relating to any of the foregoing ...."

In entering into the contracts with Wolf, Robi acknowledged: "You [i.e., Wolf] have specifically advised me [i.e., Robi] that you are not a 'talent agent' but active [*sic*] solely as a personal manager, and that you are not licensed as a 'talent agent' under the Labor Code of the State of California; you have at all times advised me that you are not licensed to seek or obtain employment or engagements for me and that you do not agree to do so, and you have made no representations to me, either oral or written, to the contrary."

Following Robi's death Martha Robi, his widow and successor in interest, licensed the manufacture of two record albums utilizing the recordings Robi and the Platters made for Jango Records.

Wolf filed this action alleging Paragraph 8 of his contract, quoted above, entitled him to a commission of 10 percent of the gross amount Robi earned from the sale of those albums. Robi filed a demurrer to the complaint which the trial court sustained and we overruled. Robi then answered the complaint raising numerous affirmative defenses. Robi's answer, however, did not include as an affirmative defense a claim Wolf's contract with Robi was void and invalid because Wolf acted under the contract to procure employment or engagements for Robi without a license to do so in violation of the Act.[3]

Although Robi did not raise the invalidity of the contract as an affirmative defense, while this action was pending in the superior court Robi did raise the invalidity issue in a Petition to Determine Controversy filed with the California Labor Commissioner pursuant to Labor Code, section 1700.44. ...

[T]he trial court found during each of the years 1983 through 1988 Wolf, acting without a talent agency license, procured and attempted to procure employment and engagements for Robi as an artist in violation of Labor Code, section 1700.5. Wolf contends these findings are not supported by substantial evidence. ...

Leaving aside Wolf's admission in his opening brief he "work[ed] through regional agents all over America to procure work for [Robi]," the record is replete with illustrations of Wolf's procurement activities on Robi's behalf.

Robi's widow, Martha, testified Robi had no contracts with talent agents in 1986 and that Wolf handled the negotiations for Robi's appearances. She recalled, for example, Wolf obtained an engagement for Robi at the Santa Clara County fair in August 1986. Donnie Brooks, a talent agent, n14 testified he represented Santa Clara in negotiating with Wolf over Robi's appearance at the fair. Brooks also testified he negotiated with Wolf to have Robi perform for one of Brooks' clients in Bristol Connecticut in April 1986. The evidence showed other occasions in 1986 in which Wolf procured or attempted to procure performance engagements for Robi. In addition, Wolf testified he sent out promotional packages "in order to solicit" engagements for Robi and

---

[3] Labor Code section 1700.4, subdivision (a) defines a talent agency as "a person or corporation who engages in the occupation of procuring, offering, promising, or attempting to procure employment or engagements for an artist ... ." Labor Code section 1700.5 states: "No person shall engage in or carry on the occupation of a talent agency without first procuring a license therefore from the Labor Commissioner." (All future statutory references are to the Labor Code unless otherwise noted.)

negotiated the details of potential performance contracts offered to him as Robi's agent by other talent agents.

The evidence also showed Wolf negotiated the Jango Records contract on behalf of Robi.

Wolf contends sending out promotional packages and negotiating performance contracts do not constitute "procuring" or "attempting to procure" employment within the meaning of Labor Code, section 1700.4, subdivision (a). If promoting an artist requires a talent agency license, Wolf argues, then public relations firms, publicists and advertising agencies all would have to be licensed as talent agencies. Wolf further maintains when personal managers negotiate performance contracts on behalf of their artist clients they are merely acting as spokespersons for the artists so the artists can concentrate on their artistry and not have to spend their time conversing with booking agents.

We need not decide in this case whether public relations firms, publicists and advertising agencies should be required to register as talent agencies because Wolf does not contend he is any of these. We note, however, a rational distinction can be drawn between promoting an artist to the public generally and "[t]he talent agent's primary function [of marketing] the artist's talent to buyers within the entertainment industry."… There is also a distinction between being the spokesperson for a client on a contract and being the negotiator for a client on a contract. The spokesperson merely passes on the client's desires or demands to the person who is contemplating engaging the client. …

California courts have uniformly held a contract under which an unlicensed party procures or attempts to procure employment for an artist in violation of the Act is void *ab initio* and the party procuring the employment is barred from recovering commissions for *any* activities under the contract. This rule applies even if, as in the present case, the contract does not call for the procuring of employment or contains an affirmative statement the party seeking compensation has not agreed to obtain employment for the artist. …

If negotiating the recording contract with Jango Records in 1986 was the only employment procurement Wolf engaged in on behalf of Robi this case would have to be decided differently because, as Wolf correctly points out, procuring recording contracts does not require a talent agency license. But the evidence shows Wolf engaged in numerous other employment procurement activities on behalf of Robi during the term of the 1986 contract. The fact procuring recording contracts without a license does not in itself violate public policy is not determinative. The same thing could be said about numerous other activities personal managers engage in which do not require a license such as counseling artists in the development of their professional careers, selecting material for their performances, managing their money, and the like. Engaging in those activities without a talent agency license does not violate public policy but those activities are nevertheless noncompensable if they are mixed in with activities which do require a license because of the overriding public policy of deterring unlicensed activities. …

Please add the following to Notes and Questions at page 155:

g. Not every claim filed against the lawyer results in liability or the barring of attorneys' fees. For a claim upholding the one-third contingency fee earned for successfully challenging the royalty residuals owed to members of Lynyrd Skynyrd, see *King v. Fox*, No. 97 Civ. 4134, 2004 U.S. Dist. LEXIS 462 (S.D.N.Y. Jan. 16, 2004).

h. How much can a lawyer do for a client before becoming a conspirator? For a recent unpublished case involving the firm of Lowy and Zucker and the firm's representations to SAG and DGA, see *Parmet v. Lapin*, 2004 Cal. App. Unpub. LEXIS 5217 (Cal. Ct. App. 2004).

i. Does the agent representing a film producer owe any fiduciary duty to the screenwriter submitting a script? See *A Slice of Pie Prods. v. Wayans Bros. Entm't*, 392 F. Supp. 2d 297 (D. Conn. 2005).

B.   Enforcement of Contracts for Minors

Please insert before New York Arts and Cultural Affairs Law § 35.03. at page 155:

Expansion of Coogan Laws

In the area of minors' contracts, the laws have improved since the first Coogan Law was passed in 1939. California updated its law in 2000 and New York adopted a Coogan Law for the first time in 2003. Jackie Coogan, who starred with Charlie Chaplin in *The Kid* at the age of four, never saw any of his childhood fortune because the adults who were supposed to be protecting him spent it.

> In California a law designed to protect the earnings of child actors, known as the Coogan Law was enacted in 1939. The law was named for child actor Jackie Coogan, who filed suit against his parents to recover the $4 million fortune he had made as a popular child actor. However the law was ineffective and the Screen Actors Guild lobbied to have it amended. California's new Coogan Law (SB 1162) became effective on January 1, 2000 and it ensures that every time young performers work under an entertainment contract, 15% of the gross earnings will be set aside for them until they reach legal majority. The bill also makes it clear that the earnings of a minor are the legal property of the minor and not his parents.

Alliance of Canadian Cinema, Television and Radio Artists, Frequently Asked Questions About the Minor's Trust, http://www.actra.ca/actra/control/mt_faq (last visited April 6, 2007).

In September 2003, New York joined California with new legislation for the protection of minors. As summarized in a press release from the Actors Equity Association, the law creates the second of the Coogan Laws:

> Similar to the California "Coogan Law," named after child star Jackie Coogan, the New York law requires that 15% of all child performers' earnings be set aside until the age of majority (18 years of age), protecting the earnings of the minor. On the education front, employers must provide a teacher, who is either New York State certified or has credentials recognized by the State, to any child performer who cannot attend school due to his or her employment (when a teacher is provided, the performers will not be marked absent from school while working). Parents will be responsible for getting work permits from the Department of Labor for their children, renewable after six months. Employers will apply to the Labor Department for certificates of eligibility to employ a child, which lasts three years. The law takes effect on March 28, 2004.

Actors Equity Association News, *Stars, Union Officials and Child Performers Celebrate Passage of NY State's New "Coogan" Law.*[4] Despite these improvements, only two states have such laws. (Florida has a much weaker provision.) In addition, there is not a pattern yet established to ensure that most child workers have their contracts treated appropriately under the new laws.

California Family Code § 6750.

(a) This chapter applies to the following contracts entered into between an unemancipated minor and any third party or parties on or after January 1, 2000:

(1) A contract pursuant to which a minor is employed or agrees to render artistic or creative services, either directly or through a third party, including, but not limited to, a personal services corporation (loan-out company), or through a casting agency. "Artistic or creative services" includes, but is not limited to, services as an actor, actress, dancer, musician, comedian, singer, stunt-person, voice-over artist, or other performer or entertainer, or as a songwriter, musical producer or arranger, writer, director, producer, production executive, choreographer, composer, conductor, or designer.

(2) A contract pursuant to which a minor agrees to purchase, or otherwise secure, sell, lease, license, or otherwise dispose of literary, musical, or dramatic properties, or use of a person's likeness, voice recording, performance, or story of or incidents in his or her life, either tangible or intangible, or any rights therein for use in motion pictures, television, the production of sound recordings in any format now known or hereafter devised, the legitimate or living stage, or otherwise in the entertainment field.

(3) A contract pursuant to which a minor is employed or agrees to render services as a participant or player in a sport.

(b) (1) If a minor is employed or agrees to render services directly for any person or entity, that person or entity shall be considered the minor's employer for purposes of this chapter.

(2) If a minor's services are being rendered through a third-party individual or personal services corporation (loan-out company), the person to whom or entity to which that third party is providing the minor's services shall be considered the minor's employer for purposes of this chapter.

(3) If a minor renders services as an extra, background performer, or in a similar capacity through an agency or service that provides one or more of those performers for a fee (casting agency), the agency or service shall be considered the minor's employer for the purposes of this chapter.

(c) (1) For purposes of this chapter, the minor's "gross earnings" shall mean the total compensation payable to the minor under the contract or, if the minor's services are being rendered through a third-party individual or personal services corporation (loan-out company), the total compensation payable to that third party for the services of the minor.

(2) Notwithstanding paragraph (1), with respect to contracts pursuant to which a minor is employed or agrees to render services as a musician, singer, songwriter, musical producer, or

---

[4] http://www.actorsequity.org/TheatreNews/coogans_11-20-2003.html (last visited April 6, 2007).

arranger only, for purposes of this chapter, the minor's "gross earnings" shall mean the total amount paid to the minor pursuant to the contract, including the payment of any advances to the minor pursuant to the contract, but excluding deductions to offset those advances or other expenses incurred by the employer pursuant to the contract, or, if the minor's services are being rendered through a third-party individual or personal services corporation (loan-out company), the total amount payable to that third party for the services of the minor.

Please replace the citation for Scott Eden Management v. Kavovit at page 156:

Scott Eden Mgt. v. Kavovit, 149 Misc. 2d 262, 563 N.Y.S.2d 1001 (1990), *aff'd* 197 A.D.2d 569 (1993).

Please add the following to Bibliography and Links at page 160:

Saira Din, *Review of Selected 2003 California Legislation: Family Chapter 667: Instituting Proper Trust Funds and Safeguarding the Earnings of Child Performers from Dissipation by Parents, Guardians and Trustees,* 35 McGeorge L. Rev. 473 (2004).

CHAPTER V: FIRST AMENDMENT ASPECTS OF THE ENTERTAINMENT INDUSTRY

A.   First Amendment Recognition of the Entertainment Industries

Please add the following to Notes and Questions at page 181:

g. The next medium impacted by expansion of First Amendment protection is video gaming. The following excerpt highlights the tension in the regulation of video game violence.

***Video Software Dealers Ass'n v. Maleng*, 325 F. Supp. 2d 1180 (W.D. Wash. 2004).**

Plaintiffs are companies and associations of persons that create, publish, distribute, sell, rent, and/or make available to the public computer and video games. Plaintiffs brought this action seeking to enjoin enforcement of Wash. Rev. Code 9.91.180 (... "the Act") on the ground that the Act violates the First Amendment by creating penalties for the distribution of computer and video games to minors based solely on their content and viewpoint. Similar disputes have erupted across the country as state and local governments have attempted to regulate the dissemination of violent video games to children. As of this date, no such regulation has passed constitutional muster. ...

The early generations of video games may have lacked the requisite expressive element, being little more than electronic board games or computerized races. The games at issue in this litigation, however, frequently involve intricate, if obnoxious, story lines, detailed artwork, original scores, and a complex narrative which evolves as the player makes choices and gains experience. All of the games provided to the Court for review are expressive and qualify as speech for purposes of the First Amendment. In fact, it is the nature and effect of the message being communicated by these video games which prompted the state to act in this sphere. As noted by the Eighth Circuit: "Whether we believe the advent of violent video games adds anything of value to society is irrelevant; guided by the First Amendment, we are obliged to recognize that 'they are as much entitled to the protection of free speech as the best of literature.'" *Interactive Digital Software Ass'n*, 329 F.3d at 958 (citing *Winters v. New York*, 333 U.S. 507 (1948)). The Court finds that the games at issue are expressive and qualify for the protections of the First Amendment.

Defendants argue that, even if the video games regulated under the Act are expressive, they fall into one of the few categories of speech that have been historically unprotected, in this case, obscenity. Defendants correctly point out that the phrase "obscene material" is not inherently limited to sexually-explicit materials. The Latin root "obscaenus" literally means "of filth" and has been defined to include that which is "disgusting to the senses" and "grossly repugnant to the generally accepted notions of what is appropriate." Graphic depictions of depraved acts of violence, such as the murder, decapitation, and robbery of women in Grand Theft Auto: Vice City, fall well within the more general definition of obscenity. Nevertheless, the Supreme Court has found that, when used in the context of the First Amendment, the word "obscenity" means material that deals with sex. Only "works which depict or describe sexual conduct" are considered obscene and therefore unprotected. State statutes designed to regulate obscene material must be drafted narrowly to cover only "works which, taken as a whole, appeal to the prurient interest in sex, which portray sexual conduct in a patently offensive way, and which, taken as a whole, do not have serious literary, artistic, political, or scientific value." ...

Finally, defendants argue that the state should be permitted to determine what speech or ideas are wholesome enough to disseminate to minors, even if the speech is protected under the First Amendment and does not satisfy the imminent lawlessness analysis of *Brandenburg v. Ohio*, 395 U.S. 444 (1969). Defendants rely heavily on *Ginsberg v. New York*, 390 U.S. 62 (1968), to support their theory that the state can regulate any speech that is "harmful to minors." Although the Supreme Court has used a "harmful to minors" analysis to broaden the definition of obscene material, the decision in Ginsberg is based on the fact that sexually-explicit material is not entitled to the protections of the First Amendment. The statute at issue in Ginsberg did not create an entirely new category of unprotected speech: rather, it adjusted the Roth definition of obscene material to capture that which is of sexual interest to minors.

Defendants have not identified, and the Court has not found, any case in which a category of otherwise protected expression is kept from children because it might do them harm. Defendants' cannot prohibit the dissemination of otherwise protected speech simply because the audience consists of minors. "Speech that is neither obscene as to youths nor subject to some other legitimate proscription cannot be suppressed solely to protect the young from ideals or images that a legislative body thinks unsuitable for them. In most circumstances, the values protected by the First Amendment are no less applicable when the government seeks to control the flow of information to minors."

Because the video and computer games at issue in this litigation are expressive speech that is entitled to the full protections of the First Amendment, strict scrutiny applies. It is undisputed that the Act seeks to regulate plaintiffs' speech based on its content (as opposed to the time, manner, and place in which it is published). Content-based regulations are presumptively invalid and are rarely permitted. Under this analysis, the Act will be upheld only if defendants can show that the regulation is necessary to serve a compelling state interest and that it is narrowly tailored to achieve that interest.

In enacting House Bill 1009, the Legislature noted two compelling interests: (1) "to curb hostile and antisocial behavior in Washington's youth" and (2) "to foster respect for public law enforcement officers." Apparently recognizing the constitutional problems associated with attempting to regulate speech because it is anti-government, defendants have merged these two purposes, arguing that "the Legislature was motivated to curb hostile and antisocial behavior of youths, including violence and aggression toward law enforcement officers." ...

The disease the Legislature apparently seeks to cure is the game-related increase in hostile and antisocial behavior in minors, particularly toward law enforcement officers. Defendants rely heavily on the Legislature's finding that "there has been an increase in studies showing a correlation between exposure to violent video and computer games and various forms of hostile and antisocial behavior." ...

Having reviewed all of the evidence provided by the parties in the light most favorable to defendants, the Court finds that defendants have presented research and expert opinions from which one could reasonably infer that the depictions of violence with which we are constantly bombarded in movies, television, computer games, interactive videos games, *etc.*, have some immediate and measurable effect on the level of aggression experienced by some viewers and that the unique characteristics of video games, such as their interactive qualities, the first-person identification aspect, and the repetitive nature of the action, makes video games potentially more harmful to the psychological well-being of minors than other forms of media. In addition, virtually all of the experts agree that prolonged exposure to violent entertainment media is one of the constellation of risk factors for aggressive or anti-social behavior (other factors include family problems, problems with peers at school and in the neighborhood, biological factors, *etc.*).

Nevertheless, the Court finds that the current state of the research cannot support the legislative determinations that underlie the Act because there has been no showing that exposure to video games that "trivialize violence against law enforcement officers" is likely to lead to actual violence against such officers. ...

In the absence of substantial evidence supporting the Legislature's prediction that the regulation of violent video games will curb hostile and anti-social behavior in youths, particularly toward law enforcement officers, it is virtually impossible to conclude that "the regulation will in fact alleviate [the identified] harms in a direct and material way." ...

As this litigation has progressed, defendants and their experts have asserted that "ultra-violent" video games cause aggression and must be regulated in order to further the state's compelling interests. The Act, however, does not simply regulate games "in which a high level of realistic violence is sustained" throughout play and is not limited to the most vile portrayals of violence. Rather, the Act regulates all "video or computer game[s] that contain[] realistic or photographic-like depictions of aggressive conflict in which the player kills, injures, or otherwise causes physical harm to a human form in the game who is depicted, by dress or other recognizable symbols, as a public law enforcement officer." This definition is expansive and does not attempt to regulate the dissemination of video games on the basis of the extremity of the violence portrayed — even the most loathsome acts are not covered as long as the victim is anyone other than a "public law enforcement officer." Where the victim is identified as a law enforcement officer, however, the distribution of games that contain even relatively common forms of violence, reflect laudable struggles against evil authority figures, depict unintentional harm, or have very limited violent content, is restricted. In short, the regulation of speech at issue here is not limited to the ultra-violent or the patently offensive and is far broader than what would be necessary to keep filth like Grand Theft Auto III and Postal II out of the hands of children. ...

h. The Illinois Violent Video Games Law and the Illinois Sexually Explicit Video Games Law were also found to violate the First Amendment. The laws protected minors from video game violence and sexually explicit materials. The Seventh Circuit found the laws vague and not narrowly tailored to meet the compelling state interest. *Entm't Software Ass'n v. Blagojevich*, 469 F.3d 641 (7th Cir. 2006). A similar law covering Minnesota's northern St. Louis County was similarly struck down in *Interactive Digital Software Ass'n v. St. Louis County*, 329 F.3d 954 (8th Cir. 2003), and a state law three years later, *Entm't Software Ass'n v. Hatch*, 443 F. Supp. 2d 1065, 1067 (D. Minn. 2006).

Additional states or municipalities have also failed to enact successful legislation. See *Am. Amusement Mach. Ass'n v. Kendrick*, 244 F.3d 572 (7th Cir. 2001) (Indianapolis, Indiana ordinance); *Video Software Dealers Ass'n v. Maleng*, 325 F. Supp. 2d 1180 (W.D. Wash. 2004) (Washington); *Video Software Dealers Ass'n v. Schwarzenegger*, 401 F. Supp. 2d 1034 (N.D. Cal. 2005) (California); *Entm't Software Ass'n v. Granholm*, 426 F. Supp. 2d 646 (E.D. Mich. 2006) (Michigan); *Entm't Software Ass'n v. Henry*, 2006 U.S. Dist. LEXIS 74186 (W.D. Okla. 2006) (Oklahoma); *Entm't Software Ass'n v. Foti*, 451 F. Supp. 2d 823 (M.D. La. 2006) (Louisiana).

i. Does the First Amendment protect the advertisements for motion pictures, even if the critic's quotes were falsified? For an interesting debate on the topic, see *Rezec v. Sony Pictures Entm't, Inc.*, 116 Cal. App. 4th 135, 10 Cal. Rptr. 3d 333 (2004).

C.   Limits on First Amendment Deference

Please add the following to Notes and Questions at page 206:

e. Because the advertising in mass transportation systems is in a designated public forum, the transportation authority has only limited discretion in which advertising to reject. Faced with challenges to a marijuana ad and a religious ad, which ad would be more likely to withstand the refusal to be displayed? See *Ridley v. Mass. Bay Transp. Auth.*, 390 F.3d 65 (1st Cir. 2004).

Please add the following to Bibliography and Links at page 207:

Clay Calvert & Robert D. Richards, *Violence and Video Games 2006: Legislation and Litigation*, 8 TEX. REV. ENT. & SPORTS L. 49 (2007).

Clay Calvert, *The First Amendment, the Media and the Culture Wars: Eight Important Lessons from 2004 About Speech, Censorship, Science and Public Policy*, 41 CAL. W. L. REV. 325 (2005).

David A. Anderson, *First Amendment Limitations on Tort Law*, 69 BROOK. L. REV. 755 (2004).

Patrick M. Garry, *Defining Speech in an Entertainment Age: The Case of First Amendment Protection for Video Games*, 57 SMU L. REV. 139 (2004).

CHAPTER VI: ATTENTION TO NON-LITERARY RIGHTS

A.   Defamation

Please add the following to Notes and Questions at page 227:

f. Defamation remains in the eye of the beholder. Described by the Ninth Circuit as a "compliment," famed daredevil Evel Knievel did not appreciate ESPN's form of attention. As the Court explained,

> Famed motorcycle stuntman Evel Knievel and his wife Krystal were photographed when they attended ESPN's Action Sports and Music Awards in 2001. The photograph depicted Evel, who was wearing a motorcycle jacket and rose-tinted sunglasses, with his right arm around Krystal and his left arm around another young woman. ESPN published the photograph on its "extreme sports" website with a caption that read "Evel Knievel proves that you're never too old to be a pimp."

Knievel v. ESPN, 393 F.3d 1068, 1070 (9th Cir. 2005). The Court reminded Knievel that an assessment of defamation must take the context of the website into account, and the remainder of the website used an "overwhelming presence of slang and non-literal language," along with such terms as ""hardcore" and "scoping," and slang phrases such as "throwing down a pose," "put a few back," and "hottie of the year....""" *Id.* at 1077.

g. One of the modern consequences of new media formats is additional republications. See *Nichols v. Moore*, 334 F. Supp. 2d 944 (E.D. Mich. 2004), for a discussion of traditional republication doctrine to new media.

h. What is based upon a true story? Given the facts and standards of the dispute between little league volunteer Robert Muzikowski and Paramount Pictures, the standard is evidently very low. In a bitterly contested defamation claim, the plaintiff objected to the conversion of the "nonfiction novel" *Hardball: A Season in the Projects* into the fictional movie *Hardball. Muzikowski v. Paramount Pictures Corp.*, 477 F.3d 899 (7th Cir. 2007). Having denied that Muzikowski is represented in any fashion in the fictionalization – to avoid the claims of defamation – Paramount claims the movie is based on the true story of the baseball team.

> Muzikowski claimed that Paramount's promotion of the *Hardball* movie as "inspired by a true story" was false because of the extent to which Muzikowski's life story was changed in the film. The district court concluded that these theories failed too, because Muzikowski had neither demonstrated that Paramount's advertisement was false nor that consumers who viewed the advertisements had been deceived.

> In order to establish a claim of false or deceptive advertising under § 43(a) of the Lanham Act, a plaintiff must show that the defendant made a material false statement of fact in a commercial advertisement and that the false statement deceived or had the tendency to deceive a substantial segment of its audience. The district court held, and we have previously assumed without deciding, that this analysis also applies to Illinois false advertising claims. Because Muzikowski does not argue to the contrary, we assume the same in this case.

In granting summary judgment to Paramount on the false advertising claims, the district court reasoned that Paramount's statement "inspired by a true story" is "literally true," observing that neither party disputes the veracity of the statement. Paramount insists that its advertisement represents the film as "the story of . . . the [Little League] team featured in Coyle's book." Muzikowski, on the other hand, contends that the advertisements "lead viewers to believe that the story is his." Since Muzikowski does not in any event contest the district court's conclusion that Paramount's advertising for *Hardball* did not contain a false statement of fact, we conclude that he has waived both this argument and his false advertising claims generally. *Id.* at 907-08.

Eighteen affidavits did little to convince the judge that a substantial portion of the viewers knew about Muzikowski or cared that it was based upon a true story, making enforcement of the "based on a true story" pronouncement much less likely. See *Id.*

i. To what extent can the use of images to illustrate a story be defamatory of those depicted in the photographs if they are not related to the story itself? See *Stanton v. Metro Corp.*, 438 F.3d 119 (1st Cir. 2006) (depicting teens at a high school party in an unrelated story about teenage promiscuity).

Please add the following to Bibliography and Links at page 241:

Sonia K. Katyal, *Privacy vs. Piracy*, 9 INT'L J. COMM. L. & POL'Y 7 (2004/2005).

Lawrence M. Friedman, *The One-Way Mirror: Law, Privacy, and the Media*, 82 WASH. U. L.Q. 319 (2004).

David Kohler, *Forty Years After New York Times v. Sullivan: The Good, the Bad, and the Ugly*, 83 OR. L. REV. 1203 (2004).

CHAPTER VII: TRADEMARKS & PUBLICITY

A.   Trademarks

Please add the following to Notes and Questions at page 250:

c. As courts continue to interpret *Dastar*, the implications are beginning to be explored. For a discussion of palming off, reverse palming off, and copyright preemption, see *Aagard v. Palomar Builders, Inc.*, 344 F. Supp. 2d 1211 (E.D. Cal. 2004) involving the theft of architectural plans. See also *A Slice of Pie Prods. v. Wayans Bros. Entm't*, 392 F. Supp. 2d 297, 323-14 (D. Conn. 2005) (unpublished screenplay); *Gen. Universal Sys., Inc. v. Lee*, 379 F.3d 131, 148-49 (5th Cir. 2004) (computer software).

d. The distinction between copyrighted works and public domain works was not made by the Supreme Court and therefore lower courts have not opted to make the distinction. Does a distinction remain regarding the corporate publisher of a work, rather than the author of the work? See *Hustlers, Inc. v. Thomasson*, 73 U.S.P.Q. 2d (BNA) 1923 (N.D. Ga. 2004).

e. How far does a trademark extend? Ishmael Butler and Maryann Vieira wrote the jazz/hip-hop song "Rebirth of Slick (Cool like Dat)." They performed in commercials for Target Stores using the song, for which they gave permission but they claim that the song title and lyrics were used in slogans and signage without permission in violation of the Lanham Act, a claim the court did not dismiss. *Butler v. Target Corp.*, 323 F. Supp. 2d 1052 (C.D. Cal. 2004).

B.   Publicity

Please add the following to Notes and Questions at page 262:

h. Drawing fine distinctions in publicity rights and the First Amendment continues to baffle courts and commentators. For example in *Doe v. TCI Cablevision*, 110 S.W.3d 363 (Mo. 2003), professional hockey player "enforcer" Tony Twist argued that his name had been co-opted by the Spawn comic for the character "Anthony 'Tony Twist' Twistelli," a mafia don and enforcer. Although the defamation claim was denied on First Amendment grounds, the right of publicity claim survived. On substantially the same facts, the Missouri Supreme Court rejected the California decision finding First Amendment protection for the comic book. The Missouri Supreme Court explained:

> Right to publicity cases, both before and after *Zacchini*, focus instead on the threshold legal question of whether the use of a person's name and identity is "expressive," in which case it is fully protected, or "commercial," in which case it is generally not protected. For instance, the use of a person's identity in news, entertainment, and creative works for the purpose of communicating information or expressive ideas about that person is protected "expressive" speech. On the other hand, the use of a person's identity for purely commercial purposes, like advertising goods or services or the use of a person's name or likeness on merchandise, is rarely protected.
>
> Several approaches have been offered to distinguish between expressive speech and commercial speech. The RESTATEMENT, for example, employs a "relatedness" test that protects the use of another person's name or identity in a work that is "related

to" that person. The catalogue of "related" uses includes "the use of a person's name or likeness in news reporting, whether in newspapers, magazines, or broadcast news . . . use in entertainment and other creative works, including both fiction and nonfiction . . . use as part of an article published in a fan magazine or in a feature story broadcast on an entertainment program . . . dissemination of an unauthorized print or broadcast biography, [and use] of another's identity in a novel, play, or motion picture . . . ." RESTATEMENT (THIRD) OF UNFAIR COMPETITION sec. 47 cmt. c at 549. The proviso to that list, however, is that "if the name or likeness is used solely to attract attention to a work that is *not related* to the identified person, the user may be subject to liability for a use of the other's identity in advertising. . . ." *Id.* (Emphasis added.)

California courts use a different approach, called the "transformative test," ... "'what is essentially a balancing test between the First Amendment and the right of publicity based on whether the work in question adds significant creative elements so as to be transformed into something more than a mere celebrity likeness or imitation.'"

The weakness of the RESTATEMENT's "relatedness" test and California's "transformative" test is that they give too little consideration to the fact that many uses of a person's name and identity have both expressive and commercial components. These tests operate to preclude a cause of action whenever the use of the name and identity is in any way expressive, regardless of its commercial exploitation. Under the relatedness test, use of a person's name and identity is actionable only when the use is solely commercial and is otherwise unrelated to that person. Under the transformative test, the transformation or fictionalized characterization of a person's celebrity status is not actionable even if its sole purpose is the commercial use of that person's name and identity. Though these tests purport to balance the prospective interests involved, there is no balancing at all - once the use is determined to be expressive, it is protected. At least one commentator, however, has advocated the use of a more balanced balancing test - a sort of predominant use test - that better addresses the cases where speech is both expressive and commercial:

> If a product is being sold that predominantly exploits the commercial value of an individual's identity, that product should be held to violate the right of publicity and not be protected by the First Amendment, even if there is some "expressive" content in it that might qualify as "speech" in other circumstances. If, on the other hand, the predominant purpose of the product is to make an expressive comment on or about a celebrity, the expressive values could be given greater weight.

Id. at 373-74, quoting Mark S. Lee, *Agents of Chaos: Judicial Confusion in Defining the Right of Publicity-Free Speech Interface*, 23 LOY. L.A. ENT. L. REV. 471, 488-98 (2003).

See also *Winters v. D.C. Comics*, 30 Cal. 4th 881, 69 P.3d 473 (2003). On remand in *Doe v. TCI Cablevision*, a St. Louis jury again found for Twist. In January 2005, the $15,000,000 verdict for Twist's publicity rights against Todd McFarlane Productions Inc. drew the Spawn publisher into bankruptcy protection.

C. Sound Alikes

Please add following *Waits v. Frito-Lay, Inc.* at page 270:

e. Modern courts continue to struggle with preemption of copyright and the extent to which the performers voice can be licensed by the sound recording company without first acquiring the performer's publicity rights in the performance. Should such claims to one's vocal performance be assigned to the sound recording company as a matter of copyright law? See *Laws v. Sony Music Entm't, Inc.*, 448 F.3d 1134 (9th Cir. 2006) *cert. denied*, __ U.S. __, 127 S. Ct. 1371 (2007).

D. Tension between Publicity and Free Speech

Please add following *Comedy III Prods., Inc. v. Gary Saderup, Inc.* at page 277:

Kirby v. Sega of America, Inc.

144 Cal. App. 4th 47, 50 Cal. Rptr. 3d 607 (2006)

A celebrity sued distributors of a video game alleging that, in creating a character in the video game, the distributors misappropriated her likeness and identity in violation of state and federal law. The distributors moved for summary judgment asserting the First Amendment provided a complete defense to each of the celebrity plaintiff's claims. The trial court agreed, granted the motions, and subsequently awarded the distributors mandatory attorney's fees, as prevailing parties under Civil Code section 3344, subdivision (a). We affirm the judgment and remand for a determination regarding the amount of attorney's fees.

From 1986 to approximately 1995, appellant Kierin Kirby, professionally known as Lady Miss Kier (hereafter, Kirby) was the lead singer of a retro-funk-dance musical group known as Deee-Lite which was popular in the early 1990's. Deee-Lite made five albums which were distributed and sold throughout the world. The band was best known for its song Groove is in the Heart from its first album released in 1990. The song's music video, which received extensive airplay on MTV, features band members clad in funky retro outfits, vivid graphics, groovy dance moves, a futuristic setting and an overall party feel.

In addition to being a musician, Kirby is a dancer, artist, choreographer and fashion designer. Kirby insists that, as Lady Kier, she developed a specific, distinctive ... look, of a fashionable, provocative, and funky diva-like artistic character. Kirby claims her unique public identity, which combines retro and futuristic visual and musical styles, results from her signature costumes and lyrical expression. Kirby's costumes included platform shoes, kneesocks, brightly colored formfitting clothes and unitards, short pleated or cheerleader-type skirts, bare midriffs, cropped tops with words or a numeral written on the chest, space or other helmets, a blue backpack, and red/pink hair worn in a page-boy flip held back by a headband, pigtails and other styles. Kirby alleges her signature lyrical expression, with which she introduces herself in the opening of the music video for Groove is in the Heart, and which is included in three of her songs, is ooh la la. Kirby claims substantial, commercially valuable goodwill in her sound, appearance, persona and likeness.

Respondents are distributors of a video game called Space Channel 5 (SC5, or the game). SC5 was created from 1997-1999 by Takashi Yuda, an employee of Sega Japan, and was released in Japan in December 1999. Yuda originally conceived the main character as a male, but changed the character to a female in order to develop a video game to appeal to girls. Yuda testified the name Ulala was a derivative of a Japanese name Urara, modified to make it easier for English-speakers to pronounce. Yuda claims he developed the Ulala character based on the anime style of Japanese cartoon characters, and denied using Kirby as a reference. Ulala has six main dance moves (up, down, right, left, forward and backward). The character's dance moves were created by Nahoko Nezu, a Japanese choreographer and dancer. Nezu's dance moves were hers alone. At the time she created the moves, Nezu did not know Kirby, and had not ever heard of her. Nezu created and performed dance moves for Ulala at Yuda's direction. He videotaped the moves and used the tapes to create Ulala's dance moves in the game. The musical theme song for SC5 is Mexican Flyer. That song, written in the 1960's, is performed by composer Ken Woodman. The music is not based on, or used in reference to, any music by Deee-Lite or Kirby.

The game, set in outer space in the 25th century, features the computer-generated image of a young, fictional, elongated and extremely thin female reporter named Ulala who works for a news channel called Space Channel 5. In the game, Ulala wears a few different costumes, but is primarily seen in an almost entirely orange outfit which includes a midriff-exposing top bearing the numeral 5, a miniskirt, elbow-length gloves, and stiletto-heeled, knee-high platform boots. Her hot pink hair is always worn in short pigtails placed high on the back of her head, and she wears a blue headset and jet pack and a blue gun holster strapped to her right thigh.

In July 2000, Kirby was contacted by PD*3 Tully Co. (PD3), a firm retained by a subsidiary of Sega Japan, in connection with its effort to launch a version of SC5 in England. PD3 was considering using one of several music videos or songs, including Groove is in the Heart, to promote the game. PD3 contacted Kirby to determine if she was interested in promoting SC5 in England and, possibly, Europe. Kirby was not.

Kirby initiated this action in April 2003. The operative second amended complaint alleges causes of action for: (1) common law infringement of the right of publicity; (2) misappropriation of likeness (Civ. Code, § 3344); (3) violation of the Lanham Act (15 U.S.C. § 1125(a)); [and overlapping state law claims]. Kirby alleged respondents wrongfully used her name, likeness and identity in developing and marketing the game and, specifically, its Ulala character. Sega, Agetec and THQ each moved for summary judgment asserting Kirby could not establish all elements of her claims and, even if she could, the First Amendment provided a complete defense to the entire action. The motions were granted after the trial court found all claims constitutionally foreclosed.

The state statutory and common law claims of appropriation.

Kirby alleges both a common law and statutory appropriation claim, a claim for violation of the Lanham Act, and several claims related to unfair competition. Her claims are predicated on the same underlying misconduct, i.e., respondents' alleged misappropriation and exploitation of Kirby's likeness or identity as depicted by the game's Ulala character.

In the context of a celebrity, the invasion of privacy tort for appropriation turns on a right of publicity arising from commercially exploitable opportunities embodied in the plaintiff's likeness. The cause of action may be both common law and statutory. The elements of a common law action are the unauthorized use of the plaintiff's identity to the defendant's advantage by appropriating the plaintiff's name, voice, likeness, etc., commercially or otherwise, and resulting injury.

The statutory claim provides: Any person who knowingly uses another's name, voice, signature, photograph, or likeness, in any manner, on or in products, merchandise, or goods, or for purposes of advertising or selling, or soliciting purchases of, products, merchandise, goods or services, without such person's prior consent, ... shall be liable for any damages sustained by the person or persons injured as a result thereof. (Civ. Code, § 3344, subd. (a) (§ 3344, subd. (a)).) The legislative prohibition against the unauthorized appropriation of one's likeness was intended to complement, not supplant, common law claims for right of publicity. The common law and statutory claims are similar but not identical, but both are involved here. A statutory cause of action for appropriation not only encompasses the common law elements, it requires a knowing use of the plaintiff's name, likeness, etc. The privacy invasion is actionable under either the statute or common law regardless of whether the purpose is commercial.

The misappropriation of one's likeness refers to a person's visual image. Ulala resembles Kirby in certain respects. Certain of Ulala's characteristics and computer-generated features resemble Kirby's. Both images are thin, and have similarly shaped eyes and faces, red lips and red or pink hair. Both wear brightly-colored, formfitting clothing, including short skirts and platform shoes in a 1960's retro style. In addition, Ulala's name is a phonetic variant of ooh la la, a phrase often used by Kirby and associated with Kirby. Finally, as the trial court pointed out, both Kirby and Ulala used the phrases groove, meow, dee-lish, and I won't give up. These similarities support Kirby's contention her identity was misappropriated.

However, Ulala and Kirby also differ in significant respects. Although Ulala dons assorted costumes in the game, she is seen most often with her hair in short, high pigtails, wearing an orange cropped top bearing the numeral 5 and orange miniskirt, orange gloves and boots with stiletto heels, a blue ray-gun holster strapped to her thigh, and a blue headset and jet pack. Kirby asserts she often wears short skirts, crop tops with numbers, elbow-length gloves, pigtails and space helmets. Kirby, as the record reflects, is found more frequently in formfitting body suits, with her hair shaped into a pageboy flip, held back with a headband. And, unlike Ulala, when Kirby wears her hair in pigtails, the pigtails not only are longer than Ulala's, but Kirby has tendrils of hair draping over her forehead which she holds back with clips. Kirby concedes she has no singular identity, her appearance and visual style are continually moving, and she is not the type of artist that wants to do the same thing every time. This lack of stasis is inconsistent with a claim of appropriation.

Notwithstanding the differences between Kirby and Ulala, we agree with the trial court that a material factual issue exists as to whether respondents misappropriated Kirby's likeness. Ulala's facial features, her clothing, hair color and style, and use of certain catch phrases are sufficiently reminiscent enough of Kirby's features and personal style to suggest imitation. In addition, although no evidence indicates Kirby's likeness was actually used to create Ulala, Kirby was specifically asked by a Sega affiliate in 2003 to endorse SC5. This solicitation suggests Sega knew of Kirby and believed her celebrity association would benefit the release of the European version of the game ... [and] to give rise to a triable factual issue on the common law claim as well.

The Lanham Act. The Lanham Act is the federal equivalent of a right of publicity claim. It protects against use of a celebrity's image or persona in connection with a product in a manner likely to falsely imply a celebrity product endorsement. Critical to a Lanham Act claim is the likelihood reasonable consumers will be confused about the celebrity's endorsement. For reasons discussed above, we agree with the trial court's finding that "[t]he same issues of fact concerning likeness and identity which support [Kirby's] appropriation claims also support her Lanham Act claim. There is a question of fact that [Kirby's] identity, though constantly evolving, has been appropriated for SC5."

The First Amendment affords a complete defense to Kirby's claims.

Respondents contend here, as they did below, that their right of free expression under the First Amendment of the United States Constitution and the even greater speech protections afforded by the California Constitution, article I, section 2, provide a complete defense to Kirby's claims. The trial court agreed, as do we. The freedom of expression protected by the First Amendment exists to preserve an uninhibited marketplace of ideas and to further individual rights of self-expression. The protections may extend to all forms of expression, including written and spoken words (fact or fiction), music, films, paintings, and entertainment, whether or not sold for a profit.

As this case illustrates, a tension frequently exists between the First Amendment's goal of fostering a marketplace of ideas and respect for individual expression, and a celebrity's right of publicity. In *Comedy III* and again in *Winter*, the Supreme Court addressed the balance between a celebrity's right to control the commercial exploitation of his or her likeness or identity and the First Amendment right of free expression. In *Comedy III*, the court held a defendant may raise the First Amendment as an affirmative defense to an allegation of appropriation if the defendant's work "adds something new, with a further purpose or different character, altering the first with new expression, meaning, or message . ...." In other words, the new work must contain significant transformative elements. The transformative test protects the right of publicity. It continues to shield celebrities from literal depictions or imitations for commercial gain by works which do not add significant new expression. Moreover, a work which has been transformed is less likely to interfere with the economic interests protected by the right of publicity, because a distorted image of a celebrity is a poor substitute for more conventional forms of celebrity depictions, and thus less likely to threaten the market for celebrity memorabilia.

The transformative test is straightforward: The inquiry is whether the celebrity likeness is one of the "raw materials" from which an original work is synthesized, or whether the depiction or imitation of the celebrity is the very sum and substance of the work in question. If the product containing celebrity's likeness is so transformed that it has become primarily the defendant's own expression of what he or she is trying to create or portray, rather than the celebrity's likeness, it is protected. (Applying this test in *Comedy III*, which involved drawings depicting The Three Stooges, and T-shirts made from those drawings, the court concluded the drawings and T-shirts were not entitled to First Amendment protection. The artist who created them, while highly skilled, contributed nothing other than a trivial variation that transformed the drawings from literal likenesses of the three actors.

The Supreme Court applied the transformative test again two years later in *Winter*. In that case, the defendant published a series of comics featuring two half-worm, half-human characters based on singers Edgar and Johnny *Winter*. Both characters had long white hair and albino features similar to the *Winter* brothers, while one wore a hat similar to one often worn by Johnny *Winter*.

The *Winter* brothers sued for statutory appropriation and lost. Applying the transformative test, the court found the comic depictions contained significant expressive content beyond the *Winters*' mere likenesses. The *Winters* were merely part of the raw material from which the comics' plot and characters were fashioned. In addition, the characters were distorted pictures of the *Winters* for the purpose of lampoon, parody or caricature. In short, and in stark contrast to the near literal depictions of the Three Stooges in *Comedy III*, the comic book characters depicted were fanciful, creative characters, not pictures of the *Winter* brothers.

Applying the comparison required by *Comedy III* and *Winter* to the evidence in the record, we agree with the trial court that, notwithstanding certain similarities, Ulala is more than a mere likeness or literal depiction of Kirby. Ulala contains sufficient expressive content to constitute a transformative work under the test articulated by the Supreme Court. First, Ulala is not a literal depiction of Kirby. As discussed above, the two share similarities. However, they also differ quite a bit: Ulala's extremely tall, slender computer-generated physique is dissimilar from Kirby's. Evidence also indicated Ulala was based, at least in part, on the Japanese style of anime. Ulala's typical hairstyle and primary costume differ from those worn by Kirby who varied her costumes and outfits, and wore her hair in several styles. Moreover, the setting for the game that features Ulala—as a space-age reporter in the 25th century—is unlike any public depiction of Kirby. Finally, we agree with the trial court that the dance moves performed by Ulala—typically short, quick movements of the arms, legs and head—are unlike Kirby's movements in any of her music videos. Taken together, these differences demonstrate Ulala is transformative, and respondents added creative elements to create a new expression.

Conceding the game adds new expression, Kirby nevertheless contends respondents violated her right of privacy because, unlike the comics in *Winter* which were intended to poke fun, the game lacks any element of caricature, lampoon, or parody. Notwithstanding the added expression, Kirby insists Ulala is no more than a look-alike, an imitation or emulation or rip-off of Lady Kier's entire persona, co-opted by respondents with the commercial objective to us[e] Lady Kier's likeness and identity and to capitalize in the game and its affiliated products on the commercial value attached to her persona. Kirby insists Ulala is nothing other than a mere emulation of Lady Kier with minor digital enhancements and manipulations. It is not entitled to First Amendment protection because the character fails to say [anything]—whether factual or critical or comedic—about a public figure. Neither contention has merit.

First, for the reasons discussed above, we reject the claim that Ulala merely emulates Kirby. Sufficient similarities preclude a conclusion that, as a matter of law, Ulala was not based in part on Kirby. However, we are similarly unable to conclude, as a matter of law, that Ulala is nothing other than an imitative character contrived of minor digital enhancements and manipulations. Respondents have added new expression, and the differences are not trivial. Ulala is not a mere imitation of Kirby.

Second, and more importantly, the transformative test specifically does not require the elements Kirby seeks to impose. The law does not require Ulala to say something—whether factual or critical or comedic about Kirby the public figure in order to receive First Amendment protection. This argument has been soundly rejected by the Supreme Court. In *Winter*, the court made clear the pivotal issue is whether the work is transformative, not the form of literary expression: It does not matter what precise literary category the work falls into. What matters is whether the work is transformative, not whether it is parody or satire or caricature or serious social commentary or any other specific form of expression. Whether the Ulala character conveys any expressive meaning is irrelevant to a First Amendment defense. All that is necessary is that respondents' work add "something new, with a further purpose or different character, altering the first with new expression, meaning, or message . ..." A work is transformative if it adds new expression. That expression alone is sufficient; it need not convey any meaning or message. The Ulala character satisfies this test.

The test simply requires the court to examine and compare the allegedly expressive work with the images of the plaintiff to discern if the defendant's work contributes significantly distinctive and expressive content; i.e., is transformative. If distinctions exist, the First Amendment bars claims based on appropriation of the plaintiff's identity or likeness; if not, the claims are not barred. As aptly summed up by the trial court, any imitation of [Kirby's] likeness or identity in Ulala is not the sum and substance of that character. Rather, the imitation is part of the raw material from which the Ulala character, and SC[5], were synthesized. As in *Winter*, Ulala is a "fanciful, creative character" who exists in the context of a unique and expressive video game. Similar facts distinguished *Winter* from *Comedy III*, and the same distinction applies here. [Respondents'] portrayal of Ulala is protected by the First Amendment.

Because Kirby's claims are subject to a First Amendment defense, and the video game is protected speech, Kirby's state common law and statutory claims fail. Kirby's Lanham Act claim is also barred. Ulala is not a literal depiction of Kirby. We agree with the trial court that any public confusion that Kirby endorses SC5, based on similarities between her and Ulala, would arise from a false assumption that the game could not contain a character resembling Kirby without her imprimatur. However, unlike the Three Stooges, Ulala is not a literal depiction of Kirby. Thus, given the many dissimilarities between the Ulala character and Kirby, any public confusion arising from a mistaken assumption is easily outweighed by the public interest in free artistic expression, so as to preclude application of the Lanham Act.

Respondents are entitled to attorney's fees.

Section 3344, subdivision (a) clearly states that [t]he prevailing party in any action under this section shall ... be entitled to attorney's fees and costs. Under this provision, respondents sought approximately $ 763,000 in attorney's fees and costs, and ultimately received an award of approximately $ 608,000. The mandatory fee provision of section 3344, subdivision (a) leaves no room for ambiguity. Whether the course is sound is not for us to say. The fee award was proper.

Respondents are awarded costs on appeal.

Please add following *Parks v. Laface Records* at page 285:

Tyne v. Time Warner Entm't Co. L.P.

901 So. 2d 802 (Fla. 2005)

We have for review a question of Florida law certified by the United States Eleventh Circuit Court of Appeals that is determinative of a cause pending in that court and for which there appears to be no controlling precedent. We have jurisdiction. See art. V, § 3(b)(6), Fla. Const.

The pertinent facts of this case, as set forth by the Eleventh Circuit, are as follows:

In October, 1991, a rare confluence of meteorological events led to a "massively powerful" weather system off the New England coast. The fishing vessel known as the Andrea Gail was caught in this storm and lost at sea. All six of the crewmembers on board the *Andrea Gail,* including Billy Tyne and Dale Murphy, Sr., were presumed to have been killed. Newspaper and television reports extensively chronicled the storm and its impact. Based on these reports, and personal interviews with meteorologists, local fisherman, and family members, Sebastian Junger penned a book, entitled *The Perfect Storm: A True Story of Men Against the Sea,* recounting the storm and the last voyage of the *Andrea Gail* and its crew. The book was published in 1997.

That same year, Warner Bros. purchased from Junger and his publisher the rights to produce a motion picture based on the book. Warner Bros. released the film, entitled *The Perfect Storm,* for public consumption in 2000. The Picture depicted the lives and deaths of Billy Tyne and Dale Murphy, Sr., who were the main characters in the film. It also included brief portrayals of each individual that is a party to this appeal. Nonetheless, Warner Bros. neither sought permission from the individuals depicted in the picture nor compensated them in any manner.

Unlike the book, the Picture presented a concededly dramatized account of both the storm and the crew of the *Andrea Gail.* For example, the main protagonist in the Picture, Billy Tyne, was portrayed as a down-and-out swordboat captain who was obsessed with the next big catch. In one scene, the Picture relates an admittedly fabricated depiction of Tyne berating his crew for wanting to return to port in Gloucester, Massachusetts. Warner Bros. took additional liberties with the land-based interpersonal relationships between the crewmembers and their families.

While the Picture did not hold itself out as factually accurate, it did indicate at the beginning of the film that "THIS FILM IS BASED ON A TRUE STORY." A disclaimer inserted during the closing credits elaborated on this point with the following statement: "This film is based on actual historical events contained in 'The Perfect Storm' by Sebastian Junger. Dialogue and certain events and characters in the film were created for the purpose of fictionalization."

On August 24, 2000, the Tyne and Murphy children, along with Tigue and Kosko, filed suit against Warner Bros. [in the United States District Court for the Middle District of Florida] seeking recompense under Florida's commercial misappropriation law [section 540.08, Florida Statutes (2000)] and for common law false light invasion of privacy.

Tyne v. Time Warner Entertainment Co., L.P., 336 F.3d 1286, 1288-89 (11th Cir. 2003).

[W]e rephrase the certified question to the specific issue that we conclude is presented by this case.

DOES THE PHRASE "FOR PURPOSES OF TRADE OR FOR ANY COMMERCIAL OR ADVERTISING PURPOSE" IN SECTION 540.08(1), FLORIDA STATUTES, INCLUDE PUBLICATIONS WHICH DO NOT DIRECTLY PROMOTE A PRODUCT OR SERVICE?

The question before this Court is a narrow one. As noted by the federal courts, the Fourth District Court of Appeal considered the applicability of section 540.08, Florida Statutes,[5] to a publication which did not directly promote a product or service, but this Court has not directly addressed this question.

---

[5] [*540.08. Unauthorized publication of name or likeness.*

(1) No person shall publish, print, display or otherwise publicly use for purposes of trade or for any commercial or advertising purpose the name, portrait, photograph, or other likeness of any natural person without the express written or oral consent to such use given by:

(a) Such person; or

(b) Any other person, firm or corporation authorized in writing by such person to license the commercial use of her or his name or likeness; or

(c) If such person is deceased, any person, firm or corporation authorized in writing to license the commercial use of her or his name or likeness, or if no person, firm or corporation is so authorized, then by any one from among a class composed of her or his surviving spouse and surviving children.

(2) In the event the consent required in subsection (1) is not obtained, the person whose name, portrait, photograph, or other likeness is so used, or any person, firm, or corporation authorized by such person in writing to license the commercial use of her or his name or likeness, or, if the person whose likeness is used is deceased, any person, firm, or corporation having the right to give such consent, as provided hereinabove, may bring an action to enjoin such unauthorized publication, printing, display or other public use, and to recover damages for any loss or injury sustained by reason thereof, including an amount which would have been a reasonable royalty, and punitive or exemplary damages.

(3) The provisions of this section shall not apply to:

(a) The publication, printing, display, or use of the name or likeness of any person in any newspaper, magazine, book, news broadcast or telecast, or other news medium or publication as part of any bona fide news report or presentation having a current and legitimate public interest and where such name or likeness is not used for advertising purposes;

(b) The use of such name, portrait, photograph, or other likeness in connection with the resale or other distribution of literary, musical, or artistic productions or other articles of merchandise or property where such person has consented to the use of her or his name, portrait, photograph, or likeness on or in connection with the initial sale or distribution thereof; or

(c) Any photograph of a person solely as a member of the public and where such person is not named or otherwise identified in or in connection with the use of such photograph.

(4) No action shall be brought under this section by reason of any publication, printing, display, or other public use of the name or likeness of a person occurring after the expiration of 40 years from and after the death of such person.

(5) As used in this section, a person's "surviving spouse" is the person's surviving spouse under the law of her or his domicile at the time of her or his death, whether or not the spouse has later remarried; and a person's "children" are her or his immediate offspring and any children legally adopted by the person. Any consent provided for in subsection (1) shall be given on behalf of a minor by the guardian of her or his person or by either parent.

(6) The remedies provided for in this section shall be in addition to and not in limitation of the remedies and rights of any person under the common law against the invasion of her or his privacy.] …

In *Loft* [*v. Fuller*, 408 So. 2d 619 (Fla. Dist. Ct. 1981)], Dorothy Loft and her two children brought an action for, among other things, violation of section 540.08 for the alleged unauthorized publication of the name and likeness of the Lofts' deceased husband and father, Robert Loft. Robert Loft had been the captain of an Eastern Airlines flight that crashed while en route from New York to Miami in 1972. The crash was followed by reports of the appearance of apparitions of the flight's crew members, including Robert Loft, on subsequent flights. Subsequent to the press stories, *The Ghost of Flight 401* was published in 1976. The book was a nonfictionalized account by the author of his investigation of the reports. A movie was also made based on this book. *Loft*, 408 So. 2d at 620.

The Fourth District held as follows:

> In our view, section 540.08, by prohibiting the use of one's name or likeness for trade, commercial or advertising purposes, is designed to prevent the unauthorized use of a name to directly promote the product or service of the publisher. Thus, the publication is harmful not simply because it is included in a publication that is sold for a profit, but rather because of the way it associates the individual's name or his personality with something else. Such is not the case here.
>
> While we agree that at least one of the purposes of the author and publisher in releasing the publication in question was to make money through sales of copies of the book and that such a publication is commercial in that sense, this in no way distinguishes this book from almost all other books, magazines or newspapers and simply does not amount to the kind of commercial exploitation prohibited by the statute. We simply do not believe that the term "commercial," as employed by Section 540.08, was meant to be construed to bar the use of people's names in such a sweeping fashion. We also believe that acceptance of appellants' view of the statute would result in substantial confrontation between this statute and the *first amendment to the United States Constitution* guaranteeing freedom of the press and of speech. Having concluded that the publication as alleged is not barred by Section 540.08, we need not decide if, under the allegations of the complaint, the book was of current and legitimate public interest, thus removing it entirely from the scope of the statute.

Loft, 408 So. 2d at 622-23 (emphasis added) (citations omitted).

We approve the Fourth District's logical construction of section 540.08 in *Loft*. This construction has been applied to cases construing the statute for more than thirty years, and the statute has remained unchanged by the Legislature for this period.

For example, in *Valentine v. C.B.S., Inc.*, 698 F.2d 430 (11th Cir. 1983), at issue was a song written by Bob Dylan and Jacques Levy depicting the murder trial of prizefighter Rubin "Hurricane" Carter. The plaintiff, a witness in the murder trial, brought an action alleging a violation of section 540.08 because the song falsely implied that she participated in a conspiracy to unjustly convict Carter. The Eleventh Circuit held that the plaintiff's claim was not actionable under section 540.08. …

We disagree with appellants' argument that to uphold the construction given to the statute in Loft renders the exceptions contained in section 540.08(3)(a) and (b) superfluous. Applying the statute to only those situations that "directly promote a product or service" does not necessarily mean that the use is in an advertisement. For example, in *Ewing v. A-1 Management, Inc.*, 481 So. 2d 99 (Fla. 1986), the defendants published the names and addresses of the plaintiffs as parents of a fugitive from justice on a wanted poster distributed by the defendant surety company after the plaintiff's son fled while on bail. The Third District Court of Appeal concluded that while this use of the plaintiffs' names fell within the scope of section 540.08(1), the use was exempted under the newsworthiness exemption of section 540.08(3)(a). Thus, as appellees argue, the newsworthiness exemption served an entirely practical, nonredundant function. ...

Moreover, it should be emphasized that the Legislature enacted section 540.08 in 1967. Since that time, the only amendment to the statute was to rephrase it in gender neutral terms. The Legislature has not amended the statute in response to the decisions that have required that the statute apply to a use that directly promotes a product or service. This inaction may be viewed as legislative acceptance or approval of the judicial construction of the statute. *Goldenberg v. Sawczak*, 791 So. 2d 1078, 1083 (Fla. 2001).

Finally, as recognized by United States District Court Judge Conway in the decision of the United States District Court, we find that defining the term "commercial purpose" in section 540.08 to apply to motion pictures or similar works raises a fundamental constitutional concern. ... It is ... clear that the Picture is entitled to First Amendment protection, and would therefore, be excepted from liability under § 540.08. This provides another basis for this Court's conclusion that Defendants are entitled to summary judgment on these claims. ...

Please add the following to Bibliography and Links at page 288:

W. Mack Webner & Leigh Ann Lindquist, *Transformation: The Bright Line Between Commercial Publicity Rights and the First Amendment*, 37 AKRON L. REV. 171 (2004).

Viva R. Moffat, *Mutant Copyrights and Backdoor Patents: The Problem of Overlapping Intellectual Property Protection*, 19 BERKELEY TECH. L.J. 1473 (2004).

CHAPTER VIII: CONTRACTS: CREDIT & CONTROL

A.   The negotiated areas for talent contracts – Credit, Compensation, & Control

Please add the following after Control at page 291:

Lee v. Marvel Enters.

386 F. Supp. 2d 235 (S.D.N.Y. 2005)

The defendant Marvel Enterprises, Inc. ("Marvel") has moved for partial summary judgment in accordance with Rule 56(a), Fed. R. Civ. P., dismissing the claims in the complaint seeking a profit participation from licensing of its characters for merchandising. The plaintiff Stan Lee ("Lee") has cross-moved for partial summary judgment declaring that he is entitled to 10% participation in profits derived by Marvel from television or movie productions, not limited by so-called "Hollywood Accounting," including film/television merchandising when the profits do not result from a fee for licensing. For the reasons set forth below, Marvel's motion is denied, and Lee's cross-motion is granted in part and denied in part.

As of the time these motions were filed, Lee continued to serve as Marvel's chairman emeritus. As discussed below, Lee has contributed significantly to Marvel's growth since his initial employment in 1940. Initially, Marvel's predominant business was publishing comic books, many of which featured characters created by Lee — e.g. Spider-Man, the Incredible Hulk, the X-Men, and the Fantastic Four. Marvel has subsequently expanded the use of its characters into movies, television, and merchandising. Lee had a contract with Marvel that permitted him to share in certain of these endeavors. Marvel then suffered the vicissitudes of a control contest and bankruptcy. When it emerged from bankruptcy with new leadership, it entered into a new contract with Lee (the "Agreement"). It is paragraph 4(f) of the Agreement, executed on November 17, 1998, that is the central focus of the present action. Paragraph 4(f) states:

> [Lee] shall be paid a participation equal to 10% of the profits derived during [his] life by Marvel (including subsidiaries and affiliates) from the profits of any live action or animation television or movie (including ancillary rights) productions utilizing Marvel Characters. This participation is not to be derived from the fee charged by Marvel for the licensing of the product or of the characters for merchandise or otherwise...

This deceptively simple language, drafted by a company and an executive both skilled and experienced in the industry, has given rise to a multimillion dollar controversy because of changes in the way Marvel has conducted business since the execution of the Agreement in November, 1998.

According to Marvel, paragraph 4(f) entitles Lee to 10% participation in only those television and motion picture production deals where Marvel has been afforded rights of net profit participation. (Such net profit participation arrangements are commonly referred to as "Hollywood Accounting" deals.[6]) Lee argues that paragraph 4(f) entitles him to 10% of all

---

[6] One commentator has provided the following description of the typical provisions of a "Hollywood accounting" deal:

profits — including gross profits or gross proceeds — derived from contingent payments to Marvel in connection with the use of Marvel characters in film or television productions.

According to Marvel, pursuant to the second sentence of paragraph 4(f), Lee is barred from any profits from merchandising. According to Lee, he is entitled to participate in all revenue from film/television merchandising with the exception of profits resulting from fees from licensing for merchandise.

Skilled counsel for both sides praise the clarity of the language of paragraph 4(f) to reach directly contrary results. What follows is an effort to clarify and determine the terms of the contractual language under the applicable principles of procedure and construction. This determination has the potential to affect substantially the financial fortunes of the parties. ...

Prior to the 1994 bankruptcy, the parties entered into an agreement granting Lee a share of Marvel's profits. In 1995, pursuant to this agreement, Marvel paid Lee a 10% participation, which was based on revenue received by Marvel under an arrangement with Danchuk Productions. Under this arrangement, Lee received a percentage of gross receipts. The payments to Marvel were characterized as "profit participation." Marvel remitted 10% ($4,994) to Lee without any deduction for costs. Marvel stated to Lee that this sum "represented your 10% of the profits." The executory portion of this prior agreement was rejected by Marvel during the bankruptcy.

After Marvel emerged from bankruptcy, the parties on November 17, 1998 executed the Agreement. In addition to paragraph 4(f), the Agreement contains other relevant provisions. Under paragraph 2, Lee is required to devote ten to fifteen hours per week to Marvel's affairs. As consideration for his services, Lee is entitled to receive an annual base salary of $810,000 for the years beginning November 1, 1998 and 1999, $850,000 for the year beginning November 1, 2000, $900,000 for the year beginning November 1, 2001, and $1,000,000 for the year beginning November 1, 2002 and each year thereafter until his death. Upon Lee's death, the Agreement provides for Lee's wife to receive survivor payments in an amount equal to 50% of Lee's base salary as of the time of his death through the time of her death, and for Lee's daughter thereafter to receive survivor payments of $100,000 per year for five years. Under paragraph 4(c) of the Agreement, Lee received 150,000 valuable stock options which Lee has already exercised for a net gain of approximately $1.4 million.

Between November 17, 1998 and today, Marvel has entered into over a thousand merchandising agreements pursuant to which it has licensed to third parties the right to use its characters in connection with various toys, games, collectibles, apparel, interactive games, arcade games and electronics, stationery and school products, health and beauty products, snack

---

The basic net profits formula subtracts from the studio's (distributor's) adjusted gross receipts the production costs, distribution expenses, and distribution fees. . . . Production costs are all costs directly attributed to the particular film (plus overhead). Production costs include the payments to all other participants in a film including the contingent compensation of gross participants. So, for example, [if a given actor] had fifteen gross points for [a given movie] (that is, he received 15[%] of the gross receipts), every dollar of revenue that the film generated pushed the net profits breakeven point back fifteen cents. Thus, if a film has significant gross participants, the breakeven point quickly recedes. Almost all the box office smashes that failed to produce net profits had significant gross participants.

Victor P. Goldberg, *The Net Profits Puzzle*, 97 COLUM. L. REV. *524, 528-529 (1997)*.

foods and beverages, sporting goods, party supplies, and amusement destinations. Merchandising has generated hundreds of millions of dollars in revenue to Marvel during this period.

In August 1998, the film *Blade*, which was based on a Marvel character, was released. Despite the fact that *Blade* apparently generated considerable profits, Marvel was not entitled to participate in these profits based on the terms of the profit-participation provision of the production agreement. This profit-participation provision, which Marvel has characterized as a "Hollywood accounting" provision, entitled Marvel to a share of *Blade's* "net profits," as that term was defined by the language of the production agreement. Marvel's Rule 30(b)(6) witness stated that "Hollywood accounting" can be interpreted "to mean that you will never see anything — you will never see — the company would not see any revenues from the studio . . . ." Marvel's chief creative officer, Avi Arad, testified that "Hollywood accounting is-is the term used to — studio's deduct everything possible out of film revenues, from cost of the movie to getting a star flowers to — you name it and its in there. And it's expensive and it's hard to monitor, and therefore I'm allergic to it."

Coincident with *Blade's* box-office success, a determination was made by Marvel to avoid "Hollywood accounting" treatment for the use of the Marvel characters. In its 2001 annual report, Marvel advised that its new movie venture agreements were either "gross profit participation 'dollar one,'" "real profit participation," or "equity (ownership) interests in the films themselves." As stated by Marvel, these new agreements "represent an exciting new source of high margin revenue and are a major departure from the past when [Marvel] made little or no money for such projects."

Marvel's contract with Sony for use of the character Spider-Man (generally regarded as Marvel's most valuable asset) contained a gross-profit participation provision. *Spider-Man: The Movie*, which was released in May, 2002, proved to be a huge box-office hit, earning $114.8 million in its opening weekend (at the time, the largest domestic opening of all time) and more than $800 million in worldwide box-office gross. Based on these receipts, the profit participation provision that Marvel negotiated with Sony has yielded more than $50,000,000 to Marvel.

In its October 30, 2002 press release announcing Marvel's quarterly financial results, Marvel's then president and CEO, Peter Cuneo ("Cuneo"), stated that "Marvel's resurgence throughout 2002 has been supported by the overwhelming popularity and success of *Spider-Man: The Movie*, which has spurred licensing and toy revenues; the expanding scope of our publishing efforts; and our strong and growing line-up of entertainment projects scheduled for release in 2003 and beyond." As set forth in its 2002 annual report, Marvel's toy division alone reported over $100 million in sales of *Spider-Man: The Movie* toys. Marvel's 2003 results were similarly strong, driven by the popularity of the films *X-Men 2*, *Daredevil*, and *Hulk*, all of which featured Marvel characters. ...

[A.] Profit Participation Pursuant To The First Sentence Of Paragraph 4(f) Is Not Limited to Net Profit Participation.

According to Lipson, Marvel's *30(b)(6)* witness, Marvel's construction of the first sentence of paragraph 4(f) is based on the plain meaning of the text. According to Lipson, Lee is entitled to participation pursuant to paragraph 4(f) only when a payment by a studio (or producer) to Marvel is the result of a calculation of profit based on "Hollywood Accounting." Marvel argues that Lee is not entitled to share in profits arising from the contingent compensation provision in the Spider-Man agreement (and others like it) because such provisions entail participation in gross receipts and not profits.

However, the first sentence of paragraph 4(f) does not state that Lee's participation is limited to net profits earned by the producer or studio. Nor is the word "profits" defined in the Agreement. Moreover, the first, and therefore preferred, dictionary definition for "profit" is "an advantageous gain or return; benefit" (The American Heritage College Dictionary (3d ed. 2000)); or "a valuable return: gain." (Merriam-Webster Online Dictionary). As demonstrated by the evidence proffered by Lee, these dictionary definitions are consistent with Marvel's own consistent practice in treating all forms of contingent compensation as profit participation.

In short, the first sentence of paragraph 4(f) is not ambiguous. It provides that Lee is entitled to share in the results of Marvel's arrangements for movie and television productions involving Marvel characters, however those arrangements may have been characterized as between Marvel and the third party, as long as there is a valuable gain or return, a benefit to Marvel.

It is also apparent that a determination of the profits to which Lee is entitled cannot be made on the basis of the present record.

[B.] "Ancillary Rights" Include Merchandising

The parties differ as to whether the term "ancillary rights," as used in the first sentence of paragraph 4(f), includes merchandising rights. According to Marvel, pursuant to the first sentence of paragraph 4(f), "ancillary rights" are properly defined as whatever rights are granted by Marvel to a licensee under a given film/television production agreement. Marvel argues that "ancillary rights" neither necessarily include nor exclude merchandising; rather, the terms of each individual film or television production agreement determines the substance of these rights. In contrast, Lee argues that the phrase "ancillary rights" describes all rights beyond a film/television production's initial intended distribution, and that such rights are understood in the entertainment industry to necessarily include merchandising. …

[T]he phrase "ancillary rights" includes rights ancillary to the basic film or television production itself. According to Lee's expert, it is understood in the motion picture and television industries that such "ancillary rights" include soundtrack, music, and merchandising revenues. Although Marvel's expert asserts that "there is no fixed and accepted definition" of the term "ancillary rights" he admits that the term is understood in the entertainment industry to include "all rights beyond the right to produce and distribute the motion picture for theatrical release." Furthermore, Marvel's expert states that "there are instances where merchandising rights are expressly excluded from the grant of ancillary rights[,]" thereby strongly suggesting that, in general, ancillary rights are understood to include merchandising.

Based on this expert testimony proffered by Lee and Marvel concerning common usage in the relevant industries, it is determined that the phrase "ancillary rights," as used in the first sentence of paragraph 4(f), necessarily includes merchandising rights. …

B.   Performer's Rights to Credit

Please add the following to Notes and Questions at page 298:

e. Additional comments relating to the implications of *Dastar* can be found on page 250 and in this supplement in the updates to those notes.

f. The Register of Copyright, Mary Beth Peters, commented on the difficulty created by *Dastar*. "[T]he longstanding understanding prior to *Dastar* [was] that section 43(a) is an important means for protecting the moral rights of attribution and integrity."[7] The importance of the § 43(a) claim is the pressure it puts on the producers of a project to provide contractual credit.

The right of attribution extends far beyond copyright. Indeed, it may very well be that performers have a much greater stake in the right to credit than do the authors of projects. The law provides little other protection to performers, so stripping them of attribution rights when the question was not before the court seems unkind as well as unnecessary. Unfortunately, the facts in the case provided a poor basis for making these determinations. The footage in *Dastar* was predominantly government war footage or anonymous stock footage. Presumably, copyright in the footage had never existed because the film was public domain governmental works, because the newsreels were never copyrighted (at a time when such formalities had to be followed), or because there had been no renewals of copyright in the stock footage incorporated into the film.

g. Do states have the ability to enforce or amend their unfair competition laws to reach the "false designation of author" or to make the intentional falsification of a credit a civil tort? What would such a statute include?

Please add the following to Bibliography and Links at page 329:

Lisa P. Ramsey, *Descriptive Trademarks and the First Amendment*, 70 TENN. L. REV. 1095 (2003).

Natalie J. Spears & S. Roberts Carter III, *This Brand is my Brand: Litigating Product Image*, 31 LITIG. 31 (2005).

---

[7] Statement of Marybeth Peters, Register of Copyrights before the Subcommittee on Courts, The Internet and Intellectual Property of the House Committee on the Judiciary, June 17, 2004, available at http://www.copyright.gov/docs/regstat061704.html.

PART II

INDUSTRY PRACTICE IN ENTERTAINMENT

CHAPTER IX: PROFESSIONAL LIVE THEATRE

C.   Playwrights

Please add the following after the Approved Production Contract at page 357:

Playwrights Licensing Antitrust Initiative Act of 2005[8]

A BILL

To modify the application of the antitrust laws to permit collective development and implementation of a standard contract form for playwrights for the licensing of their plays.

Be it enacted by the Senate and House of Representatives of the United States of America in Congress assembled,

SECTION 1. SHORT TITLE.

This Act may be cited as the 'Playwrights Licensing Antitrust Initiative Act of 2005'.

SEC. 2. NONAPPLICATION OF ANTITRUST LAWS.

(a) In General- Subject to subsection (c), the antitrust laws shall not apply to any joint discussion, consideration, review, action, or agreement for the express purpose of, and limited to, the development of a standard form contract containing minimum terms of artistic protection and levels of compensation for playwrights by means of—

> (1) meetings, discussions, and negotiations between or among playwrights or their representatives and producers or their representatives; or

> (2) joint or collective voluntary actions for the limited purposes of developing a standard form contract by playwrights or their representatives.

(b) Adoption and Implementation- Subject to subsection (c), the antitrust laws shall not apply to any joint discussion, consideration, review, or action for the express purpose of, and limited to, reaching a collective agreement among playwrights adopting a standard form contract developed pursuant to subsection (a) as the participating playwrights sole and exclusive means by which participating playwrights shall license their plays to producers.

(c) Amendment of Contract- A standard form of contract developed and implemented under subsections (a) and (b) shall be subject to amendment by individual playwrights and producers consistent with the terms of the standard form contract.

SEC. 3. DEFINITIONS.

---

[8] H.R. 532, 109th Cong. (1st Sess., 2005).

In this Act:

(1) ANTITRUST LAWS- The term 'antitrust laws' has the meaning given it in section (a) of the first section of the Clayton Act (15 U.S.C. 12), except that such term includes section 5 of the Federal Trade Commission Act (15 U.S.C. 45) to the extent that such section applies to unfair methods of competition.

(2) PLAYWRIGHT- The term 'playwright' means the author, composer, or lyricist of a dramatic or musical work intended to be performed on the speaking stage and shall include, where appropriate, the adapter of a work from another medium.

(3) PRODUCER- The term 'producer'—

> (A) means any person who obtains the rights to present live stage productions of a play; and

> (B) includes any person who presents a play as first class performances in major cities, as well as those who present plays in regional and not-for-profit theaters.

...

Statement of Gerald Schoenfeld[9]

My name is Gerald Schoenfeld. I am Chairman of the Board of The Shubert Organization, Incorporated, and also Chairman of The League of American Theatres and Producers, the legitimate theatre's trade association.

The Shubert Organization is the owner and/or operator of twenty first class legitimate theatres and one Off-Broadway theatre in the United States located in the cities of New York, Washington, DC, Philadelphia and Boston. It is also a producer of plays and musicals. Among its most recent productions are: Cats, Amour, The Heidi Chronicles, Sunday in the Park with George, Passion, The Ride Down Mount Morgan, Indiscretions, Dirty Blonde, An Inspector Calls, Amadeus, The Grapes of Wrath, The Life and Adventures of Nicholas Nickleby, Jerome Robbins' Broadway, The Most Happy Fella, Children of a Lesser God, Bob Fosse's Dancin', Whoopi Goldberg, Pygmalion, Chess, Dreamgirls, Ain't Misbehavin', The Gin Game, A Streetcar Named Desire, Lettice & Lovage, Skylight, Closer, Les Liaisons Dangereuses, Amy's View, Little Shop of Horrors, The Blue Room, and Dance of Death.

I have occupied my present position for thirty-two years and have been engaged in the negotiation of all of the various contracts involved in a theatrical production as well as in the collective bargaining agreements with the industry's unions and guilds. I am personally familiar with the Dramatists Guild and many of its members and have personal knowledge of the matters hereinafter referred to.

Obviously, the Dramatists Guild must believe it is subject to the anti-trust laws of this country, otherwise it would not be seeking an exemption from its provisions. It is also obvious

---

[9] Gerald Schoenfeld, Chairman of the Shubert Organization, Inc. and Chairman of the League of American Theatres and Producers before The United States Senate Committee on the Judiciary, April 28, 2004, available at http://judiciary.senate.gov/testimony.cfm?id=1160&wit_id=3353.

that an exemption from the anti-trust laws is rarely granted. I submit that the Guild is not an organization that is deserving of exemption.

I was significantly involved in the defense of the predecessors of The Shubert Organization in an action instituted by The United States in February, 1950 claiming alleged violations of the anti-trust laws. This case was settled by a Consent Decree entered in February, 1956.

Contractual relations between legitimate theatre producers and the Guild's members, who are the writers of dramatic plays and musicals, are incorporated in a "suggested" contract known as the Approved Production Contract [APC]. Such has been the case since 1985. Prior to 1985, an antecedent agreement incorporating many of the same provisions was promulgated by the Guild as a mandatory, rather than suggested, contract and was known as the Minimum Basic Production Contract.

The APC sets forth minimum terms and conditions regarding the production of plays and musicals written by Guild members. These terms, among other things, relate to fees and advances against royalties, territorial restrictions, participation in subsidiary rights such as stock and amateur performances, motion picture, television and radio performances, foreign productions both in English and in foreign languages. The APC is a license agreement which grants the producer the right to produce the play as written by the dramatist without any right to make any changes of any kind in the text, lyrics and/or music. It also grants the dramatist the right to approve the director , the cast, the designers and all other creative elements of the play such as the scenic, costume and lighting designers.

The territory granted by the license is restricted to The United States, Canada and The British Isles. The APC also limits the period of time that the licensed rights may be exploited by the producer as well as the duration of the producer's right to participate in subsidiary rights. The exploitation of all subsidiary rights is reserved by the dramatist as are all other rights not specifically granted to the producer pursuant to the provisions of the APC. In the event that a play or musical is initially presented in a non-profit or Off-Broadway venue in The United States or in a foreign country, the license agreement governing such presentations usually contains a provision that in the event the play or musical is thereafter presented as a first-class production in the United States it shall be subject to all of the terms, covenants and conditions contained in the APC.

Membership in the Guild is a coveted status since members will derive the benefits of the APC.

Dramatists are represented by agents who conduct the negotiations on their behalf. Certain negotiated provisions are added to the APC such as billing, per diems, travel arrangements and accommodations, types of transportation, the number of house seats, approval of venues, managers, press agents, attorneys, accountants, and certain additional financial provisions. Since the promulgation of the APC in 1985, and in order to accommodate changing economic conditions involved in the production of plays and musicals, a form of compensation for royalty participants such as authors, directors, designers, and producers was created and is known as the "royalty pool". The royalty pool provides for a certain percentage of the weekly net profits to be allocated to the royalty participants in the following manner: the total of all of the royalty percentages is the denominator of a fraction whose numerator is the percentage paid to each royalty participant, so that for example;

- if the royalty pool participants are to receive 35% percent of the weekly operating profits

- and the total royalties amount to 15%

- and the dramatist's royalty amounts to 6%,

- the dramatist would receive 6/15 of 35% of the weekly net profits.

- The dramatist and all royalty participants are entitled to receive an agreed amount of money weekly for each royalty percent regardless of whether there is any weekly net profit.

The Guild has unilaterally decreed that in no event shall the dramatist receive less than a certain specified percentage of the total weekly net profits regardless of what the dramatist might otherwise receive as a royalty pool participant. Of course, this has an impact on the ability of the producer to negotiate with other pool participants since they too are expected to receive pari-passu treatment with the dramatist.

Unfortunately, these provisions of the APC are not left to the negotiations between the agent and the producer. The ultimate party that is granted the right to approve the terms and conditions of the agreement negotiated between the producer and the dramatist(s) is reserved exclusively to the Guild. The approval process is subject to what is known as the Certification Process pursuant to which the Guild must certify that the APC, as negotiated at arm's length, conforms to the minimum terms and conditions of the APC. If the Guild does not certify, the APC provides that the agreement between the dramatist and the producer nevertheless may proceed provided that the dramatist, simultaneously with the submission of the APC to the Guild for certification, submits a letter of resignation to the Guild. This has resulted in a unilateral re-negotiation of the APC compelling compliance with its provisions upon pain of dismissal.

I know of no agreement amongst producers regarding the terms and conditions to be included in an APC. In public offerings relating to the production of plays and musicals, the significant provisions of a dramatist's agreement are set forth in the offering documents. They demonstrate no uniform provisions manifesting the existence of a conspiracy on the part of producers. Indeed, all dramatists are not equally talented yet they must receive at least the same terms and conditions of the APC.

The Guild, its members and their agents, by requiring compliance with the APC and its certification process, have had an impact upon the producer's ability to enter into a negotiation on equal terms with the Guild members. The Guild is not a labor union and thereby exempt by statute from the anti-trust laws. If they are granted exemption, then all inventors, researchers, and creators of literary property other than employees for hire would also be entitled to exemption.

Suffice it to say the conduct of the Guild and its members do not deserve an exemption but should continue to be subject to the strictures of the anti-trust laws. They are the owners of their work and the copyright holder. To ask for immunity is to seek a shield from both prior and prospective anti-trust law violations. If there are any restraints upon the production of plays and musicals they are imposed by the Guild and its members and not the producers or the venue operators.

...

Prepared Testimony of Arthur Miller[10]

Mr. Chairman. Members of the Committee. It is indeed an honor to appear before you today in support of S. 2349, The Playwrights Licensing Antitrust Initiative Act of 2004. …

It has been some time since I was last asked to testify before Congress. But, I have to tell you, today I am actually happy to appear on behalf of what I believe is truly an important topic worthy of Congressional debate and action – the future of the American theater.

I have been blessed to be lucky enough to be a successful playwright. Many of my plays, I am proud to say, have won critical acclaim – Death of a Salesman and The Crucible won a Pulitzer and a Tony award respectively.

I raise these plays, and my success, not to brag, but to emphasize an important point: I and my colleagues before you today are here not for ourselves, but for others. We are speaking on behalf of the up and coming playwrights: The Arthur Millers, the Stephen Sondheims and the Wendy Wassersteins as young playwrights. Indeed, the American theater risks losing the next generation of playwrights to other media and opportunities as the pressures on playwrights increase and their power to protect their economic and artistic interests diminish. The legislation we are advocating isn't for us, it's for them. And it's for the theater-going public.

The legislation introduced by you, Chairman Hatch and Senator Kennedy, is meant to keep the legacy of aspiring playwrights who write for the theater alive. It will help ensure that American playwrights, through the theater, can speak to the hearts and minds of the audience. That we can challenge social [mores], ideology, beliefs, or simply entertain. Drama is one of civilization's greatest art forms and we must do all that we can to promote its vitality.

The American theater has undergone enormous changes over the years. From its entrepreneurial start it has become increasingly dominated by corporate interests. Sure, business is changing in virtually every sector of our economy and there is no reason that the theater should be immune from business pressures.

But, unfortunately, in the midst of these increasing pressures, only one entity does not have a seat at the bargaining table: the playwrights. The status of the playwright is difficult to discern as it has fallen under the long shadow of questionable and conflicting legal opinions. The result is that all other entities have the collective power and ability to fight for their rights. As a result, it is the playwright who gets squeezed.

The Playwrights Licensing Antitrust Initiative Act of 2004 would provide a very limited legislative fix that would allow for the standard form contract that was last negotiated in 1982 to be updated to take account of today's market realities and intellectual property protection climate. It does not force producers to hire any playwrights, but it does allow playwrights with a willing producer to protect their economic and artistic interests.

Today many new playwrights are presented with take-it-or-leave-it contracts. In their hunger to get their plays produced, many have no choice. Others, facing the economic pressures that face all-too-many people in today's economy, are abandoning their dreams of writing for the

---

[10] Arthur Miller, The Playwrights Licensing Antitrust Initiative Act: Safeguarding the Future of American Live Theater before The United States Senate Committee on the Judiciary, April 28, 2004, available at http://judiciary.senate.gov/testimony.cfm?id=1160&wit_id=3348.

theater as they go to Hollywood or write for other media.

Some may say that this is just basic economics. But, the legislation the Chairman and Senator Kennedy have introduced is not intended to change the laws of economics. It simply says that playwrights should have a seat at the table. Failure to pass the legislation will continue the unfair bargaining situation that the playwrights find themselves in and not only will the playwright and the theater suffer, but society as a whole.

It was Senator Kennedy's brother, President Kennedy, who once said:

> "I look forward to an America which will reward achievement in the arts as we reward achievement in business or statecraft."

Unfortunately, under today's legal shadows, the up and coming playwrights must offer their wares at a discount.

I understand that antitrust exemptions are not easy to come by. And I believe that amending our laws should not be done at the drop of a hat. But, where the national interest demands that change occur, I believe it is appropriate.

Mr. Chairman. Members of the Committee. I urge your prompt approval of this legislation.

Please add the following to Notes and Questions at page 370:

g. The use of Marilyn Monroe has created quite an icon – even after her death. A playwright who featured the famous starlet in his plays claimed those plays were infringed by a television program on the same topic. To what extent can an author claim copyright in the life story of his or her subject? See *Whitehead v. CBS/Viacom, Inc.*, 315 F. Supp. 2d 1 (D.D.C. 2004).

h. The battle over joint authorship is not limited to playwrights. As comic books gain increasing economic importance, the fights have increased. The character Spawn seems to have garnered the most activity in the courtroom. See *Gaiman v. McFarlane*, 360 F.3d 644 (7th Cir. 2004) (regarding Neil Gaiman's suit against Todd McFarlane, seeking a declaration that Gaiman was a joint author with McFarlane in Spawn and certain comic-book characters.)

Please add the following to Bibliography and Links at page 374:

Kathleen Abitabile & Jeanette Picerno, *Dance and the Choreographer's Dilemma: A Legal and Cultural Perspective on Copyright Protection for Choreographic Works*, 27 CAMPBELL L. REV. 39 (2004).

CHAPTER X: FILM PRODUCTION RIGHTS, FINANCING & DISTRIBUTION

A. Overview

Please replace note "a" in Notes and Questions at page 381:

a. The Southern District of New York continues to interpret the various actions for block-booking, non-competitive licensing, monopolization claims, and related state law claims. See *Six West Retail Acquisition, Inc. v. Sony Theatre Mgmt. Corp.*, 2004-1 Trade Cas. (CCH) P74361, 2004 U.S. Dist. LEXIS 5411 (S.D.N.Y. 2004), *aff'd* 124 Fed. Appx. 73, 2005 U.S. App. LEXIS 5258 (2d Cir. 2005).

Please add the following to Notes and Questions at page 382:

d. For an interesting wrinkle on the typical claim of copyright infringement for most popular motion pictures, see *People v. Smith*, 306 A.D.2d 225, 760 N.Y.S.2d 855 (N.Y. App. Div. 2003). In *People v. Smith*, screenwriter Smith believed that the motion picture "The Cell" infringed the copyright to his original screenplay "Inner Mind's Eye." To support his claim, Smith apparently signed his own name to the actual author's screenplay and was sentenced to 2⅓ to 7 years in prison, only to have the conviction vacated on appeal. He may have fraudulently signed the screenplay, but one cannot forge one's own name. *Id.*

D. Character Licensing

Please add the following to Notes and Questions at page 412:

g. Character licensing continues to be a driving force behind motion pictures, comic books, video games, leading to some of the largest new blockbuster films and extensions into portable telephones and other devices. As a result, the litigation over such licensing has also heated up. See *Lee v. Marvel Enters.*, 386 F. Supp. 2d 235 (S.D.N.Y. 2005); *Gaiman v. McFarlane*, 360 F.3d 644 (7th Cir. 2004); and *Doe v. TCI Cablevision*, 110 S.W.3d 363 (Mo. 2003) noted elsewhere in the supplement.

E. Ratings

Please add the following after From Hays Onward at page 417:

3. Family Movie Act of 2005

TITLE II—EXEMPTION FROM INFRINGEMENT FOR SKIPPING AUDIO AND VIDEO CONTENT IN MOTION PICTURES

SEC. 201. SHORT TITLE.

This title may be cited as the "Family Movie Act of 2005."[11]

SEC. 202. EXEMPTION FROM INFRINGEMENT FOR SKIPPING AUDIO AND VIDEO CONTENT IN MOTION PICTURES.

(a) In General.—Section 110 of title 17, United States Code, is amended—

---

[11] Family Entertainment and Copyright Act, Pub. Law. No. 109-9, signed April 27, 2005.

(1) in paragraph (9), by striking "and" after the semicolon at the end;

(2) in paragraph (10), by striking the period at the end and inserting "; and";

(3) by inserting after paragraph (10) the following:

> "(11) the making imperceptible, by or at the direction of a member of a private household, of limited portions of audio or video content of a motion picture, during a performance in or transmitted to that household for private home viewing, from an authorized copy of the motion picture, or the creation or provision of a computer program or other technology that enables such making imperceptible and that is designed and marketed to be used, at the direction of a member of a private household, for such making imperceptible, if no fixed copy of the altered version of the motion picture is created by such computer program or other technology."; and

(4) by adding at the end the following:

"For purposes of paragraph (11), the term 'making imperceptible' does not include the addition of audio or video content that is performed or displayed over or in place of existing content in a motion picture.

"Nothing in paragraph (11) shall be construed to imply further rights under section 106 of this title, or to have any effect on defenses or limitations on rights granted under any other section of this title or under any other paragraph of this section.".

(b) Exemption From Trademark Infringement.—Section 32 of the Trademark Act of 1946 (15 U.S.C. 1114) is amended by adding at the end the following:

> "(3)(A) Any person who engages in the conduct described in paragraph (11) of section 110 of title 17, United States Code, and who complies with the requirements set forth in that paragraph is not liable on account of such conduct for a violation of any right under this Act. This subparagraph does not preclude liability, nor shall it be construed to restrict the defenses or limitations on rights granted under this Act, of a person for conduct not described in paragraph (11) of section 110 of title 17, United States Code, even if that person also engages in conduct described in paragraph (11) of section 110 of such title.

> "(B) A manufacturer, licensee, or licensor of technology that enables the making of limited portions of audio or video content of a motion picture imperceptible as described in subparagraph (A) is not liable on account of such manufacture or license for a violation of any right under this Act, if such manufacturer, licensee, or licensor ensures that the technology provides a clear and conspicuous notice at the beginning of each performance that the performance of the motion picture is altered from the performance intended by the director or copyright holder of the motion picture. The limitations on liability in subparagraph (A) and this subparagraph shall not apply to a manufacturer, licensee, or licensor of technology that fails to comply with this paragraph.

"(C) The requirement under subparagraph (B) to provide notice shall apply only with respect to technology manufactured after the end of the 180-day period beginning on the date of the enactment of the Family Movie Act of 2005.

"(D) Any failure by a manufacturer, licensee, or licensor of technology to qualify for the exemption under subparagraphs (A) and (B) shall not be construed to create an inference that any such party that engages in conduct described in paragraph (11) of section 110 of title 17, United States Code, is liable for trademark infringement by reason of such conduct.." ...

Statement of Marybeth Peters, Register of Copyrights[12]

The Family Movie Act would make it lawful for a person who is watching a motion picture on a DVD in the privacy of his or her own home to use software that filters out certain types of content that the person would prefer not to see or hear. As you pointed out at a hearing last month, Mr. Chairman, such software can be used by parents to assist them in preventing their children from seeing or hearing objectionable content by muting the sound or fast forwarding past objectionable material. What material is to be filtered out is determined by the provider of the software, but such software can include options that give the user the ability to select categories of material that the user prefers not to see or hear.

I do not believe that such legislation should be enacted — and certainly not at this time. As you know, litigation addressing whether the manufacture and distribution of such software violates the copyright law and the Lanham Act is currently pending in the United States District Court for the District of Colorado. A summary judgment motion is pending. The court has not yet ruled on the merits. Nor has a preliminary injunction been issued — or even sought. At the moment, providers of such software are free to sell it and consumers are free to use it. If the court ultimately rules that the making or distribution of the software is unlawful — a ruling that I believe is unlikely — the time may then be opportune to consider legislation. But meanwhile, there is every reason to believe that the proposed Family Movie Act is a solution to a problem that does not exist. ...

Let me start with a proposition that I believe everybody can agree on. I do not believe anybody would seriously argue that an individual who is watching a movie in his or her living room should be forbidden to press the mute button on a remote control in order to block out language that he or she believes is offensive. Nor should someone be forbidden to fast-forward past a scene that he or she does not wish to see. And certainly parents have the right to press the mute and fast-forward buttons to avoid exposing their children to material that they believe is inappropriate.

Does that mean that parents should be able to purchase a product that makes those decisions for them — that automatically mutes certain sounds and skips past certain images that the provider of that product believes parents would not want their children to hear or see? What if the parent is able to determine what categories of material (e.g., profanity, nudity, violence)

---

[12] Before the Subcommittee on Courts, The Internet and Intellectual Property of the House Committee on the Judiciary, Washington, DC June 17, 2004. Available at http://judiciary.house.gov/media/pdfs/printers/108th/94286.pdf.

should be blocked, and is willing to trust the provider of the filtering product to make the ultimate judgments about what material in a particular movie falls into the selected categories?

It is very tempting to say that consumers should be able to purchase such products, and that providers of such products should be permitted to develop and market them. But I have to say that I am hesitant to endorse that proposition.

First of all, I cannot accept the proposition that not to permit parents to use such products means that they are somehow forced to expose their children (or themselves) to unwanted depictions of violence, sex and profanity. There is an obvious choice – one which any parent can and should make: don't let your children watch a movie unless you approve of the content of the entire movie. Parents who have not prescreened a movie and made their own judgments can take guidance from the ratings that appear on almost all commercially released DVDs. Not only do those ratings label movies by particular classes denoting the age groups for which a particular movie is appropriate (e.g., G, PG, PG-13, R), but those ratings now also give parents additional advice about the content of a particular motion picture (e.g., "PG-13 ... Sexual Content, Thematic Material & Language" (from "The Stepford Wives") or "PG-13 ... Non-stop Creature Action Violence and Frightening Images, and for Sensuality" (from "Van Helsing")). It is appropriate that parents and other consumers should be given sufficient information to make a judgment whether a particular motion picture is suitable for their children or themselves to view. ...

Moreover, I have serious reservations about enacting legislation that permits persons other than the creators or authorized distributors of a motion picture to make a profit by selling adaptations of somebody else's motion picture. It's one thing to say that an individual, in the privacy of his or her home, should be able to filter out undesired scenes or dialog from his or her private home viewing of a movie. It's another matter to say that a for-profit company should be able to commercially market a product that alters a director's artistic vision.

That brings me to an objection that is more firmly rooted in fundamental principles of copyright, which recognize that authors have moral rights. To be sure, the state of the law with respect to moral rights is relatively undeveloped in the United States, and a recent ill-considered decision by our Supreme Court has weakened the protection for moral rights that our laws offer.[13] Moreover, I am not suggesting that enactment of the proposed legislation would violate our obligations under the Berne Convention to protect moral rights.[14] In fact, I do not believe that the Berne Convention's provision on moral rights forbids permitting the making and marketing of products that permit individual consumers to block certain undesired audio or video content from their private home viewing of motion pictures. But beyond our treaty obligations, the principles underlying moral rights are important. The right of integrity — the author's right to prevent, in the words of Article 6bis of the Berne Convention — the "distortion, mutilation, or any other modification of, or other derogatory action in relation to [his or her] work, which

---

[13] Dastar Corp. v. Twentieth Century Fox Film Corp., 539 U.S. [23], 123 S. Ct. 2041 (2003). While the Dastar decision is not the subject of this hearing, I believe that the subcommittee should examine whether section 43(a) of the Lanham Act should be amended to reflect what was the longstanding understanding prior to Dastar — that section 43(a) is an important means for protecting the moral rights of attribution and integrity. Although I will comment no further on Dastar at this hearing, and although I will not comment on the portion of the proposed legislation that would provide an exemption from liability under the Lanham Act, it is worth noting that in the wake of Dastar (and, for that matter, even under pre-Dastar law), there may be little reason to be concerned that the conduct proposed to be covered by the proposed Family Movie Act would violate the Lanham Act in any event.

[14] Berne Convention for the Protection of Literary and Artistic Works, Art. 6bis.

would be prejudicial to his honor or reputation" — is a reflection of an important principle. As one leading commentator has put it:

> Any author, whether he writes, paints, or composes, embodies some part of himself — his thoughts, ideas, sentiments and feelings — in his work, and this gives rise to an interest as deserving of protection as any of the other personal interests protected by the institutions of positive law, such as reputation, bodily integrity, and confidences. The interest in question here relates to the way in which the author presents his work to the world, and the way in which his identification with the work is maintained.[15]

I can well understand how motion picture directors may be offended when a product with which they have no connection and over which they have no control creates an altered presentation of their artistic creations by removing some of the directors' creative expression. This is more than a matter of personal preference or offense; it finds its roots in the principle underlying moral rights: that a creative work is the offspring of its author, who has every right to object to what he or she perceives as a mutilation of his or her work.

Although I acknowledge that there is some tension between principles of moral rights and the products we are discussing today, I believe that this narrowly-defined activity does not violate moral rights, for several reasons: (1) it takes place in the context of a private performance of a motion picture in which the alteration of the original motion picture is not fixed in a tangible medium of expression; (2) it consists only of omissions of limited portions of the sounds and/or images in the motion picture, rather than the addition of material or alteration of material in the motion picture; and (3) it is desired and implemented by the individual who is viewing the private performance, who is perfectly aware that there are omissions of material and that the director and studio did not consent to those omissions. But that is not to say that the creator of the motion picture does not have a legitimate artistic reason to complain — and I am very sympathetic to such complaints. ...

Analysis of Current Law

Despite my conclusion that on balance, the conduct that is addressed by the Family Movie Act should not be prohibited, I do not believe that legislation needed because it seems reasonably clear that such conduct is not prohibited under existing law. The exclusive rights of the copyright owner that might arguably be implicated are the reproduction, distribution, public performance and derivative work rights, but on examination, it seems clear that there is no infringement of any of those rights.[16]

There is no infringement of the reproduction right because no unauthorized copies of the motion pictures are made. Rather, an authorized copy of the motion picture, distributed on a DVD, is played in the same manner as it would be played on any conventional DVD player, but with some of the audio and video content of the motion picture in effect deleted from that private performance because it is muted or bypassed. The distribution right is not infringed because no copies of the motion picture are distributed, apart from the authorized, unedited DVD that the

---

[15] SAM RICKETSON, THE BERNE CONVENTION: 1886-1986 456 (1987).
[16] This brief legal analysis is based on my admittedly sketchy understanding of how the products that are the subject of the proposed legislation work. If, for example, these products actually caused copies to be made of any or all of a motion picture, my analysis might well be different.

consumer has purchased or rented. The public performance right is not infringed because the motion picture is played in the privacy of the viewer's home, a quintessential private performance.[17] ...

Because I believe that under existing law, the conduct that is addressed by this legislation is already lawful, and because I believe it is likely that the district court in Colorado will come to the same conclusion, I do not believe there is any reason to enact legislation that would make lawful that which already is lawful. ...

Please add the following to Bibliography and Links at page 420:

Barak Y. Orbach, *Antitrust and Pricing in the Motion Picture Industry*, 21 YALE J. ON REG. 317 (2004).

Jennifer J. Karangelen, *Editing Companies vs. Big Hollywood: A Hollywood Ending?*, 13 U. BALT. INTELL. PROP. L.J. 13 (2004).

---

[17] Of course, it is possible to use the filtering products to alter a performance of the motion picture in a public setting, resulting in an infringing public performance. But as I understand it, that is not the typical use, nor are the products that are the subject of this legislation marketed for such use. Moreover, if there were a public performance, it would be an act of infringement not because the performance was altered, but simply because the motion picture was performed in public without the authorization of the copyright owner.

CHAPTER XI: MUSIC PUBLISHING

B.   Publisher Agreements

Please add the following to Notes and Questions at page 430:

f. The Lion Never Sleeps - According to press reports, Disney is the first of what may be many defendants in an action to reclaim the copyright in the songs *Wimoweh* and *Mbue* for the estate of Solomon Linda, the author of the underlying composition popularized as *The Lion Sleeps Tonight*. As shown in *Folkways Music Publishers, Inc. v. Weiss*, 989 F.2d 108 (2d Cir. 1993), this has been a musical legacy fraught with intrigue.

The latest chapter stems from the application of British imperial copyright law to the claims. The Guardian reports copyright expert Dr. Dean as explaining that "all rights to a song revert[] to the composer's estate 25 years after his death."[18] The author died in 1962. He had named the song *Mbue* as the Zulu word for Lion. Pete Seeger transcribed the song for his folk band, The Weavers, who corrupted the word to *Wimoweh*. The saga continues as reported in *Folkways Music*.

Although Disney chose not to reproduce the song on the *Lion King* soundtrack album, it used the song in both the film and the live stage version of the production. The suit, in South Africa, could expose Disney and other current copyright infringers to significant liability. The South African courts have attached Disney assets in the jurisdiction pending the lawsuit. These assets are primarily the Disney trademarks. Disney has reported that it plans to defend itself vigorously. It alleges that it has licensing agreements for the song, but the question is whether the party licensing to Disney had the necessary authority to do so. If the law provided for an automatic reversion of rights, then Disney's licensor may have been in violation of the law and therefore could transfer nothing. The roaring will continue for some time.

g. In testimony before Congress, the Register of Copyright noted the congressional effort to mitigate the controlled composition clause:

> Congress also addressed the common industry practice of incorporating controlled composition clauses into a songwriter/performer's recording contract, whereby a recording artist agrees to reduce the mechanical royalty rate payable when the record company makes and distributes phonorecords including songs written by the performer. In general, the DPRA provides that privately negotiated contracts entered into after June 22, 1995, between a recording company and a recording artist who is the author of the musical work cannot include a rate for the making and distribution of the musical work below that established for the compulsory license. There is one notable exception to this general rule. A recording artist-author who effectively is acting as her own music publisher may accept a royalty rate below the statutory rate if the contract is entered into after the sound

---

[18] *Lion Takes on Mouse in Copyright Row. Poverty-stricken descendants of enduring hit song's composer could make fortune from Disney*, GUARDIAN, July 2, 2004 at http://www.buzzle.com/editorials/7-2-2004-56177.asp.

recording has been fixed in a tangible medium of expression in a form intended for commercial release. 17 U.S.C. § 115(c)(3)(E).[19]

C. Performing Rights Societies & Copyright Enforcement

Please add the following to Notes and Questions at page 445:

f. The online music industry is creating many tensions and new definitions around the various aspects of music copyright. For a discussion of the separation of public performance rights (which are subject to the licensing mechanisms of the performance rights societies) as distinct from the reproduction rights on a computer, see *Country Rd. Music, Inc. v. MP3.com, Inc.*, 279 F. Supp. 2d 325, 327-28 (S.D.N.Y. 2003) ("[T]he performing rights licenses themselves, as their name implies, explicitly authorize public performance only, do not purport to grant a reproduction right in musical compositions.... Moreover, the performing rights societies themselves do not, and do not purport to have, the authority to grant such a right.)

Please add the following to Bibliography and Links at page 468:

Cydney A. Tune, Music Licensing — *From the Basics to the Outer Limits, Part 1:* 21 ENT. & SPORTS L. 1 (Fall, 2003).

Cydney A. Tune, *Music Licensing — From the Basics to the Outer Limits, Part 2: Key Considerations for Potential Licensees and Licensors of Music*, 21 ENT. & SPORTS L. 3 (Winter, 2004).

Cydney A. Tune, *Music Licensing — From the Basics to the Outer Limits, Part 3: The Myriad World of Music Licenses*, 22 ENT. & SPORTS L. 5 (Spring, 2004).

---

[19] Statement of Marybeth Peters, The Register of Copyrights before the Subcommittee on Intellectual Property, Committee on the Judiciary, United States Senate 109th Congress, 1st Session July 12, 2005 available at http://www.copyright.gov/docs/regstat071205.html.

CHAPTER XII: SOUND RECORDING INDUSTRY

A.   Finances in the Recording Industry

Please add the following to Notes and Questions at page 472:

c. At the *2004 Midwest Art, Entertainment & Sports Law Institute – Signing and Developing Artists in a Download Economy*, attorney Peter Strand commented that a $300,000 production budget "shrinks in the dryer" so that a $30,000 production budget for an independent label would be "a good deal."[20] He explained that independent budgets often range from $15,000 to $50,000, though the upper range would be rather rare. The panel made a few additional points:

1. Less than 15% of all sound recordings released by major record companies will even make back their costs.

2. There were 38,857 albums released in 2002, 7000 from the majors and 31,857 from the [independent record labels]. Out of all of these releases, only 233 sold over 250,000 units and only 437 sold over 100,000 units. That means that less than 1% of the time for the total recording industry that an album returns makes significant sales (in terms of recouping costs and turning a clean profit). …

3. A typical album released by a major label often costs in excess of $300,000 to record plus an advance to the artists which often runs in the hundreds of thousands of dollars. In addition, for each CD released, a major label typically spends, in the aggregate, several hundred thousand dollars on marketing, promotion, and publicity (e.g., print, TV, and radio advertising, videos, independent radio promotion services, etc.), distribution and tour support for the artist. In total, the overall costs incurred in connection with a single album released by a major often runs well over a $1,000,000. Based on the odds set forth in Paragraph 2, above, it is highly unlikely that the label ever breaks even on its investment. …[21]

A.   Finances in the Recording Industry

Please add the following to Notes and Questions at page 472:

c. Despite the impression that contracts in the music business are seldom followed and rarely enforced, there can be tremendous costs for failing to abide by a contract or at least making the effort to renegotiate a new arrangement. In *Smith v. Positive Prods.*, 419 F. Supp. 2d 437 (S.D.N.Y. 2005) the district court allowed the enforcement of an arbitration provision against Jonathan "Lil Jon" Smith for twice failing to participate in a concert tour in Japan. Positive Productions, the Japanese concert promotion company, received $ 379,874 in an arbitration held under the American Arbitration Association rules. Lil Jon ignored the arbitration proceeding, but he was unsuccessful in vacating the judgment.

---

[20] *Midwest Art, Entertainment & Sports Law Institute – Signing and Developing Artists in a Download Economy*, MSBA Art & Entertainment Law Section, Minnesota State Bar Association, July 9, 2004.
[21] *Id.*

B. Producers and Copyright Ownership

Please add the following to Notes and Questions at page 481:

g. *Di minimis* sampling has been given a blow as the Sixth Circuit adopted a bright-line test that bars all sampling of unlicensed sound recordings. The Court's assessment was clear and absolute:

> If you cannot pirate the whole sound recording, can you "lift" or "sample" something less than the whole. Our answer to that question is in the negative. ... To begin with, there is ease of enforcement. Get a license or do not sample. We do not see this as stifling creativity in any significant way. It must be remembered that if an artist wants to incorporate a "riff" from another work in his or her recording, he is free to duplicate the sound of that "riff" in the studio. Second, the market will control the license price and keep it within bounds. The sound recording copyright holder cannot exact a license fee greater than what it would cost the person seeking the license to just duplicate the sample in the course of making the new recording. Third, sampling is never accidental. It is not like the case of a composer who has a melody in his head, perhaps not even realizing that the reason he hears this melody is that it is the work of another which he had heard before. When you sample a sound recording you know you are taking another's work product.

Bridgeport Music, Inc. v. Dimension Films, 401 F.3d 647, 657-58 (6th Cir. 2004), *aff'd and amended after rehearing*, 410 F.3d 792 (6th Cir. 2005).

h. Can one sell a sound recording and still exploit the underlying composition? Not through litigation. The distinction between these two aspects of a song tested the differing standards for sound recordings and the underlying musical compositions. To the extent that these standards can be compared, see *Newton v. Diamond*, 388 F.3d 1189 (9th Cir. 2004), *cert. denied*, 545 U.S. 1114 (2005).

i. When does a producer's claim of copyright ownership in the master recordings accrue? See *Diamond v. Gillis*, 357 F. Supp. 2d 1003 (E.D. Mich. 2005).

j. For a discussion of the ownership of sound master copyrights and infringement of sound recording prior to the federal copyright protection in 1972, see *Capitol Records, Inc. v. Naxos of Am., Inc. (USCOA)*, Copyright L. Rep. (CCH) ¶ 28,980, 74 U.S.P.Q. 2d (BNA) 1331 (N.Y. 2005).

D. Promotion and Exploitation of the Recording Artist

Please add the following to Notes and Questions at page 503:

e. In many cases, the recording artists deliver more songs than the number of cuts that are included on the album or CD. What happens to those previously unreleased songs? Can the record label create new albums out of unreleased songs, or should unpublished sound recordings expire after a reasonable period of time? See *Levert v. Phila. Int'l Records*, No. No. 04-1489, 2004 U.S. Dist. LEXIS 11825 (E.D. Pa. April 9, 2004) ("Plaintiffs Edward Levert and Walter Williams are singers and performers who form the musical group known as The O'Jays. The O'Jays have been recording music for more than forty years and ... recorded more than fifty records, including nine "platinum records" and ten "gold records."").

F.   Accountability under Recording Contracts

Please add the following to Notes and Questions at page 503:

e. Despite contract language limiting the audit of books to one year, misleading royalty statements may trigger the delayed discovery doctrine and toll the time provided under the contract. See *Weatherly v. Universal Music Publishing Group*, 125 Cal. App. 4th 913, 23 Cal. Rptr. 3d 157 (2004).

CHAPTER XIII: MUSIC PIRACY & TECHNOLOGY

C.   Unauthorized Distribution Using Peer-To-Peer File Sharing

Please replace MGM Studios, Inc. v. Grokster, Ltd. with the following case at page 563:

MGM Studios, Inc. v. Grokster Ltd.

545 U.S. 913 (2005)

JUSTICE SOUTER delivered the opinion of the Court.

The question is under what circumstances the distributor of a product capable of both lawful and unlawful use is liable for acts of copyright infringement by third parties using the product. We hold that one who distributes a device with the object of promoting its use to infringe copyright, as shown by clear expression or other affirmative steps taken to foster infringement, is liable for the resulting acts of infringement by third parties.

Respondents, Grokster, Ltd., and StreamCast Networks, Inc., defendants in the trial court, distribute free software products that allow computer users to share electronic files through peer-to-peer networks, so called because users' computers communicate directly with each other, not through central servers. The advantage of peer-to-peer networks over information networks of other types shows up in their substantial and growing popularity. Because they need no central computer server to mediate the exchange of information or files among users, the high-bandwidth communications capacity for a server may be dispensed with, and the need for costly server storage space is eliminated. Since copies of a file (particularly a popular one) are available on many users' computers, file requests and retrievals may be faster than on other types of networks, and since file exchanges do not travel through a server, communications can take place between any computers that remain connected to the network without risk that a glitch in the server will disable the network in its entirety. Given these benefits in security, cost, and efficiency, peer-to-peer networks are employed to store and distribute electronic files by universities, government agencies, corporations, and libraries, among others.[22]

Other users of peer-to-peer networks include individual recipients of Grokster's and StreamCast's software, and although the networks that they enjoy through using the software can be used to share any type of digital file, they have prominently employed those networks in sharing copyrighted music and video files without authorization. A group of copyright holders (MGM for short, but including motion picture studios, recording companies, songwriters, and music publishers) sued Grokster and StreamCast for their users' copyright infringements, alleging that they knowingly and intentionally distributed their software to enable users to reproduce and distribute the copyrighted works in violation of the Copyright Act, 17 U.S.C. § 101 et seq. (2000 ed. and Supp. II). MGM sought damages and an injunction.

Discovery during the litigation revealed the way the software worked, the business aims of each defendant company, and the predilections of the users. Grokster's eponymous software

---

[22] Peer-to-peer networks have disadvantages as well. Searches on peer-to-peer networks may not reach and uncover all available files because search requests may not be transmitted to every computer on the network. There may be redundant copies of popular files. The creator of the software has no incentive to minimize storage or bandwidth consumption, the costs of which are borne by every user of the network. Most relevant here, it is more difficult to control the content of files available for retrieval and the behavior of users

employs what is known as FastTrack technology, a protocol developed by others and licensed to Grokster. StreamCast distributes a very similar product except that its software, called Morpheus, relies on what is known as Gnutella technology. A user who downloads and installs either software possesses the protocol to send requests for files directly to the computers of others using software compatible with FastTrack or Gnutella. On the FastTrack network opened by the Grokster software, the user's request goes to a computer given an indexing capacity by the software and designated a supernode, or to some other computer with comparable power and capacity to collect temporary indexes of the files available on the computers of users connected to it. The supernode (or indexing computer) searches its own index and may communicate the search request to other supernodes. If the file is found, the supernode discloses its location to the computer requesting it, and the requesting user can download the file directly from the computer located. The copied file is placed in a designated sharing folder on the requesting user's computer, where it is available for other users to download in turn, along with any other file in that folder.

In the Gnutella network made available by Morpheus, the process is mostly the same, except that in some versions of the Gnutella protocol there are no supernodes. ...

Although Grokster and StreamCast do not therefore know when particular files are copied, a few searches using their software would show what is available on the networks the software reaches. MGM commissioned a statistician to conduct a systematic search, and his study showed that nearly 90% of the files available for download on the FastTrack system were copyrighted works.[23] Grokster and StreamCast dispute this figure, raising methodological problems and arguing that free copying even of copyrighted works may be authorized by the rightholders. They also argue that potential noninfringing uses of their software are significant in kind, even if infrequent in practice. Some musical performers, for example, have gained new audiences by distributing their copyrighted works for free across peer-to-peer networks, and some distributors of unprotected content have used peer-to-peer networks to disseminate files, Shakespeare being an example. Indeed, StreamCast has given Morpheus users the opportunity to download the briefs in this very case, though their popularity has not been quantified.

As for quantification, the parties' anecdotal and statistical evidence entered thus far to show the content available on the FastTrack and Gnutella networks does not say much about which files are actually downloaded by users, and no one can say how often the software is used to obtain copies of unprotected material. But MGM's evidence gives reason to think that the vast majority of users' downloads are acts of infringement, and because well over 100 million copies of the software in question are known to have been downloaded, and billions of files are shared across the FastTrack and Gnutella networks each month, the probable scope of copyright infringement is staggering.

Grokster and StreamCast concede the infringement in most downloads, and it is uncontested that they are aware that users employ their software primarily to download copyrighted files, even if the decentralized FastTrack and Gnutella networks fail to reveal which files are being copied, and when. From time to time, moreover, the companies have learned about their users' infringement directly, as from users who have sent e-mail to each company with questions about

---

[23] By comparison, evidence introduced by the plaintiffs in A & M Records, Inc. v. Napster, Inc., 239 F.3d 1004 (9th Cir. 2001), showed that 87% of files available on the Napster filesharing network were copyrighted, *id.* at 1013.

playing copyrighted movies they had downloaded, to whom the companies have responded with guidance. And MGM notified the companies of 8 million copyrighted files that could be obtained using their software.

Grokster and StreamCast are not, however, merely passive recipients of information about infringing use. The record is replete with evidence that from the moment Grokster and StreamCast began to distribute their free software, each one clearly voiced the objective that recipients use it to download copyrighted works, and each took active steps to encourage infringement.

After the notorious file-sharing service, Napster, was sued by copyright holders for facilitation of copyright infringement, StreamCast gave away a software program of a kind known as OpenNap, designed as compatible with the Napster program and open to Napster users for downloading files from other Napster and OpenNap users' computers. Evidence indicates that "it was always [StreamCast's] intent to use [its OpenNap network] to be able to capture email addresses of [its] initial target market so that [it] could promote [its] StreamCast Morpheus interface to them," indeed, the OpenNap program was engineered "'to leverage Napster's 50 million user base.'"

StreamCast monitored both the number of users downloading its OpenNap program and the number of music files they downloaded. It also used the resulting OpenNap network to distribute copies of the Morpheus software and to encourage users to adopt it. Internal company documents indicate that StreamCast hoped to attract large numbers of former Napster users if that company was shut down by court order or otherwise, and that StreamCast planned to be the next Napster. A kit developed by StreamCast to be delivered to advertisers, for example, contained press articles about StreamCast's potential to capture former Napster users, and it introduced itself to some potential advertisers as a company "which is similar to what Napster was." It broadcast banner advertisements to users of other Napster-compatible software, urging them to adopt its OpenNap. An internal e-mail from a company executive stated: "'We have put this network in place so that when Napster pulls the plug on their free service . . . or if the Court orders them shut down prior to that . . . we will be positioned to capture the flood of their 32 million users that will be actively looking for an alternative.'"

Thus, StreamCast developed promotional materials to market its service as the best Napster alternative. One proposed advertisement read: "Napster Inc. has announced that it will soon begin charging you a fee. That's if the courts don't order it shut down first. What will you do to get around it?" Another proposed ad touted StreamCast's software as the "# 1 alternative to Napster" and asked "when the lights went off at Napster . . . where did the users go?" StreamCast even planned to flaunt the illegal uses of its software; when it launched the OpenNap network, the chief technology officer of the company averred that "the goal is to get in trouble with the law and get sued. It's the best way to get in the news."

The evidence that Grokster sought to capture the market of former Napster users is sparser but revealing, for Grokster launched its own OpenNap system called Swaptor and inserted digital codes into its Web site so that computer users using Web search engines to look for "Napster" or "free filesharing" would be directed to the Grokster Web site, where they could download the Grokster software. And Grokster's name is an apparent derivative of Napster.

StreamCast's executives monitored the number of songs by certain commercial artists available on their networks, and an internal communication indicates they aimed to have a larger number of copyrighted songs available on their networks than other file-sharing networks. The point, of course, would be to attract users of a mind to infringe, just as it would be with their promotional materials developed showing copyrighted songs as examples of the kinds of files available through Morpheus. Morpheus in fact allowed users to search specifically for "Top 40" songs, which were inevitably copyrighted. Similarly, Grokster sent users a newsletter promoting its ability to provide particular, popular copyrighted materials.

In addition to this evidence of express promotion, marketing, and intent to promote further, the business models employed by Grokster and StreamCast confirm that their principal object was use of their software to download copyrighted works. Grokster and StreamCast receive no revenue from users, who obtain the software itself for nothing. Instead, both companies generate income by selling advertising space, and they stream the advertising to Grokster and Morpheus users while they are employing the programs. As the number of users of each program increases, advertising opportunities become worth more. While there is doubtless some demand for free Shakespeare, the evidence shows that substantive volume is a function of free access to copyrighted work. Users seeking Top 40 songs, for example, or the latest release by Modest Mouse, are certain to be far more numerous than those seeking a free Decameron, and Grokster and StreamCast translated that demand into dollars.

Finally, there is no evidence that either company made an effort to filter copyrighted material from users' downloads or otherwise impede the sharing of copyrighted files. Although Grokster appears to have sent e-mails warning users about infringing content when it received threatening notice from the copyright holders, it never blocked anyone from continuing to use its software to share copyrighted files. StreamCast not only rejected another company's offer of help to monitor infringement, but blocked the Internet Protocol addresses of entities it believed were trying to engage in such monitoring on its networks. …

The District Court held that those who used the Grokster and Morpheus software to download copyrighted media files directly infringed MGM's copyrights, a conclusion not contested on appeal, but the court nonetheless granted summary judgment in favor of Grokster and StreamCast as to any liability arising from distribution of the then current versions of their software. Distributing that software gave rise to no liability in the court's view, because its use did not provide the distributors with actual knowledge of specific acts of infringement.

The Court of Appeals affirmed. 380 F.3d 1154 (9th Cir. 2004). In the court's analysis, a defendant was liable as a contributory infringer when it had knowledge of direct infringement and materially contributed to the infringement. But the court read *Sony Corp. of America v. Universal City Studios, Inc.*, 464 U.S. 417 (1984), as holding that distribution of a commercial product capable of substantial noninfringing uses could not give rise to contributory liability for infringement unless the distributor had actual knowledge of specific instances of infringement and failed to act on that knowledge. The fact that the software was capable of substantial noninfringing uses in the Ninth Circuit's view meant that Grokster and StreamCast were not liable, because they had no such actual knowledge, owing to the decentralized architecture of their software. The court also held that Grokster and StreamCast did not materially contribute to their users' infringement because it was the users themselves who searched for, retrieved, and stored the infringing files, with no involvement by the defendants beyond providing the software in the first place.

The Ninth Circuit also considered whether Grokster and StreamCast could be liable under a theory of vicarious infringement. The court held against liability because the defendants did not monitor or control the use of the software, had no agreed-upon right or current ability to supervise its use, and had no independent duty to police infringement. …

MGM and many of the *amici* fault the Court of Appeals' holding for upsetting a sound balance between the respective values of supporting creative pursuits through copyright protection and promoting innovation in new communication technologies by limiting the incidence of liability for copyright infringement. The more artistic protection is favored, the more technological innovation may be discouraged; the administration of copyright law is an exercise in managing the trade-off.

The tension between the two values is the subject of this case, with its claim that digital distribution of copyrighted material threatens copyright holders as never before, because every copy is identical to the original, copying is easy, and many people (especially the young) use file-sharing software to download copyrighted works. This very breadth of the software's use may well draw the public directly into the debate over copyright policy… As the case has been presented to us, these fears are said to be offset by the different concern that imposing liability, not only on infringers but on distributors of software based on its potential for unlawful use, could limit further development of beneficial technologies.

The argument for imposing indirect liability in this case is, however, a powerful one, given the number of infringing downloads that occur every day using StreamCast's and Grokster's software. When a widely shared service or product is used to commit infringement, it may be impossible to enforce rights in the protected work effectively against all direct infringers, the only practical alternative being to go against the distributor of the copying device for secondary liability on a theory of contributory or vicarious infringement.

One infringes contributorily by intentionally inducing or encouraging direct infringement, and infringes vicariously by profiting from direct infringement while declining to exercise a right to stop or limit it.[24] Although "the Copyright Act does not expressly render anyone liable for infringement committed by another," *Sony Corp. v. Universal City Studios*, 464 U.S. at 434. …

[W]here an article is "good for nothing else" but infringement, there is no legitimate public interest in its unlicensed availability, and there is no injustice in presuming or imputing an intent to infringe. Conversely, the doctrine absolves the equivocal conduct of selling an item with

---

[24] We stated in *Sony Corp. of America v. Universal City Studios, Inc.*, 464 U.S. 417 (1984), that "'the lines between direct infringement, contributory infringement and vicarious liability are not clearly drawn' …. Reasoned analysis of [the Sony plaintiffs' contributory infringement claim] necessarily entails consideration of arguments and case law which may also be forwarded under the other labels, and indeed the parties … rely upon such arguments and authority in support of their respective positions on the issue of contributory infringement," *id.* at 435, n.17 (quoting *Universal City Studios, Inc. v. Sony Corp.*, 480 F. Supp. 429, 457-458 (C.D. Cal. 1979)). In the present case MGM has argued a vicarious liability theory, which allows imposition of liability when the defendant profits directly from the infringement and has a right and ability to supervise the direct infringer, even if the defendant initially lacks knowledge of the infringement. Because we resolve the case based on an inducement theory, there is no need to analyze separately MGM's vicarious liability theory.

substantial lawful as well as unlawful uses, and limits liability to instances of more acute fault than the mere understanding that some of one's products will be misused. It leaves breathing room for innovation and a vigorous commerce.

The parties and many of the *amici* in this case think the key to resolving it is the *Sony* rule and, in particular, what it means for a product to be "capable of commercially significant noninfringing uses." MGM advances the argument that granting summary judgment to Grokster and StreamCast as to their current activities gave too much weight to the value of innovative technology, and too little to the copyrights infringed by users of their software, given that 90% of works available on one of the networks was shown to be copyrighted. Assuming the remaining 10% to be its noninfringing use, MGM says this should not qualify as "substantial," and the Court should quantify *Sony* to the extent of holding that a product used "principally" for infringement does not qualify. As mentioned before, Grokster and StreamCast reply by citing evidence that their software can be used to reproduce public domain works, and they point to copyright holders who actually encourage copying. Even if infringement is the principal practice with their software today, they argue, the noninfringing uses are significant and will grow.

We agree with MGM that the Court of Appeals misapplied *Sony*, which it read as limiting secondary liability quite beyond the circumstances to which the case applied. *Sony* barred secondary liability based on presuming or imputing intent to cause infringement solely from the design or distribution of a product capable of substantial lawful use, which the distributor knows is in fact used for infringement. The Ninth Circuit has read *Sony*'s limitation to mean that whenever a product is capable of substantial lawful use, the producer can never be held contributorily liable for third parties' infringing use of it; it read the rule as being this broad, even when an actual purpose to cause infringing use is shown by evidence independent of design and distribution of the product, unless the distributors had "specific knowledge of infringement at a time at which they contributed to the infringement, and failed to act upon that information." Because the Circuit found the StreamCast and Grokster software capable of substantial lawful use, it concluded on the basis of its reading of *Sony* that neither company could be held liable, since there was no showing that their software, being without any central server, afforded them knowledge of specific unlawful uses.

This view of *Sony*, however, was error, converting the case from one about liability resting on imputed intent to one about liability on any theory. Because *Sony* did not displace other theories of secondary liability, and because we find below that it was error to grant summary judgment to the companies on MGM's inducement claim, we do not revisit *Sony* further, as MGM requests, to add a more quantified description of the point of balance between protection and commerce when liability rests solely on distribution with knowledge that unlawful use will occur. It is enough to note that the Ninth Circuit's judgment rested on an erroneous understanding of *Sony* and to leave further consideration of the *Sony* rule for a day when that may be required.

Sony's rule limits imputing culpable intent as a matter of law from the characteristics or uses of a distributed product. But nothing in *Sony* requires courts to ignore evidence of intent if there is such evidence, and the case was never meant to foreclose rules of fault-based liability derived from the common law. Thus, where evidence goes beyond a product's characteristics or the knowledge that it may be put to infringing uses, and shows statements or actions directed to promoting infringement, *Sony*'s staple-article rule will not preclude liability.

The classic case of direct evidence of unlawful purpose occurs when one induces commission of infringement by another, or "entices or persuades another" to infringe, Black's Law Dictionary 790 (8th ed. 2004), as by advertising. Thus at common law a copyright or patent defendant who "not only expected but invoked [infringing use] by advertisement" was liable for infringement "on principles recognized in every part of the law."

The rule on inducement of infringement as developed in the early cases is no different today.[25] Evidence of "active steps . . . taken to encourage direct infringement," such as advertising an infringing use or instructing how to engage in an infringing use, show an affirmative intent that the product be used to infringe, and a showing that infringement was encouraged overcomes the law's reluctance to find liability when a defendant merely sells a commercial product suitable for some lawful use.

For the same reasons that *Sony* took the staple-article doctrine of patent law as a model for its copyright safe-harbor rule, the inducement rule, too, is a sensible one for copyright. We adopt it here, holding that one who distributes a device with the object of promoting its use to infringe copyright, as shown by clear expression or other affirmative steps taken to foster infringement, is liable for the resulting acts of infringement by third parties. We are, of course, mindful of the need to keep from trenching on regular commerce or discouraging the development of technologies with lawful and unlawful potential. Accordingly, just as *Sony* did not find intentional inducement despite the knowledge of the VCR manufacturer that its device could be used to infringe, mere knowledge of infringing potential or of actual infringing uses would not be enough here to subject a distributor to liability. Nor would ordinary acts incident to product distribution, such as offering customers technical support or product updates, support liability in themselves. The inducement rule, instead, premises liability on purposeful, culpable expression and conduct, and thus does nothing to compromise legitimate commerce or discourage innovation having a lawful promise.

The only apparent question about treating MGM's evidence as sufficient to withstand summary judgment under the theory of inducement goes to the need on MGM's part to adduce evidence that StreamCast and Grokster communicated an inducing message to their software users. The classic instance of inducement is by advertisement or solicitation that broadcasts a message designed to stimulate others to commit violations. …

In StreamCast's case, of course, the evidence just described was supplemented by other unequivocal indications of unlawful purpose in the internal communications and advertising designs aimed at Napster users ("When the lights went off at Napster . . . where did the users go?") Whether the messages were communicated is not to the point on this record. The function of the message in the theory of inducement is to prove by a defendant's own statements that his unlawful purpose disqualifies him from claiming protection (and incidentally to point to actual violators likely to be found among those who hear or read the message). Proving that a message was sent out, then, is the preeminent but not exclusive way of showing that active steps were taken with the purpose of bringing about infringing acts, and of showing that infringing acts took place by using the device distributed. Here, the summary judgment record is replete with other evidence that Grokster and StreamCast, unlike the manufacturer and distributor in *Sony*, acted with a purpose to cause copyright violations by use of software suitable for illegal use.

---

[25] Inducement has been codified in patent law. *Ibid.*

Three features of this evidence of intent are particularly notable. First, each company showed itself to be aiming to satisfy a known source of demand for copyright infringement, the market comprising former Napster users. StreamCast's internal documents made constant reference to Napster, it initially distributed its Morpheus software through an OpenNap program compatible with Napster, it advertised its OpenNap program to Napster users, and its Morpheus software functions as Napster did except that it could be used to distribute more kinds of files, including copyrighted movies and software programs. Grokster's name is apparently derived from Napster, it too initially offered an OpenNap program, its software's function is likewise comparable to Napster's, and it attempted to divert queries for Napster onto its own Web site. Grokster and StreamCast's efforts to supply services to former Napster users, deprived of a mechanism to copy and distribute what were overwhelmingly infringing files, indicate a principal, if not exclusive, intent on the part of each to bring about infringement.

Second, this evidence of unlawful objective is given added significance by MGM's showing that neither company attempted to develop filtering tools or other mechanisms to diminish the infringing activity using their software. While the Ninth Circuit treated the defendants' failure to develop such tools as irrelevant because they lacked an independent duty to monitor their users' activity, we think this evidence underscores Grokster's and StreamCast's intentional facilitation of their users' infringement.[26]

Third, there is a further complement to the direct evidence of unlawful objective. It is useful to recall that StreamCast and Grokster make money by selling advertising space, by directing ads to the screens of computers employing their software. As the record shows, the more the software is used, the more ads are sent out and the greater the advertising revenue becomes. Since the extent of the software's use determines the gain to the distributors, the commercial sense of their enterprise turns on high-volume use, which the record shows is infringing. This evidence alone would not justify an inference of unlawful intent, but viewed in the context of the entire record its import is clear.

The unlawful objective is unmistakable. …

In sum, this case is significantly different from *Sony* and reliance on that case to rule in favor of StreamCast and Grokster was error. *Sony* dealt with a claim of liability based solely on distributing a product with alternative lawful and unlawful uses, with knowledge that some users would follow the unlawful course. The case struck a balance between the interests of protection and innovation by holding that the product's capability of substantial lawful employment should bar the imputation of fault and consequent secondary liability for the unlawful acts of others. …

There is substantial evidence in MGM's favor on all elements of inducement, and summary judgment in favor of Grokster and StreamCast was error. On remand, reconsideration of MGM's motion for summary judgment will be in order. The judgment of the Court of Appeals is vacated, and the case is remanded for further proceedings consistent with this opinion.

---

[26] Of course, in the absence of other evidence of intent, a court would be unable to find contributory infringement liability merely based on a failure to take affirmative steps to prevent infringement, if the device otherwise was capable of substantial noninfringing uses. Such a holding would tread too close to the *Sony* safe harbor.

[The precise role of *Sony* continues to be debated. The Court split between concurrences by Justices Ginsburg and Breyer on whether Grokster's product is "capable of 'substantial' or 'commercially significant' noninfringing uses." Each concurrence had three votes.]

Please add the following to Notes and Questions at page 577:

g. The reframing of *Grokster* to use the "inducement of infringement" doctrine has the potential to separate out interesting new technologies and well-intended companies from those sham enterprises that provide noninfringing activities as a smokescreen for the business of profiting from other parties' copyright infringement.

h. On remand, the district court applied the "inducement doctrine" to the claim. "Plaintiffs need prove only that StreamCast distributed the product with the intent to encourage infringement. Since there is no dispute that StreamCast did distribute an infringement-enabling technology, the inquiry focuses on the defendant's intent, which can be shown by evidence of the defendant's expression or conduct." The district court found sufficient intent and issued the injunction. *MGM Studios, Inc. v. Grokster Ltd.*, 454 F. Supp. 2d 966, 985 (C.D. Cal. 2006).

i. An example of this attempt to distinguish between infringement and technical copyright noncompliance was demonstrated in *Chamberlain Group, Inc. v. Skylink Techs., Inc.*, 292 F. Supp. 2d 1040 (N.D. Ill. 2003), *cert. denied*, 544 U.S. 923 (2005). Here, a garage door manufacturer used encrypted coding to tie its remote door opener to the door mechanism. The court rejected the tying:

> Under Chamberlain's theory, any customer who loses his or her Chamberlain transmitter, but manages to operate the opener either with a non-Chamberlain transmitter or by some other means of circumventing the rolling code, has violated the DMCA. In this court's view, the statute does not require such a conclusion. GDO transmitters are similar to television remote controls in that consumers of both products may need to replace them at some point due to damage or loss, and may program them to work with other devices manufactured by different companies. In both cases, consumers have a reasonable expectation that they can replace the original product with a competing, universal product without violating federal law.

Id. at 1046. The distinction is not grounded in copyright or fair use, but in the reasonable expectations of consumers. While this is a proper outcome, to what extent can consumer expectation provide a guide for common law development of copyright policy?

D. Consumer Services & Electronics

Please add the following to Notes and Questions at page 586:

d. Perhaps one of the fastest growing new media phenomenon is the explosion of Podcasting. Apple Computer and other companies are rushing to create directories and search engines to provide the public a mechanism for accessing this growing, low-cost distribution channel. This grassroots medium may become the new leading edge for content development, and as a result it will be closely watched by the large media companies for trends and future stars. See Nick Wingfield, *Podcasting for Dummies, Apple's iTunes Adds Directory of Internet Audio Programs, Boosting Fledgling Technology*, WALL ST. J., June 29, 2005 at D1.

E. Digital Audio Transmissions

Please add the following after Webcasting Rates and Terms for Statutory License at page 594:

Music Licensing Reform

Statement of Marybeth Peters
The Register of Copyrights before the Subcommittee
on Intellectual Property, Committee on the Judiciary, United States Senate
109th Congress, 1st Session July 12, 2005.[27]

Section 115 governs the compulsory licensing of the reproduction and distribution rights for nondramatic musical works by means of physical phonorecords and digital phonorecord deliveries. This compulsory license has been in effect for 96 years. However, the means to provide music to the public have changed radically in the last decade, necessitating changes in the law to protect the rights of copyright owners while at the same time meeting the needs of the users in a digital world. The present language of section 115 is outdated, particularly as applied to the online environment. Reform is necessary not only to promote the availability of a wide variety of music to the listening public, but also to assist in the music industry's continuing fight against piracy. ...

Evolution of the Compulsory Mechanical License

1. Mechanical Licensing under the 1909 Copyright Act

Starting in 1905, copyright owners began seeking legislative changes which would grant them the exclusive right to authorize the mechanical reproduction of their works. The impetus for this movement was the emergence of the player piano and the ambiguity surrounding the extent of copyright owners' right to control the making of copies of their works on piano rolls. Then, in 1908, the Supreme Court held in *White-Smith Publishing Co. v. Apollo Co.*[28] that perforated piano rolls were not "copies" under the copyright statute in force at that time, but rather parts of devices which performed the work. This decision spurred Congress to take action and, in 1909, Congress granted copyright owners' wish in part by adding to the Copyright Act the right, but not an exclusive right, for copyright owners to make and distribute, or authorize others to make and distribute, mechanical reproductions (known today as phonorecords) of their nondramatic musical works.[29]

However, due to concerns about potential monopolistic behavior, Congress also created a compulsory license to allow anyone to make and distribute a mechanical reproduction of a nondramatic musical work without the consent of the copyright owner provided that the person

---

[27] Available at http://www.copyright.gov/docs/regstat071205.html.

[28] 209 U.S. 1 (1908).

[29] The music industry construed the reference in Section 1(e) of the 1909 Act as referring only to a nondramatic musical work as opposed to music contained in dramatico-musical works. See, Melville B. Nimmer, Nimmer on Copyright § 16.4 (1976). Congress expressly incorporated this interpretation into the law with the adoption of the 1976 Act. 17 U.S.C. § 115(a)(1). It is important to keep in mind that a "musical work" refers to a composition (e.g., the specification of notes and lyrics, such as written on a page of sheet music) while a "sound recording" refers to the fixation of a particular performance of a composition such as on an audio compact disc. However, to reproduce a recorded song, one needs to obtain licenses both as to the musical work as well as to the sound recording.

adhered to the provisions of the license, most notably paying a statutorily established royalty to the copyright owner. Section 1(e) of the 1909 Act allowed any person to make "similar use" of the nondramatic musical work upon payment of a royalty of two cents for "each such part manufactured." However, no one could take advantage of the compulsory license until the copyright owner had authorized the first mechanical reproduction of the work. ... The license had the effect of capping the amount of money a composer could receive for the mechanical reproduction of his work. The two cent rate set in 1909 remained in effect until January 1, 1978, and acted as a ceiling for the rate in privately negotiated licenses. Such stringent requirements for use of the compulsory license did not foster wide use of the license. ... [U]p to this day, the Copyright Office receives very few notices of intention.

2. The Mechanical License under the 1976 Copyright Act

... Congress adopted a number of new conditions and clarifications in section 115 of the Copyright Act of 1976, including:

- making the license available only after a phonorecord has been distributed to the public in the United States with the authority of the copyright owner and only to someone whose primary intent is to distribute phonorecords to the public for private use (§ 115(a)(1));

- disallowing the duplication of a sound recording embodying the nondramatic musical work without the authorization of the copyright owner of the sound recording (§ 115(a)(1));

- allowing for the rearrangement of a nondramatic musical work "to the extent necessary to conform it to the style or manner of the interpretation of the performance involved," provided that the rearrangement "does not change the basic melody or fundamental character of the work" (§ 115(a)(2));

- allowing a licensee to file its notice of intention with the Copyright Office in the case where the public records of the Copyright Office do not identify the copyright owner and include an address (§ 115(b)(1));

- requiring service of the notice of intention on the copyright owner "before or within thirty days after making, and before distributing any phonorecords of the work" (§ 115(b)(1));

- requiring payment only on those made[30] and distributed[31] after the copyright owner is identified in the registration or other public records of the Copyright Office (§ 115(c)(1));[32]

---

[30] Congress intended the term "made" "to be broader than 'manufactured' and to include within its scope every possible manufacturing or other process capable of reproducing a sound recording in phonorecords." H. Rep. No. 1476, at 110 (1976). Although originally enacted to address the reproduction of musical compositions on perforated player piano rolls, the compulsory license has for most of the past century been used primarily for the making and distribution of phonorecords and, more recently, for the digital delivery of music online.

[31] For purposes of section 115, "the concept of 'distribution' comprises any act by which the person exercising the compulsory license voluntarily relinquishes possession of a phonorecord (considered as a fungible unit), regardless of whether the distribution is to the public, passes title, constitutes a gift, or is sold, rented, leased, or loaned, unless it is actually returned and the transaction cancelled." *Id.*

[32] This provision replaced the earlier requirement in the 1909 law that a copyright owner must file a notice of use with the Copyright Office in order to be eligible to receive royalties generated under the compulsory license.

- establishment of an independent rate setting body to adjust the rates;[33] and

- allowing for termination of the license for failure to pay monthly royalties if a user fails to make payment within thirty days of the receipt of a written notice from the copyright owner advising the user of the default (§ 115(c)(6)). …

3. The Digital Performance Right in Sound Recordings Act of 1995

By 1995, Congress recognized that "digital transmission of sound recordings [was] likely to become a very important outlet for the performance of recorded music."[34] Moreover, it realized that "[t]hese new technologies also may lead to new systems for the electronic distribution of phonorecords with the authorization of the affected copyright owners."[35] For these reasons, Congress made further changes to section 115 to meet the challenges of providing music in a digital format when it enacted the Digital Performance Right in Sound Recordings Act of 1995 ("DPRA"), Pub. L. 104-39, 109 Stat. 336.[36] The amendments to section 115 clarified the reproduction and distribution rights of copyright owners of musical works as well as clarifying the role of producers and distributors of sound recordings, especially with respect to what the amended section 115 termed "digital phonorecord deliveries." Specifically, Congress wanted to reaffirm the mechanical rights of songwriters and music publishers in the new world of digital technology.

To accomplish this goal, Congress expanded the scope of the compulsory license to include the making and distribution by means of digital transmissions of phonorecords and, in doing so, adopted a new term of art, the "digital phonorecord delivery" ("DPD"), to describe the delivery to a consumer of a phonorecord by means of a digital transmission, which requires the payment of a statutory royalty under section 115. …

The Need for Reform

At its inception, the compulsory license facilitated the availability of music to the listening public. However, the evolution of technology and business practices has eroded the effectiveness of this provision. Despite several attempts to amend the compulsory license and the Copyright Office's regulations[37] in order to keep pace with advancements in the music industry and in technology, the use of the section 115 compulsory license, other than as a de facto ceiling on privately negotiated rates, has remained at an almost non-existent level. …

---

[33] In 1993, Congress passed the Copyright Royalty Tribunal Reform Act of 1993, Pub. L. No. 103-198, 107 Stat. 2304, which eliminated the Copyright Royalty Tribunal and replaced it with a system of ad hoc Copyright Arbitration Royalty Panels (CARPs) administered by the Librarian of Congress. Late last year, Congress passed the Copyright Royalty and Distribution Reform Act of 2004, Pub. L. No. 108-419, 118 Stat. 2341,which replaced the CARP system with three full-time Copyright Royalty Judges appointed by the Librarian of Congress.

[34] S. Rep. No. 104-128, at 14 (1995).

[35] *Id.*

[36] The DRPA also granted copyright owners of sound recordings an exclusive right to perform their works publicly by means of a digital audio transmission, 17 U.S.C. § 106(6), subject to certain limitations. See, 17 U.S.C. § 114.

[37] See Notice and Recordkeeping for Making and Distributing Phonorecords, 64 Fed. Reg. 41286 (1999); Mechanical and Digital Phonorecord Delivery Compulsory License, 66 Fed. Reg. 14099 (2001); Compulsory License for Making and Distributing Phonorecords, Including Digital Phonorecord Deliveries, 66 Fed. Reg. 45241 (2001); Compulsory License for Making and Distributing Phonorecords, Including Digital Phonorecord Deliveries, 69 Fed. Reg. 34578 (2004).

Two of the issues highlighted at that hearing – issues that we at the Copyright Office have been hearing about for several years – involve problems arising when online music services wish to license activities that involve both reproduction and public performance, leading to demands for payment to two separate agents for the same copyright owner (i.e., the "double-dipping" concern); and the contrast between the relatively efficient licensing process for performance rights and the unsatisfactory process for licensing reproduction and distribution rights. While the three performing rights societies – the American Society of Composers, Authors and Publishers ("ASCAP"), Broadcast Music, Inc. ("BMI") and SESAC, Inc. – collectively are able to license public performances of virtually all nondramatic musical works, a significant percentage of nondramatic musical works cannot be licensed from the main licensing agent for the reproduction and distribution rights – the Harry Fox Agency, Inc. ("HFA"). For this and other reasons, some of which I will address below, online music services that wish to obtain licenses to make available as many nondramatic musical works as possible find it impossible to obtain the necessary reproduction and distribution rights. ...

Proposed Legislative Solutions

Any solution to the crisis in music licensing must make it easy for licensees to obtain, from a single source or at least a manageable number of sources, all the necessary rights for all the musical compositions licensees wish to offer to the public. Such "one-stop shopping" is essentially available today with respect to performance rights.[38] However, nothing approaching "one-stop shopping" exists with respect to reproduction and distribution rights. And as noted above, a music service must obtain separate licenses for (1) the performance and (2) the reproduction and distribution of the same musical works, even when the performance, reproduction and distribution all take place in the course of a single transmission. True "one-stop shopping" would involve (1) all the musical compositions one wishes to license, and (2) all necessary rights one wishes to license.

As I see it, there are two ways to accomplish such "one-stop shopping." First, a solution along the lines of our discussions last year, transforming the section 115 compulsory license into a section 114-style blanket license with royalty payments funneled through a single designated agent could simplify the licensing process. Alternatively, the section 115 compulsory license could be abandoned – at least with respect to digital phonorecord deliveries – and replaced with a system of collective licensing similar to systems in place in many other countries. ...

1. Expansion of the Section 115 Compulsory License

a. A Blanket Compulsory License

Section 114 of the Copyright Act may provide a useful model for licensing of reproduction and distribution of nondramatic musical works. Under section 114, an eligible music service may obtain a license to transmit certain kinds of performances of all sound recordings by filing a single notice of intent to use the statutory license with the Copyright Office. Royalty rates and terms of payments are established by the Copyright Royalty Judges through the mechanism set

---

[38] In actuality, the performing rights societies - ASCAP, BMI and SESAC - offer "three-stop shopping": A music service that wishes to license the rights to all nondramatic musical compositions must obtain a license from each of the three societies. But that has not proved to be a significant burden with respect to the licensing of performance rights.

forth in Chapter 8 of the Copyright Act. The royalty payments are made to a designated agent of copyright owners and performers (currently SoundExchange, which is controlled equally by record companies and performers), which distributes the royalties to the copyright owners and performers.

A similar mechanism under section 115 would permit a digital music service to obtain a license to make digital phonorecord deliveries of any musical composition (or at least of any musical composition that has been distributed to the public in the United States under the authority of the copyright owner; see, 17 U.S.C. § 115(a)(1)) simply by serving or filing a notice of intent to use the statutory license. Royalty payments would be made to a single entity which would then redistribute those royalties to the copyright owners, and the royalty rates and terms of payment would be established under the Copyright Royalty Judge system. ...

The two points of agreement among the interested parties seem to be a desire to have a blanket licensing scheme with one designated agent and a single notice procedure regardless of the number of musical works to be utilized pursuant to the statutory license. I agree with the consensus on these two fundamental points.

One of the main points of contention, however, is the envisioned scope of the compulsory license. ... [A]t a minimum the compulsory license should be clarified to expressly include within its scope all intermediate reproductions of a nondramatic musical work made within the course of any digital phonorecord delivery, including buffer, cache and server copies.[39] ...

Another option to consider is eliminating the section 115 compulsory license and perhaps replacing it with a collective licensing structure. ... The Copyright Office has long taken the position that statutory licenses should be enacted only in exceptional cases, when the marketplace is incapable of working. ... Our compulsory license in the United States is also an anomaly. Virtually all other countries that at one time provided for this compulsory license have eliminated it in favor of private negotiations and collective licensing administration. Many countries permit these organizations to license both the public performance right and the reproduction and distribution rights for a musical composition, thereby creating "one-stop shopping" for music licensees and streamlined royalty processing for copyright owners.[40] (24) ...

b. Simple Repeal of the Compulsory License

Should the concept of free marketplace negotiations for reproduction and distribution rights for nondramatic musical works appear to be desirable, then a variation on this legislative concept might also be worthwhile to explore. One might ask whether it would further benefit the industry as a whole simply to repeal, yet not replace, the section 115 compulsory license. Then reproduction and distribution rights would truly be left to marketplace negotiations. A sunset

---

[39] Technically, these are phonorecords rather than copies, see 17 U.S.C. § 101 (definitions of "copies" and "phonorecords"), but terms such as "buffer copy" and "server copy" have entered common parlance.

[40] See, David Sinacore-Guinn, COLLECTIVE ADMINISTRATION OF COPYRIGHTS AND NEIGHBORING RIGHTS: INTERNATIONAL PRACTICES, PROCEDURES, AND ORGANIZATIONS § 17.9.3 (1993) (citing 45 countries which permit collective licensing organizations to license both rights, including Argentina, Brazil, Chile, France, Germany, Greece, Hong Kong, India, Israel, Italy, Japan, Mexico, South Korea and Spain). The European Union has recently recognized that there may be value in one-stop shopping in the form of EU-wide licensing of online music. See, Huw Jones, *EU Weighs Plan to Help Online Music Marketsource*, Reuters (June 30, 2005), available at http://today.reuters.co.uk/news/newsArticle.aspx?type=internetNews&storyID=005-6-30T04025Z 01_MOR038309_RTRIDST_0_OUKIN-MEDIA-EU-COPYRIGHT.XML, visited July 8, 2005.

period of several years would likely be prudent to permit the industry to develop a smooth transition. My prediction would be that music publishers would voluntarily coalesce into music rights organizations, or perhaps would create a single online clearinghouse (or a handful of such clearinghouses) which would permit one-stop shopping while nevertheless permitting each publisher to set its own rates. It might be wise to couple repeal of section 115 with incentives designed to promote one of these alternatives that would result in one-stop shopping or something close to it. ...

Exemption to Prohibition on Circumvention of Copyright Protection Systems for Access Control Technologies The Recommendation of the Register of Copyrights[41]

The Digital Millennium Copyright Act ("DMCA"), Pub. L. No. 105-304 (1998), was enacted to comply with the WIPO Copyright Treaty (WCT) and WIPO Performances and Phonograms Treaty (WPPT). It established "a wide range of rules that will govern not only copyright owners in the marketplace for electronic commerce, but also consumers, manufacturers, distributors, libraries, educators, and on-line service providers" and "define[d] whether consumers and businesses may engage in certain conduct, or use certain devices, in the course of transacting electronic commerce."

Title I of the Act, which added a new Chapter 12 to Title 17 U.S.C., prohibits circumvention of technological measures employed by or on behalf of copyright owners to protect their works ("access controls"). Specifically, § 1201(a)(1)(A) provides, in part, that "No person shall circumvent a technological measure that effectively controls access to a work protected under this title." In order to ensure that the public will have continued ability to engage in noninfringing uses of copyrighted works, such as fair use, subparagraph (B) limits this prohibition. It provides that the prohibition against circumvention "shall not apply to persons who are users of a copyrighted work which is in a particular class of works, if such persons are, or are likely to be in the succeeding three-year period, adversely affected by virtue of such prohibition in their ability to make noninfringing uses of that particular class of works under this title" as determined in a rulemaking proceeding.

The rulemaking proceeding is conducted by the Register of Copyrights, who is to provide notice of the rulemaking, seek comments from the public, consult with the Assistant Secretary for Communications and Information of the Department of Commerce, and recommend final regulations to the Librarian of Congress. The regulations, to be issued by the Librarian of Congress, announce "any class of copyrighted works for which the Librarian has determined, pursuant to the rulemaking conducted under subparagraph (C), that noninfringing uses by persons who are users of a copyrighted work are, or are likely to be, adversely affected, and the prohibition contained in subparagraph (A) shall not apply to such users with respect to such class of works for the ensuing 3-year period."

---

[41] http://www.copyright.gov/1201/1201_recommendation.html. See Exemption to Prohibition on Circumvention of Copyright Protection Systems for Access Control Technologies 37 C.F.R. 201 (2006).

This is the third § 1201 rulemaking. The first rulemaking culminated in the Librarian's announcement on October 27, 2000, that announced noninfringing users of two classes of works would not be subject to the prohibition against circumvention of access controls.

…

Statement of the Librarian of Congress Relating to Section 1201 Rulemaking[42]

In accordance with section 1201(a)(1) of the copyright law, I am issuing a final rule that sets out six classes of works that will be subject to exemptions for the next three years from the statute's prohibition against circumvention of technology that effectively controls access to a copyrighted work. This is the third time that I have issued such a rule, which the Digital Millennium Copyright Act (DMCA) requires that I do every three years. These exemptions expire after three years, unless proponents prove their case once again. …

It is important to understand the purposes of this rulemaking, as stated in the law, and the role I have in it. This is not a broad evaluation of the successes or failures of the DMCA. The purpose of the proceeding is to determine whether current technologies that control access to copyrighted works are diminishing the ability of individuals to use works in lawful, noninfringing ways. The DMCA does not forbid the act of circumventing copy controls, and therefore this rulemaking proceeding is not about technologies that control copying. Nor is this rulemaking about the ability to make or distribute products or services used for purposes of circumventing access controls, which are governed by a different part of section 1201.

In this rulemaking, 74 individuals or organizations proposed classes of works for exemption (many of them duplicative) and 35 submitted comments on those proposals. The Copyright Office conducted four days of public hearings in March and April: three in Washington and one in Palo Alto, California. Transcripts of the hearings, copies of all of the comments and reply comments, and copies of other information received by the Copyright Office have been posted on the Office's website.

The Register of Copyrights and her staff have conducted a careful and extensive evaluation of the entire record in the proceeding and determined that proponents of exemptions have demonstrated that the prohibition on circumventing access controls has had a substantial adverse effect on the ability of people to make noninfringing uses of six particular classes of copyrighted works. The Register has given me her analysis and recommendation, and today I have signed a document providing that persons making noninfringing uses of these six classes of works will not be subject to the prohibition against circumventing access controls during the next three years. The six classes of works are:

> 1. Audiovisual works included in the educational library of a college or university's film or media studies department, when circumvention is accomplished for the purpose of making compilations of portions of those works for educational use in the classroom by media studies or film professors.

> 2. Computer programs and video games distributed in formats that have become obsolete and that require the original media or hardware as a condition of access, when circumvention is accomplished for the purpose of preservation or

---

[42] http://www.copyright.gov/1201/docs/2006_statement.html.

archival reproduction of published digital works by a library or archive. A format shall be considered obsolete if the machine or system necessary to render perceptible a work stored in that format is no longer manufactured or is no longer reasonably available in the commercial marketplace.

3. Computer programs protected by dongles that prevent access due to malfunction or damage and which are obsolete. A dongle shall be considered obsolete if it is no longer manufactured or if a replacement or repair is no longer reasonably available in the commercial marketplace.

4. Literary works distributed in ebook format when all existing ebook editions of the work (including digital text editions made available by authorized entities) contain access controls that prevent the enabling either of the book's read-aloud function or of screen readers that render the text into a specialized format.

5. Computer programs in the form of firmware that enable wireless telephone handsets to connect to a wireless telephone communication network, when circumvention is accomplished for the sole purpose of lawfully connecting to a wireless telephone communication network.

6. Sound recordings, and audiovisual works associated with those sound recordings, distributed in compact disc format and protected by technological protection measures that control access to lawfully purchased works and create or exploit security flaws or vulnerabilities that compromise the security of personal computers, when circumvention is accomplished solely for the purpose of good faith testing, investigating, or correcting such security flaws or vulnerabilities.

Three of these classes of works are very similar to the classes of works that were exempted three years ago, but with modifications to take into account the somewhat different cases that were presented to the Register this year. The new classes of works will enable film and media studies professors to make compilations of film clips for classroom instruction, make it easier for owners of wireless telephone handsets to continue to use those handsets when they switch to new wireless carriers, and permit the testing, investigation and correction of security vulnerabilities on compact discs that are distributed with access control technology that compromises the security of personal computers.

Please add the following to Bibliography and Links at page 595:

Mark S. Nadel, *How Current Copyright Law Discourages Creative Output: The Overlooked Impact of Marketing*, 19 BERKELEY TECH. L.J. 785 (2004).

Craig A. Grossman, *From* Sony *to* Grokster, *The Failure of the Copyright Doctrines of Contributory Infringement and Vicarious Liability to Resolve the War Between Content and Destructive Technologies*, 53 BUFF. L. REV. 141 (2005).

Peter K. Yu, *P2P and the Future of Private Copying*, 76 U. COLO. L. REV. 653 (2005).

Shae Yatta Harvey, *National, Multi-District Preliminary Tour Injunctions: Why the Hesitation?*, 40 IDEA 195 (2000).

CHAPTER XIV: TELEVISION & CABLE PRODUCTION AGREEMENTS

A.   Television Writer Agreements

Please add the following to Notes and Questions at page 613:

e. In July 2005, the once successful independent television producer, Carsey-Werner Co., announced it was closing the company. The producer of hits including *The Cosby Show, Roseanne, Third Rock from the Sun*, and *That 70's Show* explained that in the current production climate, there is little room for independent producers.

Covering the story, The Wall Street Journal explained the context for the changing business:

> Until the mid-1990s, regulatory restrictions on broadcasters forced the networks to go outside their own operations for most of the shows they put on the air. But 10 years ago, the Federal Communications Commission phased out the so-called financial interest and syndication rules. The elimination of the rules, known as fin-syn, paved the way for the networks to create their own production shops, and to merge with television studios.

> Since then, the six broadcast networks have increasingly made programming choices primarily based on who owns the show, with a strong preference for buying in-house content, rather than on the quality of the material. Most networks today produce or co-produce half of their own shows, up significantly from five years ago. [43]

With the end of regulations and consent decrees separating the ownership of television production from the ownership of its distribution, the consolidation was swift and inevitable. Ironically, even as the network consolidation is completed, the divestiture of cable networks is gaining steam. For example, Liberty Media Corp. is spinning off its stake in Discovery Communications, paving the way for greater independence of the company that owns Discovery Channel, TLC and Animal Planet. Although it will be owned 50% by Cox Communications Inc. and Advance/Newhouse Communications Inc., the move will allow greater autonomy. [44]

In the future, it may be likely that creative development turns increasingly to the smaller cable channels and the companies that once grew as independent producers will instead reach out to control cable channels. Stay tuned.

f. The FCC is required under § 628(g) of the Communications Act of 1934, as amended (Communications Act) to provide an annual report to congress on the status of television, cable, and satellite competition. The 2004 Report to Congress noted that for the first time, cable viewership exceeded broadcast television viewership:

---

[43] Joe Flint, *Television Suffers From Loss of Independent Producers. With Just a Few Companies Creating Content, Prime-Time Line-Up Blurs*, WALL ST. J., July 6, 2005 at "The Small Screen." http://online.wsj.com/article/0,,SB112057535281877372,00.html?mod=home_us_inside_today.

[44] See *Liberty Media Sets July Date to Spin Off Its Stake in Discovery*, WALL ST. J., July 6, 2005 at A2.

During the 2003-2004 television season, the combined audience share[45] of all nonbroadcast networks[46] was higher than the combined audience share of all broadcast television stations[47] for both all day viewing and prime time viewing.[48] For all day viewing, the combined audience share of all nonbroadcast networks was 56, and the combined audience share of all broadcast television stations was 44. For prime time viewing, the combined audience share of all nonbroadcast networks was 52, and the combined audience share of all broadcast television stations was 48. According to NCTA, the seven national commercial broadcast networks (ABC, CBS, NBC, FOX, UPN, WB, and PAX) accounted for a 38 share of all day viewing in 2003, and all nonbroadcast networks accounted for a 63 share of all day viewing.[49] **According to NCTA, the 2003–2004 television season (September 2003–May 2004) was the first time that the combined nonbroadcast networks' share of prime time viewing was greater than the combined national broadcast networks' share of prime time viewing.[50]**

Federal Communications Commission, *Annual Assessment of the Status of Competition in the Market for the Delivery of Video, Eleventh Annual Report*, January 14, 2005 at 26 (*emphasis added*).

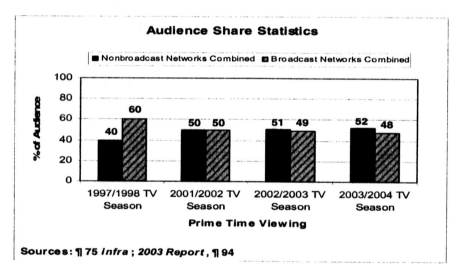

Id. at 14.

---

[45] A share is the percent of all households using television during the time period that are viewing the specified station(s) or network(s). Due to simultaneous multiple set viewing, Nielsen reports audience shares that exceed 100 percent when totaled. We have normalized audience shares to equal 100 percent.

[46] Nonbroadcast network shares include basic (BST and CPST) networks, premium networks, and PPV networks distributed by MVPDs.

[47] Broadcast shares include network affiliates, independent, and public television stations.

[48] Prime time viewing is Monday through Saturday, 8 p.m.-11 p.m., and Sunday, 7 p.m.-11 p.m. Nielsen Media Research, *Broadcast Calendar (TV Season) Share of Audience Report, Prime time and Total Day*, Sept. 2004. *See also* NCTA Comments at 45–46. The most popular nonbroadcast networks continue to receive a lower audience share for all day viewing and prime time viewing than any of the major broadcast television networks. Nielsen Media Research.

[49] NCTA Comments at 45. NCTA's numbers do not include PBS and independent commercial broadcast stations.

[50] *Id*. at 46.

B. TV Substantial Similarity

Please add the following to Notes and Questions at page 625:

d. To what extent is the Fox reality show, *Trading Spouses*, a copy of the British made and ABC-acquired *Wife Swap?* The world may never know. Trademark, trade dress, and bad etiquette claims were dismissed, though the copyright claim was allowed. See *RDF Media Ltd. v. Fox Broad. Co.*, 372 F. Supp. 2d 556 (C.D. Cal. 2005).

e. Who wants to share in being a millionaire? On the issue of fair dealing when self-dealing syndication and related rights, see *Celador International Ltd. v. The Walt Disney Co.*, 347 F. Supp. 2d 846, (C.D. Cal. 2004). Owners of "Who Wants to Be a Millionaire" can bring claims for an alleged breach of the covenant of good faith and fair dealing when selling rights to other entities or divisions commonly owned by a party to the agreement.

CHAPTER XV: TELEVISION REGULATION

A. Overview

Please add the following to Notes and Questions at page 661:

e. To fully understand the philosophical debate regarding the government's role in regulating the airwaves, it is helpful to begin with John F. Kennedy's FCC Chairman, Newton N. Minow and his famous indictment that "when television is bad, nothing is worse. ... I can assure you that you will observe a vast wasteland." The speech is reprinted at Appendix, page 103.

B. Content Regulation

Please add the following to Notes and Questions at page 679:

d. Clear Channel Communication has become the largest owner of radio stations and networks in the United States. On June 4, 2004 it entered into a consent decree with the FCC regarding a large number of ongoing complaints against its personalities and D.J.s. The consent decree provides in part:

> 1. The Commission has been investigating whether Clear Channel Communications, Inc. and its direct and indirect subsidiaries that hold FCC authorizations ("Clear Channel") may have violated restrictions on the broadcast of obscene, indecent or profane material.[51] ...

> 4. Based on the record before us, in particular Clear Channel's admission that some of the material it broadcast was indecent in violation of 47 C.F.R. § 73.3999, the significant remedial efforts that Clear Channel has already taken and the additional remedial efforts to which Clear Channel has agreed, we conclude that there are no substantial and material questions of fact in regard to these matters as to whether Clear Channel possesses the basic qualifications, including its character qualifications, to hold or obtain any FCC licenses or authorizations. ...

> ### Consent Decree

> 1. The Federal Communications Commission and Clear Channel Communications, Inc., for itself and on behalf of its direct and indirect subsidiaries that hold FCC authorizations, hereby enter into this Consent Decree for the purpose of resolving and terminating certain forfeiture proceedings, investigations and complaints currently being conducted by, or pending before, the Commission relating to possible violations of the Indecency Laws by Clear Channel Stations. ...

> 9. Clear Channel represents that it has adopted, and is currently in the process of implementing, a company-wide compliance plan for the purpose of preventing the broadcast of material violative of the Indecency Laws. A summary of that plan is set forth in the Attachment. Clear Channel agrees, to the extent it has not already done so, to implement this compliance plan within thirty (30) days

---

[51] 18 U.S.C. § 1464; 47 C.F.R. § 73.3999 (2004).

of the Effective Date and to keep such compliance plan in effect for three (3) years after the Effective Date. Clear Channel reserves the right to revise the plan from time to time, provided that the Commission shall be given not less than thirty (30) days advance written notice of any revisions to the plan. …

11. Clear Channel waives any and all rights it may have to seek administrative or judicial reconsideration, review, appeal or stay, or to otherwise challenge or contest the validity of this Consent Decree and the Adopting Order, provided no modifications are made to the Consent Decree adverse to Clear Channel or any Clear Channel Station. If the Commission, or the United States acting on its behalf, brings a judicial action to enforce the terms of the Adopting Order or this Consent Decree, or both, Clear Channel will not contest the validity of this Consent Decree or of the Adopting Order and will waive any statutory right to a trial de novo. If Clear Channel brings a judicial action to enforce the terms of the Adopting Order or this Consent Decree, or both, the Commission will not contest the validity of this Consent Decree or of the Adopting Order. …

Federal Communications Commission, *In the Matter of Clear Channel Communications, Inc.*, FCC 04-128, adopted June 4, 2004.[52]

The concern raised by the Clear Channel consent decree flows from the risks associated with the strategic attempt to chill this marketplace. Company-wide compliance encouraged against the threat of substantial punishment for past and future practices creates the ideal governmental control over the broadcaster. As the largest company in the field, its compliance with the FCC will certainly impact all programming. The consent decree also removes a major source of financial support for other stations which are unwilling to enter into agreements with the government.

e. The marketplace has also been incorporated into content control regarding the end of Don Imus longstanding radio show on CBS. After thirty years of rude, offensive shock humor, the leader of the genre was toppled in days after YouTube rebroadcasts of his offensive comments regarding the Rutgers University women's basketball team galvanized the public and advertisers. Robin Abcarian and Meg James, *The Imus Scandal: Firing By CBS; A talk powerhouse is shut down; The firing of Don Imus by CBS brings an abrupt end to a radio forum that attracted media and political heavies*, L.A. TIMES, April 13, 2007 at 1.

f. The recent increase in the FCC's interest in stopping indecency on television has led to the fining of stations for "fleeting expletives" since 2003. This approach was dealt a serious blow by the Second Circuit.

We find that the FCC's new policy regarding "fleeting expletives" represents a significant departure from positions previously taken by the agency and relied on by the broadcast industry. We further find that the FCC has failed to articulate a reasoned basis for this change in policy. Accordingly, we hold that the FCC's new policy regarding "fleeting expletives" is arbitrary and capricious under the Administrative Procedure Act. …

We also note that the FCC's indecency test raises the separate constitutional

---

[52] Available at http://hraunfoss.fcc.gov/edocs_public/attachmatch/FCC-04-128A1.pdf.

question of whether it permits the FCC to sanction speech based on its subjective view of the merit of that speech. It appears that under the FCC's current indecency regime, any and all uses of an expletive is presumptively indecent and profane with the broadcaster then having to demonstrate to the satisfaction of the Commission, under an unidentified burden of proof, that the expletives were "integral" to the work. In the licensing context, the Supreme Court has cautioned against speech regulations that give too much discretion to government officials.

Finally, we recognize there is some tension in the law regarding the appropriate level of First Amendment scrutiny. In general, restrictions on First Amendment liberties prompt courts to apply strict scrutiny. Outside the broadcasting context, the Supreme Court has consistently applied strict scrutiny to indecency regulations. At the same time, however, the Supreme Court has also considered broadcast media exceptional. "[B]ecause broadcast regulation involves unique considerations, our cases . . . have never gone so far as to demand that such regulations serve 'compelling' governmental interests."

Restrictions on broadcast "speech" have been upheld "when we [are] satisfied that the restriction is narrowly tailored to further a substantial governmental interest."

The Networks contend that the bases for treating broadcast media "different[ly]" have "eroded over time," particularly because 86 percent of American households now subscribe to cable or satellite services. ... Whatever merit these arguments may have, they cannot sway us in light of Supreme Court precedent. Nevertheless, we would be remiss not to observe that it is increasingly difficult to describe the broadcast media as uniquely pervasive and uniquely accessible to children, and at some point in the future, strict scrutiny may properly apply in the context of regulating broadcast television. ...

Fox TV Stations, Inc. v. FCC, __ F.3d __ 2007 U.S. App. LEXIS 12868, *4-63 (2d Cir. 2007).

C.   Must Carry and Ownership Legislation

Please add the following to Notes and Questions at page 707:

f. Given the continuing problems facing digital piracy, the FCC had attempted to intercede with antipiracy technology that prohibits the redistribution of a broadcast signal. The FCC tried to "assure that DTV broadcast content will not be indiscriminately redistributed over the Internet, while protecting consumers' ability to view and record video content in a manner to which they have become accustomed."[53] The broadcast flag allowed a digital signal to be copied once, but would block a second copying of that program. The regulation, however, has been judged to greatly exceed the FCC's regulatory authority.

It is axiomatic that administrative agencies may issue regulations only pursuant to authority delegated to them by Congress. The principal question presented by this case is whether Congress delegated authority to the Federal Communications

---

[53] *In the Matter of: Digital Broadcast Content Protection,* 18 FCC Rcd 23550 (2003) (Broadcast Flag Order).

Commission ("Commission" or "FCC") in the Communications Act of 1934, ("Communications Act" or "Act"), to regulate apparatus that can receive television broadcasts when those apparatus are not engaged in the process of receiving a broadcast transmission. In the seven decades of its existence, the FCC has never before asserted such sweeping authority. Indeed, in the past, the FCC has informed Congress that it lacked any such authority. In our view, nothing has changed to give the FCC the authority that it now claims. ...

In November 2003, the Commission adopted "broadcast flag" regulations, requiring that digital television receivers and other devices capable of receiving digital television broadcast signals, manufactured on or after July 1, 2005, include technology allowing them to recognize the broadcast flag. The broadcast flag is a digital code embedded in a DTV broadcasting stream, which prevents digital television reception equipment from redistributing broadcast content. The broadcast flag affects receiver devices only *after* a broadcast transmission is complete. ...

In this case, all relevant materials concerning the FCC's jurisdiction - including the words of the Communications Act of 1934, its legislative history, subsequent legislation, relevant case law, and Commission practice - confirm that the FCC has no authority to regulate consumer electronic devices that can be used for receipt of wire or radio communication when those devices are not engaged in the process of radio or wire transmission.

Am. Library Ass'n v. FCC, 406 F.3d 689, 691, 708 (D.C. Cir. 2005) (citations omitted).

Please add the following to Bibliography and Links at page 708:

Joel Timmer, *The Seven Dirty Words you can say on Cable and DBS: Extending Broadcast Indecency Regulation and the First Amendment*, 10 COMM. L. & POL'Y 179 (2005).

Mark Cenite, *Federalizing or Eliminating Online Obscenity Law as an Alternative to Contemporary Community Standards*, 9 COMM. L. & POL'Y 25 (2004).

Patrick M. Garry, *The Flip Side of the First Amendment: A Right to Filter*, 2004 MICH. ST. L. REV. 57 (2004).

CHAPTER XVI: PUBLISHING

A.   Overview

Please add the following to Overview at page 711:

5. Decline of Readership

A recent report by the National Endowment for the Arts raised dramatic concerns regarding the literary competency of the adult American population. The size of the active reading audience being lost poses profound and dangerous implications for U.S. society:

Fewer Than Half of American Adults Now Read Literature

New York, N.Y. - Literary reading is in dramatic decline with fewer than half of American adults now reading literature, according to a National Endowment for the Arts (NEA) survey released today. *Reading at Risk: A Survey of Literary Reading in America* reports drops in all groups studied, with the steepest rate of decline - 28 percent - occurring in the youngest age groups.

The study also documents an overall decline of 10 percentage points in literary readers from 1982 to 2002, representing a loss of 20 million potential readers. The rate of decline is increasing and, according to the survey, has nearly tripled in the last decade. The findings were announced today by NEA Chairman Dana Gioia during a news conference at the New York Public Library. ...

National Endowment for the Arts News Room, Literary Reading in Dramatic Decline, According to National Endowment for the Arts Survey *(July 8, 2004).*[54]

Ironically, publishing revenues for the same period are up as a result of non-book sales.

D.   Ownership of Editorial Content

Please add the following to Notes and Questions at page 739:

e. The case of *Faulkner v. Nat'l Geographic Enters.*, 294 F. Supp. 2d 523 (S.D.N.Y. 2003), was affirmed, *Faulkner v. Nat'l Geographic Enters.*, 409 F.3d 26 (2d Cir. 2005), though the ongoing litigation continued through numerous additional opinions. In affirming the district court decision, the Second Circuit explained:

> [W]e hold that, because the original context of the Magazines is omnipresent in the CNG and because it is a new version of the Magazine, the CNG is a privileged revision.
>
> "'Revision' denotes a new 'version,' and a version is, in this setting, a "'distinct form of something regarded by its creator or others as one work.'" [*N.Y. Times Co. v. Tasini*, 533 U.S. 483, 500 (2001)] (quoting Webster's Third New International Dictionary 1944, 2545 (1976)). "In determining whether the [underlying works] have been reproduced and distributed 'as part of' a 'revision'

---

[54] Available at http://www.nea.gov/news/news04/ReadingAtRisk.html.

of the collective works in issue, we focus on the [underlying works] as presented to, and perceptible by, the user of the [CNG]." *Id.* at 499 (citations omitted). The CNG presents the underlying works to users in the same context as they were presented to the users in the original versions of the Magazine. The CNG uses the almost identical "selection, coordination, and arrangement" of the underlying works as used in the original collective works. *Tasini*, 206 F.3d at 168. The CNG presents an electronic replica of the pages of the Magazine. Pages are presented two at a time, with the gutter (that is, the Magazine fold) in the middle, and with the page numbers in the lower outside corners, just as they are presented in the written format. In addition, the contents of the CNG, including the authors' contributions, are in the same positions relative to the other contributions in the Magazine. To be sure, a CNG user can focus on particular pages or parts of pages. However, a user of a microfilm of a collective work can do the same thing, as, indeed can a reader of an original magazine by opening to a particular page. In contrast, the databases at issue in *Tasini* precluded readers from viewing the underlying works in their original context.

Moreover, because the Section 201(c) privilege of reproduction and distribution extends to that collective work and any revision of that collective work, a permissible revision may contain elements not found in the original — for example, a collection of bound volumes of past issues with a copyrightable index to the entire collection. … In the case of the CNG, some images found in the original version of the Magazines are blacked out, and it contains additional elements …. However, these changes do not substantially alter the original context which, unlike that of the works at issue in *Tasini*, is immediately recognizable. The presentation does not, therefore, affect the CNG's status as a revision.

Faulkner v. Nat'l Geographic Enters., 409 F.3d 26, 38 (2d Cir. 2005).

f. To what extent can the sleuthing needed to find previously unpublished works become a part of a compiler's copyright? When Stuart Silverstein published a book of Dorothy Parker's uncollected poems, he did not expect Penguin Books to first reject his manuscript and then publish the same poems in its own anthology. But sleuthing and compiling may not be the same. See *Silverstein v. Penguin Putnam, Inc.*, 368 F.3d 77 (2d Cir. 2004).

g. With the rise of new technology and self-publishing technology, anyone can serve as a publishing house. At what point do the promises of a successful print and promotional campaign become contractual guarantees? For insight into this issue and the risks of interference with an author's rights, see *Lee v. Mt. Ivy Press, L.P.*, 63 Mass. App. Ct. 538, 827 N.E.2d 727 (Mass. App. Ct. 2005).

h. Amazon.com had entered into an agreement with Borders Books to operate Borders.com and eventually Waldens.com because Borders was unsuccessful at running its online book business. Borders hoped to reduce its losses through the Amazon arrangement while maintaining an Internet presence. The district court rejected claims of a *per se* antitrust challenge to the relationship, since the sales prices of two companies were not fixed by agreement and the pricing was ancillary to the overall legitimate purposes of the agreement. See *Gerlinger v. Amazon.com, Inc.*, 311 F. Supp. 2d 838 (N.D. Cal. 2004).

E.   Fair use in Publishing

Please add the following to Notes and Questions at page 749:

e. Secrecy in publishing is generally inconsistent with copyright registration. In the area of copyrighted test books, the two areas conflict a great deal. To what extent can a newspaper "report" the content of such a copyrighted but nonpublic test book? See *Chi. Bd. of Educ. v. Substance, Inc.*, 354 F.3d 624 (7th Cir. 2004). For a discussion regarding competing test preparation companies, see *Mulcahy v. Cheetah Learning LLC*, 386 F.3d 849 (8th Cir. 2004).

Please add the following to Bibliography and Links at page 750:

Jane C. Ginsburg, *The Right to Claim Authorship in U.S. Copyright and Trademarks Law*, 41 HOUS. L. REV. 263 (2004).

Diane Leenheer Zimmerman, *Authorship Without Ownership: Reconsidering Incentives in a Digital Age*, 52 DEPAUL L. REV. 1121 (2003).

Please add the following chapter at page 752:

CHAPTER XVII: VISUAL ARTS AND CULTURAL ARTIFACTS

Although somewhat different than the more commercial areas of entertainment law, fine art, visual arts, sculpture, and cultural artifacts play a similar role in society of entertaining and educating the public. Similarly, the laws of copyright, trademark, publicity rights, First Amendment law, contract law and labor law shape the world of art and the operations of museums in much the same way as the other entertainment industries.

The museum experience is a key part of our education and cultural heritage. Eighty percent of parents include the museum experience as part of their upbringing. Unfortunately, according to a recent report, "[o]ne in five parents has never taken his or her child to a museum; most frequent objections are that it's too far to travel (51 percent), takes too much time (48 percent), and costs too much (28 percent)"[55]

This chapter provides an introduction to a group of issues unique to the fields of visual arts and cultural artifacts. The topic is the subject of entire courses, so these materials are designed to illustrate its intersection with entertainment law and to highlight the stark differences which derive from the unique management obligations of museums and the international issues related to art theft, forgery and trafficking in stolen or illegally obtained artifacts.

A. Overview of Copyright for Pictoral, Graphic, or Sculptural Arts

Bleistein v. Donaldson Lithographing Co.

188 U.S. 239 (1903)

MR. JUSTICE HOLMES delivered the opinion of the court.

The alleged infringements consisted in the copying in reduced form of three chromolithographs prepared by employees of the plaintiffs for advertisements of a circus owned by one Wallace. Each of the three contained a portrait of Wallace in the corner and lettering bearing some slight relation to the scheme of decoration, indicating the subject of the design and the fact that the reality was to be seen at the circus. One of the designs was of an ordinary ballet, one of a number of men and women, described as the Stirk family, performing on bicycles, and one of groups of men and women whitened to represent statutes. The Circuit Court directed a verdict for the defendant on the ground that the chromolithographs were not within the protection of the copyright law, and this ruling was sustained by the Circuit Court of Appeals. …

We shall do no more than mention the suggestion that painting and engraving unless for a mechanical end are not among the useful arts, the progress of which Congress is empowered by the Constitution to promote. The Constitution does not limit the useful to that which satisfies immediate bodily needs. It is obvious also that the plaintiffs' case is not affected by the fact, if it be one, that the pictures represent actual groups – visible things. They seem from the testimony to have been composed from hints or description, not from sight of a performance. But even if they had been drawn from the life, that fact would not deprive them of protection. The opposite proposition would mean that a portrait by Velasquez or Whistler was common property because others might try their hand on the same face. Others are free to copy the original. They are not

---

[55] *Museum; factoids Research Alert*, IAC Newsletter Database, October 6, 2006 at Pg. 4(1).

free to copy the copy. The copy is the personal reaction of an individual upon nature. Personality always contains something unique. It expresses its singularity even in handwriting, and a very modest grade of art has in it something irreducible, which is one man's alone. That something he may copyright unless there is a restriction in the words of the act.

If there is a restriction it is not to be found in the limited pretensions of these particular works. ... We assume that the construction of Rev. Stat. § 4952 ... provides that "in the construction of this act the words 'engraving,' 'cut' and 'print' shall be applied only to pictorial illustrations or works connected with the fine arts." We see no reason for taking the words "connected with the fine arts" as qualifying anything except the word "works," but it would not change our decision if we should assume further that they also qualified "pictorial illustrations," as the defendant contends.

These chromolithographs are "pictorial illustrations." The word "illustrations" does not mean that they must illustrate the text of a book, and that the etchings of Rembrandt or Steinla's engraving of the Madonna di San Sisto could not be protected to-day if any man were able to produce them. Again, the act however construed, does not mean that ordinary posters are not good enough to be considered within its scope. The antithesis to "illustrations or works connected with the fine arts" is not works of little merit or of humble degree, or illustrations addressed to the less educated classes; it is "prints or labels designed to be used for any other articles of manufacture." Certainly works are not the less connected with the fine arts because their pictorial quality attracts the crowd and therefore gives them a real use – if use means to increase trade and to help to make money. A picture is none the less a picture and none the less a subject of copyright that it is used for an advertisement. And if pictures may be used to advertise soap, or the theatre, or monthly magazines, as they are, they may be used to advertise a circus. Of course, the ballet is as legitimate a subject for illustration as any other. A rule cannot be laid down that would excommunicate the paintings of Degas. ...

It would be a dangerous undertaking for persons trained only to the law to constitute themselves final judges of the worth of pictorial illustrations, outside of the narrowest and most obvious limits. At the one extreme some works of genius would be sure to miss appreciation. Their very novelty would make them repulsive until the public had learned the new language in which their author spoke. It may be more than doubted, for instance, whether the etchings of Goya or the paintings of Manet would have been sure of protection when seen for the first time. At the other end, copyright would be denied to pictures which appealed to a public less educated than the judge. Yet if they command the interest of any public, they have a commercial value – it would be bold to say that they have not an aesthetic and educational value – and the taste of any public is not to be treated with contempt. It is an ultimate fact for the moment, whatever may be out hopes for a change. That these pictures had their worth and their success is sufficiently shown by the desire to reproduce them without regard to the plaintiffs' rights. We are of opinion that there was evidence that the plaintiffs have rights entitled to the protection of the law.

The judgment of the Circuit Court of Appeals is reversed; the judgment of the Circuit Court is also reversed and the cause remanded to that court with directions to set aside the verdict and grant a new trial.

DISSENT: MR. JUSTICE HARLAN, with whom concurred MR. JUSTICE McKENNA, dissenting.

[Quoting the Court of Appeals] "What we hold is this: That if a chromo, lithograph, or other print, engraving, or picture has no other use than that of a mere advertisement, and no value aside from this function, it would not be promotive of the useful arts, within the meaning of the constitutional provision, to protect the 'author' in the exclusive use thereof, and the copyright statute should not be construed as including such a publication, if any other construction is admissible.... It must have some connection with the fine arts to give it intrinsic value, and that it shall have is the meaning which we attach to the act of June 18, 1874, amending the provisions of the copyright law. We are unable to discover anything useful or meritorious in the design copyrighted by the plaintiffs in error other than as an advertisement of acts to be done or exhibited to the public in Wallace's show. No evidence, aside from the deductions which are to be drawn from the prints themselves, was offered to show that these designs had any original artistic qualities." ... The clause of the Constitution giving Congress power to promote the progress of science and useful arts, by securing for limited terms to authors and inventors the exclusive right to their respective works and discoveries, does not, as I think, embrace a mere advertisement of a circus.

Notes and Questions

a. Initially, the courts must grapple with the definition of art in a number of contexts. As Justice Learned Hand explained, "It is true that 'works of art' is a loose phrase whose perimeter is hard to define; nevertheless ... the mere fact that the meaning of the phrase, 'works of art,' admits of debate does not make it different from many statutes whose interpretation is every day regarded as reviewable by the courts." *Vacheron Watches, Inc. v. Benrus Watch Co.*, 260 F.2d 637, 640 (2d Cir. 1958).

b. Congress and the courts did not hesitate to recognize fine art as within the ambit of copyright protection. The courts extended this protection to artistic photographs as writings within the meaning of the Constitution. *Burrow-Giles Lithographic Co. v. Sarony*, 111 U.S. 53 (1884). Despite this expansion, however, questions remained regarding the scope of this protection and the meaning of author for purposes of copyright.

c. To what extent does the reproduction of a public domain work of art entitle the new artist to copyright in the completed work? Compare L. *Batlin & Son, Inc. v. Snyder*, 536 F.2d 486 (2d Cir. 1976) (*en banc*), with *Durham Indus., Inc. v. Tomy Corp.*, 630 F.2d 905 (2d Cir. 1980) and *Entertainment Research Group, Inc. v. Genesis Creative Group, Inc.*, 122 F.3d 1211, 1219 (9th Cir. 1997).

B.   Artists Rights to Attribution and Integrity

Introduction

The law protecting visual artists builds on the legal protections afforded to all copyright owners, those protected by § 43(a) of the Lanham Act as well as the state law protections for publicity rights. In addition to these protections, select works of visual art are protected by the Visual Artists Rights Act, providing protection for an artist's rights of attribution and integrity.

Article 6[bis] of the Berne Convention states the international standard for the protection of moral rights.

Independently of the author's economic rights, and even after the transfer of the said rights, the author shall have the right to claim authorship of the work and to object to any distortion, mutilation or other modification of, or other derogatory action in relation to, the said work, which would be prejudicial to his honor or reputation.

Berne Convention for the Protection of Literary and Artistic Works, September 9, 1886, art. 6[bis], S. Treaty Doc. No. 27, 99th Cong., 2d Sess. 41 (1986).

In the United States, the moral rights of attribution regarding the identity of the author or artist of a work and the moral right of integrity protecting the work from destruction or mutilation are not explicitly recognized under copyright law, except as provided in the Visual Artists Rights Act of 1990, 17 U.S.C. § 106(a) (2000) (VARA).

Despite this, courts prior to 1990 and courts adjudicating copyright claims outside the coverage of VARA have sometimes recognized aspects of the moral rights of attribution and integrity through an interpretation of contractual provisions, Lanham Act § 43(a) unfair competition claims, or various state law claims. In a report on VARA, the Register of Copyrights provides a useful history of this litigation:

> Although moral rights were not recognized in U.S. copyright law prior to enactment of VARA, some state legislatures had enacted moral rights laws, and a number of judicial decisions accorded some moral rights protection under theories of copyright, unfair competition, defamation, invasion of privacy, and breach of contract. Such cases have continued relevance, not only for historical interest, but also for precedential value because state and common law moral rights protection was not entirely preempted by VARA. Arguably, state laws of defamation, invasion of privacy, contracts, and unfair competition by "passing off" are not preempted. Further, VARA rights endure only for the artist's life, after which preemption ceases.
>
> In *Vargas v. Esquire* [164 F.2d 522, 526 (7th Cir. 1947)], artist Antonio Vargas created for Esquire magazine a series of calendar girl illustrations, some of which were published without his signature or credit-line. The U.S. Court of Appeals for the Seventh Circuit ruled that the rights of the parties were determined by the contract in which Vargas agreed as independent contractor to furnish pictures and granted all rights in the artwork to Esquire. The court rejected theories of implied contract, moral rights, and unfair competition.
>
> In *Granz v. Harris* [198 F.2d 585 (2d Cir. 1952)], a jazz concert was re-recorded with a reduced playing time and content, such that a full eight minutes was omitted. The contract required the defendant to use a credit-line attributing the plaintiff-producer, who sued. The Second Circuit decided that selling abbreviated recordings with the original credit line constituted unfair competition and breach of contract. Whether by contract or by tort, the plaintiff could prevent publication "as his, of a garbled version of his uncopyrighted product."
>
> In *Gilliam v. American Broadcasting Cos.* [538 F.2d 14 (2d Cir. 1976)], ABC broadcast the first of two 90-minute specials, consisting of three 30-minute Monty Python shows each, but cut 24 of the original 90 minutes. Monty Python sued for

an injunction and damages. The Second Circuit ruled that ABC's actions contravened contractual provisions limiting the right to edit the program and that a licensee's unauthorized use of an underlying work by publication in a truncated version was a copyright infringement. In a theory akin to moral rights, the court said that a distorted version of a writer's or performer's work may violate rights protected by the Lanham Act and may present a cause of action under that statute. The concurrence cautioned against employing the Lanham Act as a substitute for moral rights, and believed the court should restrict its opinion to contract and copyright issues.

Another case, *Wojnarowicz v. American Family Association* [772 F. Supp. 201 (S.D.N.Y. 1991)], involved a group that protested an artist's work by reproducing 14 fragments in a pamphlet. The U.S. District Court for the Southern District of New York found for the artist under the New York Artists' Authorship Rights Act, but dismissed claims under the Copyright and Lanham Acts.[56]

Carter v. Helmsley-Spear, Inc.

71 F.3d 77 (2d Cir. 1995)

Defendants 474431 Associates and Helmsley-Spear, Inc. (defendants or appellants), as the owner and managing agent respectively, of a commercial building in Queens, New York, appeal from an order of the United States District Court for the Southern District of New York (Edelstein, J.), entered on September 6, 1994 following a bench trial. The order granted plaintiffs, who are three artists, a permanent injunction that enjoined defendants from removing, modifying or destroying a work of visual art that had been installed in defendants' building by plaintiffs-artists commissioned by a former tenant to install the work. See *Carter v. Helmsley-Spear, Inc.*, 861 F. Supp. 303 (S.D.N.Y. 1994). Defendants also appeal from the dismissal by the trial court of their counterclaim for waste. Plaintiffs cross-appeal from the dismissal of their cause of action for tortious interference with contractual relations and from the denial of their requests to complete the work and for an award of attorney's fees and costs.

On this appeal we deal with an Act of Congress that protects the rights of artists to preserve their works. One of America's most insightful thinkers observed that a country is not truly civilized "where the arts, such as they have, are all imported, having no indigenous life." 7 WORKS OF RALPH WALDO EMERSON, SOCIETY AND SOLITUDE, CHAPT. II CIVILIZATION 34 (AMS. ed. 1968). From such reflection it follows that American artists are to be encouraged by laws that protect their works. Although Congress in the statute before us did just that, it did not mandate the preservation of art at all costs and without due regard for the rights of others.

For the reasons that follow, we reverse and vacate the grant of injunctive relief to plaintiffs and affirm the dismissal by the district court of plaintiffs' other claims and its dismissal of defendants' counterclaim for waste.

---

[56] Waiver of Moral Rights in Visual Artworks, Executive Summary, Report of the Copyright Office (October 1996), *available at* http://www.copyright.gov/reports/exsum.html.

BACKGROUND

Defendant 474431 Associates (Associates) is the owner of a mixed use commercial building located at 47-44 31st Street, Queens, New York, which it has owned since 1978. Associates is a New York general partnership. The general partners are Alvin Schwartz and Supervisory Management Corp., a wholly-owned subsidiary of Helmsley Enterprises, Inc. Defendant Helmsley-Spear, Inc. is the current managing agent of the property for Associates.

On February 1, 1990 Associates entered into a 48-year net lease, leasing the building to 47-44 31st Street Associates, L.P. (Limited Partnership), a Delaware limited partnership. From February 1, 1990 until June 1993, Irwin Cohen or an entity under his control was the general partner of the Limited Partnership, and managed the property through Cohen's SIG Management Company (SIG). Corporate Life Insurance Company (Corporate Life) was a limited partner in the Limited Partnership. In June 1993 SIG ceased its involvement with the property and Corporate Life, through an entity controlled by it, became the general partner of the Limited Partnership. The property was then managed by the Limited Partnership, through Theodore Nering, a Corporate Life representative. There is no relationship, other than the lease, between Associates, the lessor, and the Limited Partnership, the lessee.

Plaintiffs John Carter, John Swing and John Veronis (artists or plaintiffs) are professional sculptors who work together and are known collectively as the "Three-J's" or "Jx3." On December 16, 1991 SIG entered into a one-year agreement with the plaintiffs "engaging and hiring the Artists . . . to design, create and install sculpture and other permanent installations" in the building, primarily the lobby. Under the agreement plaintiffs had "full authority in design, color and style," and SIG retained authority to direct the location and installation of the artwork within the building. The artists were to retain copyrights to their work and SIG was to receive 50 percent of any proceeds from its exploitation. On January 20, 1993 SIG and the artists signed an agreement extending the duration of their commission for an additional year. When Corporate Life became a general partner of the Limited Partnership, the Limited Partnership assumed the agreement with plaintiffs and in December 1993 again extended the agreement.

The artwork that is the subject of this litigation is a very large "walk-through sculpture" occupying most, but not all, of the building's lobby. The artwork consists of a variety of sculptural elements constructed from recycled materials, much of it metal, affixed to the walls and ceiling, and a vast mosaic made from pieces of recycled glass embedded in the floor and walls. Elements of the work include a giant hand fashioned from an old school bus, a face made of automobile parts, and a number of interactive components. These assorted elements make up a theme relating to environmental concerns and the significance of recycling.

The Limited Partnership's lease on the building was terminated on March 31, 1994. It filed for bankruptcy one week later. The property was surrendered to defendant Associates on April 6, 1994 and defendant Helmsley-Spear, Inc. took over management of the property. Representatives of defendants informed the artists that they could no longer continue to install artwork at the property, and instead had to vacate the building. These representatives also made statements indicating that defendants intended to remove the artwork already in place in the building's lobby.

As a result of defendants' actions, artists commenced this litigation. On April 26, 1994 the district court issued a temporary restraining order enjoining defendants from taking any action to alter, deface, modify or mutilate the artwork installed in the building. In May 1994 a hearing was held on whether a preliminary injunction should issue. The district court subsequently granted a preliminary injunction enjoining defendants from removing the artwork pending the resolution of the instant litigation.

A bench trial was subsequently held in June and July 1994, at the conclusion of which the trial court granted the artists the permanent injunction prohibiting defendants from distorting, mutilating, modifying, destroying and removing plaintiffs' artwork. The injunction is to remain in effect for the lifetimes of the three plaintiffs. Plaintiffs' other claims, including their cause of action for tortious interference and a request for an award of costs and attorney's fees and that they be allowed to continue to add to the artwork in the lobby, as well as defendants' counterclaim for waste, were all dismissed with prejudice. This appeal and cross-appeal followed.

DISCUSSION

I. Artists' Moral Rights

A. History of Artists' Moral Rights

Because it was under the rubric of the Visual Artists Rights Act of 1990 that plaintiffs obtained injunctive relief in the district court, we must explore, at least in part, the contours of that Act. In doing so it is necessary to review briefly the concept of artists' moral rights and the history and development of those rights in American jurisprudence, which led up to passage of the statute we must now examine.

The term "moral rights" has its origins in the civil law and is a translation of the French *le droit moral*, which is meant to capture those rights of a spiritual, non-economic and personal nature. The rights spring from a belief that an artist in the process of creation injects his spirit into the work and that the artist's personality, as well as the integrity of the work, should therefore be protected and preserved. Because they are personal to the artist, moral rights exist independently of an artist's copyright in his or her work.

While the rubric of moral rights encompasses many varieties of rights, two are protected in nearly every jurisdiction recognizing their existence: attribution and integrity. See Art Law at 420. The right of attribution generally consists of the right of an artist to be recognized by name as the author of his work or to publish anonymously or pseudonymously, the right to prevent the author's work from being attributed to someone else, and to prevent the use of the author's name on works created by others, including distorted editions of the author's original work. The right of integrity allows the author to prevent any deforming or mutilating changes to his work, even after title in the work has been transferred.

In some jurisdictions the integrity right also protects artwork from destruction. Whether or not a work of art is protected from destruction represents a fundamentally different perception of the purpose of moral rights. If integrity is meant to stress the public interest in preserving a nation's culture, destruction is prohibited; if the right is meant to emphasize the author's personality, destruction is seen as less harmful than the continued display of deformed or mutilated work that misrepresents the artist and destruction may proceed.

Although moral rights are well established in the civil law, they are of recent vintage in American jurisprudence. Federal and state courts typically recognized the existence of such rights in other nations, but rejected artists' attempts to inject them into U.S. law. Nonetheless,

American courts have in varying degrees acknowledged the idea of moral rights, cloaking the concept in the guise of other legal theories, such as copyright, unfair competition, invasion of privacy, defamation, and breach of contract.

In the landmark case of *Gilliam v. American Broadcasting Companies, Inc.*, 538 F.2d 14 (2d Cir. 1976), we relied on copyright law and unfair competition principles to safeguard the integrity rights of the "Monty Python" group, noting that although the law "seeks to vindicate the economic, rather than the personal rights of authors . . . the economic incentive for artistic . . . creation . . . cannot be reconciled with the inability of artists to obtain relief for mutilation or misrepresentation of their work to the public on which the artists are financially dependent." Because decisions protecting artists rights are often "clothed in terms of proprietary right in one's creation," we continued, "they also properly vindicate the author's personal right to prevent the presentation of his work to the public in a distorted form."

Artists fared better in state legislatures than they generally had in courts. California was the first to take up the task of protecting artists with the passage in 1979 of the California Art Preservation Act, Cal. Civ. Code § 987 et seq. (West 1982 & Supp. 1995), followed in 1983 by New York's enactment of the Artist's Authorship Rights Act, N.Y. Arts & Cult. Aff. Law § 14.03 (McKinney Supp. 1995). Nine other states have also passed moral rights statutes, generally following either the California or New York models.

B. Visual Artists Rights Act of 1990

Although bills protecting artists' moral rights had first been introduced in Congress in 1979, they had drawn little support. The issue of federal protection of moral rights was a prominent hurdle in the debate over whether the United States should join the Berne Convention, the international agreement protecting literary and artistic works. Article 6[bis] of the Berne Convention protects attribution and integrity, stating in relevant part:

> Independently of the author's economic rights, and even after the transfer of the said rights, the author shall have the right to claim authorship of the work and to object to any distortion, mutilation or other modification of, or other derogatory action in relation to, the said work, which would be prejudicial to his honor or reputation.

Berne Convention for the Protection of Literary and Artistic Works, September 9, 1886, art. 6[bis], S. Treaty Doc. No. 27, 99th Cong., 2d Sess. 41 (1986).

The Berne Convention's protection of moral rights posed a significant difficulty for U.S. adherence. See Copyright Law at 1022 ("The obligation of the United States to provide droit moral . . . was the single most contentious issue surrounding Berne adherence."); Nimmer at 8D-15 ("During the debate over [the Berne Convention Implementation Act], Congress faced an avalanche of opposition to moral rights, including denunciations of moral rights by some of the bill's most vociferous advocates."); H.R. Rep. No. 514, 101st Cong., 2d Sess. 7 (1990), reprinted in 1990 U.S.C.C.A.N. 6915, 6917 ("After almost 100 years of debate, the United States joined the Berne Convention . . . . Consensus over United States adherence was slow to develop in large part because of debate over the requirements of Article 6[bis].").

Congress passed the Berne Convention Implementation Act of 1988, Pub. L. No. 100-568, 102 Stat. 2853 (1988), and side-stepped the difficult question of protecting moral rights. It declared that the Berne Convention is not self-executing, existing law satisfied the United States' obligations in adhering to the Convention, its provisions are not enforceable through any action brought pursuant to the Convention itself, and neither adherence to the Convention nor the implementing legislation expands or reduces any rights under federal, state, or common law to claim authorship of a work or to object to any distortion, mutilation, or other modification of a work.

Two years later Congress enacted the Visual Artists Rights Act of 1990 (VARA or Act), Pub. L. No. 101-650 (tit. VI), 104 Stat. 5089, 5128-33 (1990). Construing this Act constitutes the subject of the present appeal. The Act

> protects both the reputations of certain visual artists and the works of art they create. It provides these artists with the rights of "attribution" and "integrity." . . .
>
> These rights are analogous to those protected by Article 6bis of the Berne Convention, which are commonly known as "moral rights." The theory of moral rights is that they result in a climate of artistic worth and honor that encourages the author in the arduous act of creation.

H.R. Rep. No. 514 at 5 (internal quote omitted). The Act brings to fruition Emerson's insightful observation.

Its principal provisions afford protection only to authors of works of visual art – a narrow class of art defined to include paintings, drawings, prints, sculptures, or photographs produced for exhibition purposes, existing in a single copy or limited edition of 200 copies or fewer. 17 U.S.C. § 101 (Supp. III 1991). With numerous exceptions, VARA grants three rights: the right of attribution, the right of integrity and, in the case of works of visual art of "recognized stature," the right to prevent destruction. 17 U.S.C. § 106A (Supp. III 1991). For works created on or after June 1, 1991 – the effective date of the Act – the rights provided for endure for the life of the author or, in the case of a joint work, the life of the last surviving author. The rights cannot be transferred, but may be waived by a writing signed by the author. Copyright registration is not required to bring an action for infringement of the rights granted under VARA, or to secure statutory damages and attorney's fees. 17 U.S.C. §§ 411, 412 (1988 & Supp. III 1991). All remedies available under copyright law, other than criminal remedies, are available in an action for infringement of moral rights. 17 U.S.C. § 506 (1988 & Supp. III 1991). With this historical background in hand, we pass to the merits of the present litigation.

II Work of Visual Art

Because VARA is relatively new, a fuller explication of it is helpful. In analyzing the Act, therefore, we will follow in order the definition set forth in § 101, as did the district court when presiding over this litigation. The district court determined that the work of art installed in the lobby of Associates' building was a work of visual art as defined by VARA; that distortion, mutilation, or modification of the work would prejudice plaintiffs' honor and reputations; that the work was of recognized stature, thus protecting it from destruction (including removal that would result in destruction); and that Associates consented to or ratified the installation of the work in its building. The result was that defendants were enjoined from removing or otherwise altering the work during the lifetimes of the three artists.

A. Singleness of the Work

As a preliminary matter, we must determine whether the trial court correctly found that the work is a single piece of art, to be analyzed under VARA as a whole, rather than separate works to be considered individually. This finding was a factual one reviewed under the clearly erroneous standard. For purposes of framing the issues at trial the parties entered into a joint stipulation relating to numerous facts, including a definition of "the Work." This stipulated definition contained a long, detailed list of all the sculptural elements contained in the building's lobby. The district court found that, with a few precise exceptions determined to be separate works of art, the artwork created by plaintiffs in the lobby was a single work. This finding was based on testimony, credited by the trial judge, of the artists themselves and of their expert witnesses.

The trial court found further support for its conclusion in the method by which the artists created the work – each additional element of the sculpture was based on the element preceding it so that they would mesh together. The result was a thematically consistent, interrelated work whose elements could not be separated without losing continuity and meaning. The record evidence of singleness was confirmed at the request of the parties by the district court's own inspection of the work.

Appellants' primary contention is that the finding of singleness is inconsistent with a finding that certain works of art were separate from the work that is the subject of this appeal. This assertion rests on the mistaken belief that the parties' joint stipulation to a definition of "the Work" precluded an ultimate determination by the factfinder that most but not all of the work installed in the lobby was a single artwork. In other words, according to appellants, either every component in the stipulated definition is part of a single work or every component is an individual work; there is no middle ground. Appellants' goal is to have VARA applied to each element of the sculpture individually, so that components that may not be visual art standing alone cannot be considered visual art when they are combined by the artists to create a whole that has a nature different than the mere sum of its parts.

Appellants' goal is not attainable. The parties stipulated that when they used the term "the Work" it included a list of sculptural components. The result was that during the trial there was no dispute as to the parties' meaning when referring to "the Work." The trial court was free to find that a few items of "the Work" were separate works of art, while the remainder of "the Work" was a single, interrelated, indivisible work of art. The finding of singleness was based on determinations of witness credibility as well as the district court's own inspection of the artwork. We cannot say that such a finding was clearly erroneous.

B. The Statutory Definition

A "work of visual art" is defined by the Act in terms both positive (what it is) and negative (what it is not). In relevant part VARA defines a work of visual art as "a painting, drawing, print, or sculpture, existing in a single copy" or in a limited edition of 200 copies or fewer. 17 U.S.C. § 101. Although defendants aver that elements of the work are not visual art, their contention is foreclosed by the factual finding that the work is a single, indivisible whole. Concededly, considered as a whole, the work is a sculpture and exists only in a single copy. Therefore, the work satisfies the Act's positive definition of a work of visual art. We next turn to the second part of the statutory definition – what is not a work of visual art.

The definition of visual art excludes "any poster, map, globe, chart, technical drawing, diagram, model, applied art, motion picture or other audio-visual work." 17 U.S.C. § 101. Congress meant to distinguish works of visual art from other media, such as audio-visual works and motion pictures, due to the different circumstances surrounding how works of each genre are created and disseminated. See H.R. Rep. No. 514 at 9. Although this concern led to a narrow definition of works of visual art,

> the courts should use common sense and generally accepted standards of the artistic community in determining whether a particular work falls within the scope of the definition. Artists may work in a variety of media, and use any number of materials in creating their works. Therefore, whether a particular work falls within the definition should not depend on the medium or materials used.

Id. at 11.

"Applied art" describes "two- and three-dimensional ornamentation or decoration that is affixed to otherwise utilitarian objects." Defendants' assertion that at least parts of the work are applied art appears to rest on the fact that some of the sculptural elements are affixed to the lobby's floor, walls, and ceiling – all utilitarian objects. Interpreting applied art to include such works would render meaningless VARA's protection for works of visual art installed in buildings. A court should not read one part of a statute so as to deprive another part of meaning.

Appellants do not suggest the entire work is applied art. The district court correctly stated that even if components of the work standing alone were applied art, "nothing in VARA proscribes protection of works of visual art that incorporate elements of, rather than constitute, applied art." VARA's legislative history leaves no doubt that "a new and independent work created from snippets of [excluded] materials, such as a collage, is of course not excluded" from the definition of a work of visual art. H.R. Rep. No. 514 at 14. The trial judge correctly ruled the work is not applied art precluded from protection under the Act.

III Work Made for Hire

Also excluded from the definition of a work of visual art is any work made for hire. A "work made for hire" is defined in the Copyright Act, in relevant part, as "a work prepared by an employee within the scope of his or her employment." Appellants maintain the work was made for hire and therefore is not a work of visual art under VARA. The district court held otherwise, finding that the plaintiffs were hired as independent contractors.

A. Reid Tests

The Copyright Act does not define the terms "employee" or "scope of employment." In *Community for Creative Non-Violence v. Reid*, 490 U.S. 730 (1989), the Supreme Court looked to the general common law of agency for guidance. It held that a multi-factor balancing test was required to determine if a work was produced for hire (by an employee) or was produced by an independent contractor. The Court elaborated 13 specific factors:

> the hiring party's right to control the manner and means by which the product is accomplished. . . . the skill required; the source of the instrumentalities and tools; the location of the work; the duration of the relationship between the parties; whether the hiring party has the right to assign additional projects to the hired party; the extent of the hired party's discretion over when and how long to work; the method of payment; the hired party's role in hiring and paying assistants; whether the work is part of the regular business of the hiring party; whether the hiring party is in business; the provision of employee benefits; and the tax treatment of the hired party.

Reid, 490 U.S. at 751-52. While all of these factors are relevant, no single factor is determinative. Instead, the factors are weighed by referring to the facts of a given case.

The district court determined that the sculpture was not "work for hire" and therefore not excluded from the definition of visual art. The Reid test is a list of factors not all of which may come into play in a given case. The Reid test is therefore easily misapplied. We are usually reluctant to reverse a district court's factual findings as to the presence or absence of any of the Reid factors and do so only when the district court's findings are clearly erroneous. By contrast, the ultimate legal conclusion as to whether or not the sculpture is "work for hire" is reviewed de novo. The district court correctly stated the legal test. But some of its factual findings, we think, were clearly erroneous.

B. Factors Applied

The district court properly noted that *Aymes* established five factors which would be relevant in nearly all cases: the right to control the manner and means of production; requisite skill; provision of employee benefits; tax treatment of the hired party; whether the hired party may be assigned additional projects. Analysis begins with a discussion of these factors. [*Aymes v. Bonelli*, 980 F.2d 857, 861 (2d Cir. 1992).]

First, plaintiffs had complete artistic freedom with respect to every aspect of the sculpture's creation. Although the artists heeded advice or accepted suggestions from building engineers, architects, and others, such actions were not a relinquishment of their artistic freedom. The evidence strongly supports the finding that plaintiffs controlled the work's "manner and means." This fact, in turn, lent credence to their contention that they were independent contractors. While artistic freedom remains a central factor in our inquiry, the Supreme Court has cautioned that "the extent of control the hiring party exercises over the details of the product is not dispositive." *Reid*, 490 U.S. at 752. Hence, resolving the question of whether plaintiffs had artistic freedom does not end the analysis.

The district court also correctly found the artists' conception and execution of the work required great skill in execution. Appellants' contention that the plaintiffs' reliance on assistants in some way mitigates the skill required for this work is meritless, particularly because each of the plaintiffs is a professional sculptor and the parties stipulated that professional sculpting is a highly skilled occupation. The right to control the manner and means and the requisite skill needed for execution of this project were both properly found by the district court to weigh against "work for hire" status.

The trial court erred, however, when it ruled that the defendants could not assign the artists additional projects. First, the employment agreement between SIG Management Company and the artists clearly states that the artists agreed not only to install the sculpture but also to "render such other related services and duties as may be assigned to [them] from time to time by the Company." By the very terms of the contract the defendants and their predecessors in interest had the right to assign other related projects to the artists. The district court incorrectly decided that this language supported the artists' claim to be independent contractors. While the artists' obligations were limited to related services and duties, the defendants nonetheless did have the right to assign to plaintiffs work other than the principal sculpture.

Further, the defendants did, in fact, assign such other projects. The district court concedes as much, explaining that "plaintiffs did create art work on the property other than that in the

Lobby." The record shows the artists performed projects on the sixth floor of the building, on the eighth floor, and in the boiler room. Thus, on at least three different occasions the plaintiffs were assigned additional projects, which they completed without further compensation. ...

We must also consider factors the district court correctly found to favor finding the sculpture to be work for hire. Specifically, the provision of employee benefits and the tax treatment of the plaintiffs weigh strongly in favor of employee status. The defendants paid payroll and social security taxes, provided employee benefits such as life, health, and liability insurance and paid vacations, and contributed to unemployment insurance and workers' compensation funds on plaintiffs' behalf. Moreover, two of the three artists filed for unemployment benefits after their positions were terminated, listing the building's management company as their former employer. Other formal indicia of an employment relationship existed. For instance, each plaintiff was paid a weekly salary. The artists also agreed in their written contract that they would work principally for the defendants for the duration of their agreement on a 40-hour per week basis and they would only do other work to the extent that it would not "interfere with services to be provided" to the defendants. All of these facts strongly suggest the artists were employees. ...

C. Employee Status

Our review of the legal conclusion drawn from balancing the various Reid factors persuades us that the factors that weigh in favor of finding the artists were employees outweigh those factors supporting the artists' claim that they were independent contractors. ... These factors, properly considered and weighed with the employee benefits granted plaintiffs and the tax treatment accorded them, are more than sufficient to demonstrate that the artists were employees, and the sculpture is therefore a work made for hire as a matter of law.

IV Defendants' Counterclaim and Plaintiffs' Cross-appeal

Finally, since we have determined that the work is one made for hire and therefore outside the scope of VARA's protection, we need not discuss that Act's broad protection of visual art and the protection it affords works of art incorporated into a building. Also, as plaintiffs' sculpture was not protected from removal because the artists were employees and not independent contractors, we need not reach the defendants' Fifth Amendment takings argument.

Moreover, because the sculpture is not protected by VARA from removal resulting in its destruction or alteration, we do not address plaintiffs' contentions that VARA entitles them to complete the "unfinished" portion of the work, that they are entitled to reasonable costs and attorney's fees, and that appellants tortiously interfered with the artists' contract with SIG and the Limited Partnership. Finally, the district court dismissed defendants' counterclaim against the artists for waste, finding, inter alia, that such a cause of action under New York law may only be brought by a landlord against a tenant. Appellants have failed to persuade us that it was error to dismiss this counterclaim.

CONCLUSION

Accordingly, the district court's order insofar as it held the work was one not made for hire is reversed and the injunction vacated. In all other respects, the order of the district court is affirmed. Each party to bear its own costs.

Martin v. City of Indianapolis

192 F.3d 608 (7th Cir. 1999)

We are not art critics, do not pretend to be and do not need to be to decide this case. A large outdoor stainless steel sculpture by plaintiff Jan Martin, an artist, was demolished by the defendant as part of an urban renewal project. Plaintiff brought a one-count suit against the City of Indianapolis (the "City") under the Visual Artists Rights Act of 1990 ("VARA"), 17 U.S.C. § 101 *et seq.* The parties filed cross-motions for summary judgment. The district court granted plaintiff's motion and awarded plaintiff statutory damages in the maximum amount allowed for a non-willful statutory violation. …

Plaintiff is an artist, but in this instance more with a welding torch than with a brush. He offered evidence to show, not all of it admitted, that his works have been displayed in museums, and other works created for private commissions, including a time capsule for the Indianapolis Museum of Art Centennial. He has also done sculptured jewelry for the Indiana Arts Commission. In 1979, at the Annual Hoosier Salem Art Show, plaintiff was awarded the prize for best of show in any medium. He holds various arts degrees from Purdue University, the Art Institute of Chicago and Bowling Green State University in Ohio. Plaintiff had been employed as production coordinator for Tarpenning-LaFollette Co. (the "Company"), a metal contracting firm in Indianapolis. It was in this position that he turned his artistic talents to metal sculpture fabrication.

In 1984, plaintiff received permission from the Indianapolis Metropolitan Development Commission to erect a twenty-by-forty-foot metal sculpture on land owned by John LaFollette, chairman of the Company. The Company also agreed to furnish the materials. The resulting Project Agreement between the City and the Company granted a zoning variance to permit the erection of plaintiff's proposed sculpture. An attachment to that agreement and the center of this controversy provided as follows:

> Should a determination be made by the Department of Metropolitan Development that the subject sculpture is no longer compatible with the existing land use or that the acquisition of the property is necessary, the owner of the land and the owner of the sculpture will receive written notice signed by the Director of the Department of Metropolitan Development giving the owners of the land and sculpture ninety (90) days to remove said sculpture. Subject to weather and ground conditions.

Plaintiff went to work on the project and in a little over two years it was completed. He named it "Symphony # 1," but as it turns out in view of this controversy, a more suitable musical name might have been "1812 Overture." Because of the possibility that the sculpture might someday have to be removed, as provided for in the Project Agreement, Symphony # 1 was engineered and built by plaintiff so that it could be disassembled for removal and later reassembled. The sculpture did not go unnoticed by the press, public or art community. Favorable comments admitted into evidence and objected to by the City are now an issue on appeal and their admissibility will be considered hereinafter.

The trouble began in April 1992 when the City notified LaFollette that there would be public hearings on the City's proposed acquisition of various properties as part of an urban renewal plan. One of the properties to be acquired was home to Symphony # 1. Kim Martin, president of the Company and plaintiff's brother, responded to the City. He reminded the City that the

Company had paid for Symphony # 1, and had signed the agreement with the Metropolitan Development Corporation pertaining to the eventuality of removal. Martin stated that if the sculpture was to be removed, the Company would be willing to donate it to the City provided the City would bear the costs of removal to a new site, but that plaintiff would like some input as to where his sculpture might be placed. Plaintiff also personally appeared before the Metropolitan Development Commission and made the same proposal. This was followed by a letter from plaintiff to the Mayor reiterating the removal proposal. The Mayor responded that he was referring plaintiff's proposal to his staff to see what could be done.

The City thereafter purchased the land. At the closing, plaintiff again repeated his proposal and agreed to assist so Symphony # 1 could be saved and, if necessary, moved without damage. The City's response was that plaintiff would be contacted in the event the sculpture was to be removed. Shortly thereafter, the City awarded a contract to demolish the sculpture, and demolition followed, all without prior notice to plaintiff or the Company. This lawsuit resulted in which summary judgment was allowed for plaintiff. However, his victory was not entirely satisfactory to him, nor was the City satisfied. The City appealed, and plaintiff cross-appealed.

VARA seems to be a stepchild of our copyright laws, but does not require copyright registration. Some remedies under the Copyright Act, however, including attorney's fees, are recoverable. 17 U.S.C. §§ 504-05. VARA provides: "The author of a work of visual art . . . shall have the right . . . to prevent any destruction of a work of recognized stature, and any intentional or grossly negligent destruction of that work is a violation of that right." The district court considered Symphony # 1 to be of *recognized stature"* under the evidence presented and thus concluded that the City had violated plaintiff's rights under VARA. That finding is contested by the City.

"Recognized stature" is a necessary finding under VARA in order to protect a work of visual art from destruction. In spite of its significance, that phrase is not defined in VARA, leaving its intended meaning and application open to argument and judicial resolution. The only case found undertaking to define and apply "recognized stature" is *Carter v. Helmsley-Spear, Inc.*, 861 F. Supp. 303 (S.D.N.Y. 1994), *aff'd in part, vacated in part, rev'd in part*, 71 F.3d 77 (2nd Cir. 1995). Involved was an unusual work of art consisting of interrelated sculptural elements constructed from recycled materials, mostly metal, to decorate the lobby of a commercial building in a borough of New York City. Part of the work was "a giant hand fashioned from an old school bus, [and] a face made of automobile parts . . . ." Although the Second Circuit reversed the district court and held that the work was not a work of visual art protected by VARA, the district court presented an informative discussion in determining whether a work of visual art may qualify as one of "recognized stature." That determination is based greatly on the testimony of experts on both sides of the issue, as would ordinarily be expected.

The stature test formulated by the New York district court required:

> (1) that the visual art in question has "stature," i.e. is viewed as meritorious, and (2) that this stature is "recognized" by art experts, other members of the artistic community, or by some cross-section of society. In making this showing, plaintiffs generally, but not inevitably, will need to call expert witnesses to testify before the trier of fact.

Carter I, 861 F. Supp. at 325.

Even though the district court in this present case found that test was satisfied by the plaintiff's evidence, plaintiff argues that the *Carter v. Helmsley-Spear* test may be more rigorous than Congress intended. That may be, but we see no need for the purposes of this case to endeavor to refine that rule. Plaintiff's evidence, however, is not as complete as in *Carter v. Helmsley-Spear*, possibly because Symphony # 1 was destroyed by the City without the opportunity for experts to appraise the sculpture in place.

The City objects to the "stature" testimony that was offered by plaintiff as inadmissible hearsay. If not admitted, it would result in plaintiff's failure to sustain his burden of proof. It is true that plaintiff offered no evidence of experts or others by deposition, affidavit or interrogatories. Plaintiff's evidence of "stature" consisted of certain newspaper and magazine articles, and various letters, including a letter from an art gallery director and a letter to the editor of *The Indianapolis News*, all in support of the sculpture, as well as a program from the show at which a model of the sculpture won "Best of Show." After reviewing the City's objection, the district court excluded plaintiff's "programs and awards" evidence as lacking adequate foundation, but nevertheless found Martin had met his "stature" burden of proof with his other evidence.

Included in the admitted evidence, for example, was a letter dated October 25, 1982 from the Director of the Herron School of Art, Indiana University, Indianapolis. It was written to the Company and says in part, "The proposed sculpture is, in my opinion, an interesting and aesthetically stimulating configuration of forms and structures." *The Indianapolis Star*, in a four-column article by its visual arts editor, discussed public sculpture in Indianapolis. This article included a photograph of Symphony # 1. The article lamented that the City had "been graced by only five pieces of note, "but that two more had been added that particular year, one being plaintiff's sculpture. It noted, among other things, that Symphony # 1 had been erected without the aid of "federal grants" and without the help of any committee of concerned citizens. Other public sculptures came in for some criticism in the article. However, in discussing Symphony # 1, the author wrote: "Gleaming clean and abstract, yet domestic in scale and reference, irregularly but securely cabled together, the sculpture shows the site what it might be. It unites the area, providing a nexus, a marker, a designation, an identity and, presumably, a point of pride." …

Next the City claims that the Project Agreement entered into pre-VARA by plaintiff and the City encompassed many of plaintiff's rights under VARA. Therefore, the City argues, that whereas plaintiff failed to remove his work within the time allowed in the contract, plaintiff waived any cause of action he might have had under VARA. That failure was the City's, not plaintiff's, as under the Agreement the City was obligated to give the owners of the land and the sculpture ninety days to remove the sculpture. The City, after discussing with the Company and plaintiff possible other uses for the tract and the removal proposal, failed to give the required notice and went ahead and demolished the sculpture. Nothing had happened between the parties prior to that which could constitute a waiver of any rights by the Company or plaintiff. Plaintiff had no notice of the City letting a contract for Symphony # 1's demolition and no notice when that demolition would actually occur. After the preliminary and ongoing discussions plaintiff and the Company had with the City, when there was no immediate threat of imminent demolition, plaintiff had the right to continue to rely on the specific notice provided in the Agreement, unless it had been waived, which it was not.

Plaintiff and the Company had proposed a solution if the sculpture was to be moved. That proposal was still pending when the surprise destruction of Symphony # 1 occurred. Prior to the demolition, nothing more had been heard from anyone, including the Mayor. Bureaucratic ineptitude may be the only explanation. Under 17 U.S.C. § 106A(e)(1), an artist may waive VARA rights "in a written instrument signed by the author," specifying to what the waiver applies. There is no written waiver instrument in this case which falls within the VARA requirements. We regard this argument to be without merit.

In spite of the City's conduct resulting in the intentional destruction of the sculpture, we do not believe under all the circumstances, particularly given the fact that the issue of VARA rights had not been raised until this suit, that the City's conduct was "willful," as used in VARA, 17 U.S.C. § 504(c)(2), so as to entitle the plaintiff to enhanced damages. This appears to be a case of bureaucratic failure within the City government, not a willful violation of plaintiff's VARA rights. As far as we can tell from the record, those VARA rights were unknown to the City. The parties proceeded under their pre-VARA agreement which the City breached. However, plaintiff retained his VARA rights. As unfortunate as the City's unannounced demolition of Symphony # 1 was, it does not qualify plaintiff for damages under VARA....

Being fully satisfied with the district court's careful resolution of these unique issues and the resulting judgment, the district court's finding is affirmed in all respects.

DISSENT: MANION, *Circuit Judge*, concurring in part and dissenting in part. Like my colleagues, I am not an art critic. So I begin with the well-worn adage that one man's junk is another man's treasure. No doubt Jan Martin treasured what the city's bulldozers treated as junk. At this point in the litigation this court is not in a position to attach either label (or perhaps one falling somewhere in between) to Symphony # 1. For the Martin sculpture to receive protection under the Visual Arts Rights Act (VARA), it has to rise to the statutory level of "recognized stature." Because at this summary judgment stage, at least, it has clearly not merited the protection that goes with that description, I respectfully dissent.

Another well-worn adage advises that you should never look a gift horse in the mouth. Of course anyone who has ever accepted a gift horse that turns out to be lame or otherwise infirm quickly understands the error of that advice when the feed and veterinary bills arrive. When the City acquired several tracts of land for urban renewal, Martin's Symphony # 1 remained in place on one of the tracts. Martin offered to donate the sculpture to the City if it would remove and relocate it to another site. The City examined this "gift" and determined it would have cost it $8,000 to relocate, so it declined the offer. But it did agree to notify Martin in advance of any renewal project so he could remove Symphony # 1 if he so chose. Although it appears that Martin was fully aware that the sculpture's days were numbered, the City did not send him an official notice before the bulldozer moved in. If this were a simple breach of contract claim (albeit not a federal case), damages could well be in order. Instead, this is a federal claim under VARA, and different standards apply.

I dissent, however, because summary judgment is not appropriate here. A plaintiff cannot satisfy his burden of demonstrating recognized stature through old newspaper articles and unverified letters, some of which do not even address the artwork in question. Rather, as the district court stated in *Carter*, in "making this showing [of recognized stature] plaintiffs generally, but not inevitably, will need to call expert witnesses to testify before the trier of fact." Instances where expert testimony on this point is not necessary will be rare, and this is not one of those exceptional cases where something of unquestioned recognition and stature was destroyed. Furthermore, where newspaper articles are admitted into evidence only to acknowledge recognition but not for the truth of the matter asserted (that the art in question was good or bad), a plaintiff needs more to overcome *a defendant's* motion for summary judgment on a VARA claim, much less prevail on his own summary judgment motion. While the very publication of newspaper articles on a work of art may have bearing on the "recognized" element, there has to be some evidence that the art had stature (i.e., that it met a certain high level of quality). ...

For now, however, those who are purchasers or donees of art had best beware. To avoid being the perpetual curator of a piece of visual art that has lost (or perhaps never had) its luster, the recipient must obtain at the outset a waiver of the artist's rights under VARA. Before awarding building permits for erection of sculptures, municipalities might be well advised to obtain a written waiver of the artist's rights too. If not, once destroyed, art of questionable value may acquire a minimum worth of $20,000.00 under VARA.

Report Waiver of Moral Rights in Visual Artworks

Executive Summary, Report of the Copyright Office (October 1996)[57]

On June 10, 1992, eighteen months after VARA's enactment, the [Copyright Office (Office)] published a Request for Information in the Federal Register seeking comments on artists' bargaining power relative to that of commercial users of artworks, on parties' awareness of the VARA rights and their inclusion of waiver provisions in contracts, on the contractual compliance with the law's requirements that works and uses subject to waivers be specifically identified, on the actual exercise of waivers, and on the relative numbers of waivers granted for rights of attribution and integrity for moveable works of visual art and for art works incorporated into buildings. We asked for empirical evidence on the kinds of contracts that include waivers and on the economic impact of those waivers; and we requested parties' assessment of whether the artist's renown affected his or her waiver of rights, and on what factors influence artists' decisions to waive rights. Finally, we asked for comments on possible constitutional problems that might arise if waivers were prohibited. ...

More than 1,000 persons filed written responses to the survey. Responses were received from 47 states and the District of Columbia, and 955 respondents were self-described visual artists. Most artists grossed less that $10,000 annually from their artwork and most had multiple sources of income.

About three-fourths of the respondents claimed awareness of moral rights, although many who elaborated in written comments stressed the need for more education of artists. Fewer than half knew that moral rights could be waived. Seven percent of those who answered the question said waiver clauses were routinely included in artists' contracts, but nearly 40 percent said waiver clauses were part of contracts for commissioned works.

Nearly one quarter of artists covered by VARA knew of artists who had been asked to waive their moral rights. Thirteen percent of artists covered by VARA said they had refused contracts because they included waivers and a similar number had insisted that a waiver clause be struck from a contract. These artists were generally those who earned more than $25,000 annually from their art or who were represented by an agent. More than half of those who had rejected a request

---

[57] *Id.*

for waiver said such rejection voided the deal. In general, those participants who filed written commentary believe that VARA does little to enhance the artist's inferior bargaining position relative to the buyer.

More than half of the respondents who had experienced waivers said they complied with the specificity requirements of VARA, and about one-third said contracts contained a separate price for the waiver of moral rights. However, most art contracts continue to be oral and therefore cannot contain valid waiver clauses under the terms of VARA. Many artists decried the complexity of art contracts and stated that legal requirements were too burdensome and legal advice too costly. ...

On June 21, 1995, the Copyright Office held a public hearing to solicit comments on the effect of the waiver of moral rights provision of VARA. ... Most saw the need for the sec. 113 waiver provisions for works incorporated into buildings. For one attorney, however, the fact that most contracts for major commissions will now routinely require waivers means that the sec. 113 waiver provision should be tightened, if not repealed. ...

Many panelists believed that repeal of sec. 113 waiver would result in a chilling effect on creation of art, since property owners may be unwilling to commit to a permanent structure. On the other hand, there may be a chilling effect even if building owners have secured a waiver: several artists reported that, had they been operating under a waiver, they would have undertaken the project, but with a different scale and design. Some predicted a standard term in landlord-tenant contracts requiring tenants to get waivers or refrain from installing art.

Other recommendations were made for VARA. For example, several parties agreed that one joint author should not have the ability to waive for all co-authors. Others believed VARA should apply to print or broadcast reproductions of works, thus covering distortions in books, magazines and electronic media. ...

Notes and Questions

a. To what extent do the cases identified by the Register of Copyright regarding the U.S. moral rights law compare to the treaty obligation to adhere to Article 6^{Bis} of the Berne Convention?

b. The Supreme Court has significantly revised the role that Lanham Act § 43(a) can play with regard to protection for the attribution of a motion picture video cassette, providing that the source of goods is the distributor of those cassettes. Does the same source of goods analysis apply to the creation of a work of art? Does it matter whether the work is incorporated into a utilitarian object (such as the base of a lamp or a piece of jewelry) or if the work is a more traditional oil painting or photograph? See *Dastar Corp. v. Twentieth Century Fox Film Corp.*, 539 U.S. 23 (2003).

c. When an artist's clay model for a sculpture is left outdoors, does this constitute a violation of VARA? In this case the model was a 35-foot clay model for a statue's head made for the "purpose of memorializing the life of Catherine of Braganza, Princess of Portugal and Queen of England in the mid-seventeenth century and namesake of the borough of Queens." The statue was to become "a monument to Queen Catherine to be installed at a prominent place within the Hunters Point Redevelopment Project in Queens." What result from the weather damage or the work by a second artist who attempted the restoration? See *Flack v. Friends of Queen Catherine, Inc.*, 139 F. Supp. 2d 526 (S.D.N.Y. 2001).

d. What attributes constitute the artwork? Often, sculptural works are designed for particular locations. To what extent does the spatial environment define the work and become part of the installation for purposes of VARA protection? See *Phillips v. Pembroke Real Estate, Inc.*, 459 F.3d 128 (1st Cir. 2006).

e. What constitutes a work was art of a sufficiently recognized stature to gain VARA protection? Compare *Pollara v. Seymour*, 344 F.3d 265 (2d Cir. 2003); *Martin v. City of Indianapolis*, 192 F.3d 608 (7th Cir. 1999); and *Scott v. Dixon*, 309 F. Supp. 2d 395 (E.D.N.Y. 2004).

f. A church mural depicting a very masculine Christ met with increasing consternation by the congregation, which had the mural covered over. The artist sued under Article 6[Bis] of the Berne Convention but could not establish that the treaty applied to New York real property law. See *Crimi v. Rutgers Presbyterian Church*, 194 Misc. 570, 89 N.Y.S.2d 813 (1949).

g. In addition to VARA, states including California, New York and Massachusetts have state legislation involving the protection of moral rights for authors. Some states also provide ongoing economic rights to artists such as *droit de suite* (a royalty for visual artists). See *Phillips v. Pembroke Real Estate, Inc.*, 459 F.3d 128 (1st Cir. 2006); Massachusetts Art Preservation Act, Mass. Gen. Laws ch. 231, § 85S; California Art Preservation Act, Cal. Civ. Code § 987 (1979).

h. To what extent does VARA preempt the previous state statutes that provide moral rights or economic resale rights? See This statute is still on the books in New York, but has been declared expressly preempted by VARA. See *Board of Managers of Soho International Arts Condominium v. City of New York*, 2003 WL 21403333 (S.D.N.Y. 2003) (unreported), *reconsideration denied*, 2003 WL 21767653 (S.D.N.Y. 2003) reviewing N.Y. Art & Cult Affr § 14.03 (McKinney 1984). The Court explains the standard copyright preemption standard that a "statute pre-empts a state law if two conditions are met: 1) if the work to which the rights under the state statute falls within the "subject matter" of copyright as specified in 17 U.S.C. §§ 102 and 103 and 2) if the right is the same or "equivalent" to those granted by [the state law]." *Id.* (internal citations omitted).

Problem XVII-B

Bryce has been in pre-production for a feature-length film. The director of photography hopes to shoot a location that is described in the screenplay and based on a true historical story. To shoot the location, a mural painted in 2001 would need to be covered during the shooting. Bryce has been assured by the set designer that the mural can be covered with a paint that can easily be removed. Bryce has contacted the building owners for permission to temporarily cover the mural in order to make the film. Because of the historical importance of the location and potential marketing opportunities, the building's owners would like the film to be shot, but they are concerned that the temporary covering of the mural would interfere with the artist's rights under VARA. Please advise Bryce on the obligations the mural owners have to the artist under VARA. If Bryce were to remove the image in post-production rather than by covering it, explain any VARA or other copyright issues.

C. Government Regulation of Content in the Visual Arts

National Endowment for the Arts v. Finley

524 U.S. 569 (1998)

JUSTICE O'CONNOR delivered the opinion of the Court. The National Foundation on the Arts and Humanities Act, as amended in 1990, requires the Chairperson of the National Endowment for the Arts (NEA) to ensure that "artistic excellence and artistic merit are the criteria by which [grant] applications are judged, *taking into consideration general standards of decency and respect for the diverse beliefs and values of the American public.*" 20 U.S.C. § 954(d)(1). In this case, we review the Court of Appeals' determination that § 954(d)(1), on its face, impermissibly discriminates on the basis of viewpoint and is void for vagueness under the First and Fifth Amendments. We conclude that § 954(d)(1) is facially valid, as it neither inherently interferes with First Amendment rights nor violates constitutional vagueness principles.

With the establishment of the NEA in 1965, Congress embarked on a "broadly conceived national policy of support for the . . . arts in the United States," pledging federal funds to "help create and sustain not only a climate encouraging freedom of thought, imagination, and inquiry but also the material conditions facilitating the release of . . . creative talent." The enabling statute vests the NEA with substantial discretion to award grants; it identifies only the broadest funding priorities, including "artistic and cultural significance, giving emphasis to American creativity and cultural diversity," "professional excellence," and the encouragement of "public knowledge, education, understanding, and appreciation of the arts."

Applications for NEA funding are initially reviewed by advisory panels composed of experts in the relevant field of the arts. Under the 1990 Amendments to the enabling statute, those panels must reflect "diverse artistic and cultural points of view" and include "wide geographic, ethnic, and minority representation," as well as "lay individuals who are knowledgeable about the arts." The panels report to the 26-member National Council on the Arts (Council), which, in turn, advises the NEA Chairperson. The Chairperson has the ultimate authority to award grants but may not approve an application as to which the Council has made a negative recommendation.

Since 1965, the NEA has distributed over three billion dollars in grants to individuals and organizations, funding that has served as a catalyst for increased state, corporate, and foundation support for the arts. Congress has recently restricted the availability of federal funding for individual artists, confining grants primarily to qualifying organizations and state arts agencies, and constraining sub-granting. By far the largest portion of the grants distributed in fiscal year 1998 were awarded directly to state arts agencies. In the remaining categories, the most substantial grants were allocated to symphony orchestras, fine arts museums, dance theater foundations, and opera associations.

Throughout the NEA's history, only a handful of the agency's roughly 100,000 awards have generated formal complaints about misapplied funds or abuse of the public's trust. Two provocative works, however, prompted public controversy in 1989 and led to congressional revaluation of the NEA's funding priorities and efforts to increase oversight of its grant-making procedures. The Institute of Contemporary Art at the University of Pennsylvania had used $30,000 of a visual arts grant it received from the NEA to fund a 1989 retrospective of photographer Robert Mapplethorpe's work. The exhibit, entitled *The Perfect Moment*, included homoerotic photographs that several Members of Congress condemned as pornographic. Members also denounced artist Andres Serrano's work *Piss Christ*, a photograph of a crucifix immersed in urine. Serrano had been awarded a $15,000 grant from the Southeast Center for Contemporary Art, an organization that received NEA support.

When considering the NEA's appropriations for fiscal year 1990, Congress reacted to the controversy surrounding the Mapplethorpe and Serrano photographs by eliminating $45,000 from the agency's budget, the precise amount contributed to the two exhibits by NEA grant recipients. Congress also enacted an amendment providing that no NEA funds "may be used to promote, disseminate, or produce materials which in the judgment of [the NEA] may be considered obscene, including but not limited to, depictions of sadomasochism, homoeroticism, the sexual exploitation of children, or individuals engaged in sex acts and which, when taken as a whole, do not have serious literary, artistic, political, or scientific value." The NEA implemented Congress' mandate by instituting a requirement that all grantees certify in writing that they would not utilize federal funding to engage in projects inconsistent with the criteria in the 1990 appropriations bill. That certification requirement was subsequently invalidated as unconstitutionally vague by a Federal District Court, and the NEA did not appeal the decision.

In the 1990 appropriations bill, Congress also agreed to create an Independent Commission of constitutional law scholars to review the NEA's grant-making procedures and assess the possibility of more focused standards for public arts funding. The Commission's report, issued in September 1990, concluded that there is no constitutional obligation to provide arts funding, but also recommended that the NEA rescind the certification requirement and cautioned against legislation setting forth any content restrictions. Instead, the Commission suggested procedural changes to enhance the role of advisory panels and a statutory reaffirmation of "the high place the nation accords to the fostering of mutual respect for the disparate beliefs and values among us." ...

Ultimately, Congress adopted the Williams/Coleman Amendment, a bipartisan compromise between Members opposing any funding restrictions and those favoring some guidance to the agency. In relevant part, the Amendment became § 954(d)(1), which directs the Chairperson, in establishing procedures to judge the artistic merit of grant applications, to "take into consideration general standards of decency and respect for the diverse beliefs and values of the American public."[58]

The NEA has not promulgated any official interpretation of the provision, but in December 1990, the Council unanimously adopted a resolution to implement § 954(d)(1) merely by

---

[58] Title 20 U.S.C. § 954(d) provides in full that:

"No payment shall be made under this section except upon application therefor which is submitted to the National Endowment for the Arts in accordance with regulations issued and procedures established by the Chairperson. In establishing such regulations and procedures, the Chairperson shall ensure that –

"(1) artistic excellence and artistic merit are the criteria by which applications are judged, taking into consideration general standards of decency and respect for the diverse beliefs and values of the American public; and

"(2) applications are consistent with the purposes of this section. Such regulations and procedures shall clearly indicate that obscenity is without artistic merit, is not protected speech, and shall not be funded."

ensuring that the members of the advisory panels that conduct the initial review of grant applications represent geographic, ethnic, and aesthetic diversity. John Frohnmayer, then Chairperson of the NEA, also declared that he would "count on [the] procedures" ensuring diverse membership on the peer review panels to fulfill Congress' mandate.

The four individual respondents in this case, Karen Finley, John Fleck, Holly Hughes, and Tim Miller, are performance artists who applied for NEA grants before § 954(d)(1) was enacted. An advisory panel recommended approval of respondents' projects, both initially and after receiving Frohnmayer's request to reconsider three of the applications. A majority of the Council subsequently recommended disapproval, and in June 1990, the NEA informed respondents that they had been denied funding. Respondents filed suit, alleging that the NEA had violated their First Amendment rights by rejecting the applications on political grounds, had failed to follow statutory procedures by basing the denial on criteria other than those set forth in the NEA's enabling statute, and had breached the confidentiality of their grant applications through the release of quotations to the press, in violation of the Privacy Act of 1974, 5 U.S.C. § 552(a). Respondents sought restoration of the recommended grants or reconsideration of their applications, as well as damages for the alleged Privacy Act violations. When Congress enacted § 954(d)(1), respondents, now joined by the National Association of Artists' Organizations (NAAO), amended their complaint to challenge the provision as void for vagueness and impermissibly viewpoint based.

The District Court denied the NEA's motion for judgment on the pleadings, and, after discovery, the NEA agreed to settle the individual respondents' statutory and as-applied constitutional claims by paying the artists the amount of the vetoed grants, damages, and attorney's fees.

The District Court then granted summary judgment in favor of respondents on their facial constitutional challenge to § 954(d)(1) and enjoined enforcement of the provision. The court rejected the argument that the NEA could comply with § 954(d)(1) by structuring the grant selection process to provide for diverse advisory panels. The provision, the court stated, "fails adequately to notify applicants of what is required of them or to circumscribe NEA discretion." Reasoning that "the very nature of our pluralistic society is that there are an infinite number of values and beliefs, and correlatively, there may be no national 'general standards of decency,'" the court concluded that § 954(d)(1) "cannot be given effect consistent with the Fifth Amendment's due process requirement." Drawing an analogy between arts funding and public universities, the court further ruled that the First Amendment constrains the NEA's grant-making process, and that because § 954(d)(1) "clearly reaches a substantial amount of protected speech," it is impermissibly overbroad on its face. The Government did not seek a stay of the District Court's injunction, and consequently the NEA has not applied § 954(d)(1) since June 1992. A divided panel of the Court of Appeals affirmed the District Court's ruling. ... We granted certiorari and now reverse the judgment of the Court of Appeals.

Respondents raise a facial constitutional challenge to § 954(d)(1), and consequently they confront "a heavy burden" in advancing their claim. Facial invalidation "is, manifestly, strong medicine" that "has been employed by the Court sparingly and only as a last resort." To prevail, respondents must demonstrate a substantial risk that application of the provision will lead to the suppression of speech.

Respondents argue that the provision is a paradigmatic example of viewpoint discrimination because it rejects any artistic speech that either fails to respect mainstream values or offends standards of decency. The premise of respondents' claim is that § 954(d)(1) constrains the agency's ability to fund certain categories of artistic expression. The NEA, however, reads the provision as merely hortatory, and contends that it stops well short of an absolute restriction. Section 954(d)(1) adds "considerations" to the grant-making process; it does not preclude awards to projects that might be deemed "indecent" or "disrespectful," nor place conditions on grants, or even specify that those factors must be given any particular weight in reviewing an application. Indeed, the agency asserts that it has adequately implemented § 954(d)(1) merely by ensuring the representation of various backgrounds and points of view on the advisory panels that analyze grant applications.

We do not decide whether the NEA's view – that the formulation of diverse advisory panels is sufficient to comply with Congress' command – is in fact a reasonable reading of the statute. It is clear, however, that the text of § 954(d)(1) imposes no categorical requirement. The advisory language stands in sharp contrast to congressional efforts to prohibit the funding of certain classes of speech. When Congress has in fact intended to affirmatively constrain the NEA's grant-making authority, it has done so in no uncertain terms.

Furthermore, like the plain language of § 954(d), the political context surrounding the adoption of the "decency and respect" clause is inconsistent with respondents' assertion that the provision compels the NEA to deny funding on the basis of viewpoint discriminatory criteria. The legislation was a bipartisan proposal introduced as a counterweight to amendments aimed at eliminating the NEA's funding or substantially constraining its grant-making authority. The Independent Commission had cautioned Congress against the adoption of distinct viewpoint-based standards for funding, and the Commission's report suggests that "additional criteria for selection, if any, should be incorporated as part of the selection process (perhaps as part of a definition of 'artistic excellence'), rather than isolated and treated as exogenous considerations." In keeping with that recommendation, the criteria in § 954(d)(1) inform the assessment of artistic merit, but Congress declined to disallow any particular viewpoints. As the sponsors of § 954(d)(1) noted in urging rejection of the Rohrabacher Amendment, "if we start down that road of prohibiting categories of expression, categories which are indeed constitutionally protected speech, where do we end? Where one Member's aversions end, others with different sensibilities and with different values begin."; see also *id.*, at 28663 (statement of Rep. Williams) (arguing that the Rohrabacher Amendment would prevent the funding of Jasper Johns' flag series, "The Merchant of Venice," "Chorus Line," "Birth of a Nation," and the "Grapes of Wrath"). In contrast, before the vote on § 954(d)(1), one of its sponsors stated: "If we have done one important thing in this amendment, it is this. We have maintained the integrity of freedom of expression in the United States."

That § 954(d)(1) admonishes the NEA merely to take "decency and respect" into consideration, and that the legislation was aimed at reforming procedures rather than precluding speech, undercut respondents' argument that the provision inevitably will be utilized as a tool for invidious viewpoint discrimination. In cases where we have struck down legislation as facially unconstitutional, the dangers were both more evident and more substantial. In *R. A. V. v. St. Paul*, 505 U.S. 377 (1992), for example, we invalidated on its face a municipal ordinance that defined as a criminal offense the placement of a symbol on public or private property "'which one knows or has reasonable grounds to know arouses anger, alarm, or resentment in others on the basis of race, color, creed, religion, or gender.'" That provision set forth a clear penalty, proscribed views on particular "disfavored subjects," and suppressed "distinctive ideas, conveyed by a distinctive message."

In contrast, the "decency and respect" criteria do not silence speakers by expressly "threatening censorship of ideas." Thus, we do not perceive a realistic danger that § 954(d)(1) will compromise First Amendment values. As respondents' own arguments demonstrate, the considerations that the provision introduces, by their nature, do not engender the kind of directed viewpoint discrimination that would prompt this Court to invalidate a statute on its face. Respondents assert, for example, that "one would be hard-pressed to find two people in the United States who could agree on what the 'diverse beliefs and values of the American public' are, much less on whether a particular work of art 'respects' them"; and they claim that "'decency' is likely to mean something very different to a septegenarian in Tuscaloosa and a teenager in Las Vegas." The NEA likewise views the considerations enumerated in § 954(d)(1) as susceptible to multiple interpretations. Accordingly, the provision does not introduce considerations that, in practice, would effectively preclude or punish the expression of particular views. Indeed, one could hardly anticipate how "decency" or "respect" would bear on grant applications in categories such as funding for symphony orchestras.

Respondents' claim that the provision is facially unconstitutional may be reduced to the argument that the criteria in § 954(d)(1) are sufficiently subjective that the agency could utilize them to engage in viewpoint discrimination. Given the varied interpretations of the criteria and the vague exhortation to "take them into consideration," it seems unlikely that this provision will introduce any greater element of selectivity than the determination of "artistic excellence" itself. And we are reluctant, in any event, to invalidate legislation "on the basis of its hypothetical application to situations not before the Court." *FCC v. Pacifica Foundation*, 438 U.S. 726, 743, 57 L. Ed. 2d 1073, 98 S. Ct. 3026 (1978).

The NEA's enabling statute contemplates a number of indisputably constitutional applications for both the "decency" prong of § 954(d)(1) and its reference to "respect for the diverse beliefs and values of the American public." Educational programs are central to the NEA's mission. And it is well established that "decency" is a permissible factor where "educational suitability" motivates its consideration.

Permissible applications of the mandate to consider "respect for the diverse beliefs and values of the American public" are also apparent. In setting forth the purposes of the NEA, Congress explained that "it is vital to democracy to honor and preserve its multicultural artistic heritage." The agency expressly takes diversity into account, giving special consideration to "projects and productions . . . that reach, or reflect the culture of, a minority, inner city, rural, or tribal community," § 954(c)(4), as well as projects that generally emphasize "cultural diversity," § 954(c)(1). Respondents do not contend that the criteria in § 954(d)(1) are impermissibly applied when they may be justified, as the statute contemplates, with respect to a project's intended audience.

We recognize, of course, that reference to these permissible applications would not alone be sufficient to sustain the statute against respondents' First Amendment challenge. But neither are we persuaded that, in other applications, the language of § 954(d)(1) itself will give rise to the suppression of protected expression. Any content-based considerations that may be taken into account in the grant-making process are a consequence of the nature of arts funding. The NEA has limited resources and it must deny the majority of the grant applications that it receives, including many that propose "artistically excellent" projects. The agency may decide to fund particular projects for a wide variety of reasons, "such as the technical proficiency of the artist, the creativity of the work, the anticipated public interest in or appreciation of the work, the work's contemporary relevance, its educational value, its suitability for or appeal to special audiences (such as children or the disabled), its service to a rural or isolated community, or even simply that the work could increase public knowledge of an art form." As the dissent below noted, it would be "impossible to have a highly selective grant program without denying money to a large amount of constitutionally protected expression." The "very assumption" of the NEA is that grants will be awarded according to the "artistic worth of competing applications," and absolute neutrality is simply "inconceivable."

Respondent's reliance on our decision in *Rosenberger v. Rector and Visitors of Univ. of Va.*, 515 U.S. 819 (1995), is therefore misplaced. In *Rosenberger*, a public university declined to authorize disbursements from its Student Activities Fund to finance the printing of a Christian student newspaper. We held that by subsidizing the Student Activities Fund, the University had created a limited public forum, from which it impermissibly excluded all publications with religious editorial viewpoints. Although the scarcity of NEA funding does not distinguish this case from *Rosenberger*, the competitive process according to which the grants are allocated does. In the context of arts funding, in contrast to many other subsidies, the Government does not indiscriminately "encourage a diversity of views from private speakers." The NEA's mandate is to make aesthetic judgments, and the inherently content-based "excellence" threshold for NEA support sets it apart from the subsidy at issue in *Rosenberger* – which was available to all student organizations that were "'related to the educational purpose of the University,'" – and from comparably objective decisions on allocating public benefits, such as access to a school auditorium or a municipal theater, or the second class mailing privileges available to "'all newspapers and other periodical publications.'"

It is so ordered.

CONCUR: JUSTICE SCALIA, with whom JUSTICE THOMAS joins, concurring in the judgment.

"The operation was a success, but the patient died." What such a procedure is to medicine, the Court's opinion in this case is to law. It sustains the constitutionality of 20 U.S.C. § 954(d)(1) by gutting it. The most avid congressional opponents of the provision could not have asked for more. I write separately because, unlike the Court, I think that § 954(d)(1) must be evaluated as written, rather than as distorted by the agency it was meant to control. By its terms, it establishes content- and viewpoint-based criteria upon which grant applications are to be evaluated. And that is perfectly constitutional. … One can regard [the statute] as either suggesting that decency and respect are elements of what Congress regards as artistic excellence and merit, or as suggesting that decency and respect are factors to be taken into account *in addition to* artistic excellence and merit. But either way, it is entirely, 100% clear that decency and respect are to be taken into account in evaluating applications. …

This is so apparent that I am at a loss to understand what the Court has in mind (other than the gutting of the statute) when it speculates that the statute is merely "advisory." …The statute requires the decency and respect factors to be considered in evaluating *all* applications – not, for example, just those applications relating to educational programs, *ante*, at 13, or intended for a particular audience. ...

Section 954(d)(1) is no more discriminatory, and no less constitutional, than virtually every other piece of funding legislation enacted by Congress. "The Government can, without violating the Constitution, selectively fund a program to encourage certain activities it believes to be in the public interest, without at the same time funding an alternative program . . . ." *Rust v. Sullivan*, 500 U.S. 173 (1991). As we noted in *Rust*, when Congress chose to establish the National Endowment for Democracy it was not constitutionally required to fund programs encouraging competing philosophies of government – an example of funding discrimination that cuts much closer than this one to the core of *political* speech which is the primary concern of the First Amendment. It takes a particularly high degree of chutzpah for the NEA to contradict this proposition, since the agency itself discriminates – and is required by law to discriminate – in favor of artistic (as opposed to scientific, or political, or theological) expression. Not all the common folk, or even all great minds, for that matter, think that is a good idea. In 1800, when John Marshall told John Adams that a recent immigration of Frenchmen would include talented artists, "Adams denounced all Frenchmen, but most especially 'schoolmasters, painters, poets, &C.' He warned Marshall that the fine arts were like germs that infected healthy constitutions." Surely the NEA itself is nothing less than an institutionalized discrimination against that point of view. Nonetheless it is constitutional, as is the congressional determination to favor decency and respect for beliefs and values over the opposite. Because such favoritism does not "abridge" anyone's freedom of speech. ...

DISSENT: JUSTICE SOUTER, dissenting.

The question here is whether the italicized segment of this statute is unconstitutional on its face: "artistic excellence and artistic merit are the criteria by which applications [for grants from the National Endowment for the Arts] are judged, *taking into consideration general standards of decency and respect for the diverse beliefs and values of the American public*." 20 U.S.C. § 954(d) (emphasis added). It is.

The decency and respect proviso mandates viewpoint-based decisions in the disbursement of government subsidies, and the Government has wholly failed to explain why the statute should be afforded an exemption from the fundamental rule of the First Amendment that viewpoint discrimination in the exercise of public authority over expressive activity is unconstitutional. The Court's conclusions that the proviso is not viewpoint based, that it is not a regulation, and that the NEA may permissibly engage in viewpoint-based discrimination, are all patently mistaken. Nor may the question raised be answered in the Government's favor on the assumption that some constitutional applications of the statute are enough to satisfy the demand of facial constitutionality, leaving claims of the proviso's obvious invalidity to be dealt with later in response to challenges of specific applications of the discriminatory standards. This assumption is irreconcilable with our long standing and sensible doctrine of facial overbreadth, applicable to claims brought under the First Amendment's speech clause. I respectfully dissent. ...

One need do nothing more than read the text of the statute to conclude that Congress's purpose in imposing the decency and respect criteria was to prevent the funding of art that conveys an offensive message; the decency and respect provision on its face is quintessentially viewpoint based, and quotations from the Congressional Record merely confirm the obvious legislative purpose. In the words of a cosponsor of the bill that enacted the proviso, "works which deeply offend the sensibilities of significant portions of the public ought not to be supported with public funds." … In the face of such clear legislative purpose, so plainly expressed, the Court has its work cut out for it in seeking a constitutional reading of the statute. …

Because "the normal definition of 'indecent' . . . refers to nonconformance with accepted standards of morality," restrictions turning on decency, especially those couched in terms of "general standards of decency," are quintessentially viewpoint based: they require discrimination on the basis of conformity with mainstream mores. The Government's contrary suggestion that the NEA's decency standards restrict only the "mode, form, or style" of artistic expression, not the underlying viewpoint or message, may be a tempting abstraction (and one not lacking in support). But here it suffices to realize that "form, mode, or style" are not subject to abstraction from artistic viewpoint, and to quote from an opinion just two years old: "In artistic . . . settings, indecency may have strong communicative content, protesting conventional norms or giving an edge to a work by conveying otherwise inexpressible emotions. . . . Indecency often is inseparable from the ideas and viewpoints conveyed, or separable only with loss of truth or expressive power." *Denver Area Ed. Telecommunications Consortium, Inc.* v. *FCC*, 518 U.S. 727, 805 (1996) (concurrence). …

Brooklyn Inst. of Arts & Sciences v. New York & Rudolph W. Giuliani

64 F. Supp. 2d 184 (E.D.N.Y. 1999)

The Mayor of the City of New York has decided that a number of works in the Brooklyn Museum's currently showing temporary exhibit "Sensation: Young British Artists from the Saatchi Collection" are "sick" and "disgusting" and, in particular, that one work, a painting entitled "The Holy Virgin Mary" by Chris Ofili, is offensive to Catholics and is an attack on religion. As a result, the City has withheld funds already appropriated to the Museum for operating expenses and maintenance and, in a suit filed in New York State Supreme Court two days after the Museum filed its suit in this court, seeks to eject the Museum from the City-owned land and building in which the Museum's collections have been housed for over one hundred years.

The Museum seeks a preliminary injunction barring the imposition of penalties by the Mayor and the City for the Museum's exercise of its First Amendment rights. … For the reasons that follow, defendants' motion is denied, and plaintiff's motion is granted. …

Upon completion of construction of a wing of the new building, the City of Brooklyn entered into a building lease and contract (the "Contract") [in 1893] with the Institute, for a term coextensive with the Lease, to house the Institute's collections. The City of New York is the successor to the City of Brooklyn under the Lease and the Contract. The parties agree that, upon the expiration of the original term of the Lease agreement in December 1993, the Museum remained a tenant in possession of the land and the building on the same terms and conditions as contained in the Lease and Contract. ... The Contract provides that "[the City] shall pay to the [Institute] each year such sum as may be necessary for the maintenance of said Museum Building, or as may be authorized by law or be apportioned or appropriated by [the City]." The Contract specifically defines "maintenance" to include: (1) repairs and alterations; (2) fuel; (3) waste removal; (4) wages of employees providing essential maintenance, custodial, security and other basic services; (5) cleaning and general care; (6) tools and supplies; and (7) insurance for the building, furniture and fixtures.

Consistent with the applicable statutes, the Lease, and the Contract, as well as with historical practices, the City's Procedures Manual specifies that public funds are provided to designated cultural institutions to help meet costs for general maintenance, security and energy, and in some instances to support education programs. City funds generally "are not used for direct curatorial or artistic services." The City also approves certain capital expenditures as part of its program "to protect and ensure the continued existence of New York City's most precious assets, its cultural institutions, for local communities, the general public and the artistic community." The City's Fiscal Year 2000 appropriation of approximately $5.7 million to the Museum specifies that the funding contributes to "maintenance, security, administration, curatorial, educational services and energy costs." The City was not asked to fund the controversial exhibit giving rise to this action. The City's Fiscal Year 2000 appropriation to the Brooklyn Children's Museum is approximately $1.6 million.

Nothing in the City's lengthy annual final report and budget request form, which each institution must supply, asks for detailed information concerning the individual works in exhibits. Instead, the form is designed to determine, among other things: the general purposes and plans of the institution; "brief descriptions" (emphasis in original) of immediate past and future programming; accomplishments and plans for educational programs for children, educators and the general public; and detailed financial information.

The Sensation Exhibit was first shown in 1997 at the Royal Academy of Art in London, where it drew record crowds for a contemporary art exhibit and generated controversy and some protest demonstrations. The Brooklyn Museum's Director, Arnold Lehman, viewed the Exhibit in London and decided to attempt to bring it to New York after its scheduled showing at a museum in Berlin. The Exhibit includes approximately ninety works of some forty contemporary British artists, a number of whom have received recognition by the artistic community. Chris Ofili, Damien Hirst, and Rachel Whiteread, for example, have received the Turner Award from the Tate Gallery. After being shown in Brooklyn, the Exhibit is scheduled to be shown at the National Gallery of Australia, and the Toyota City Museum outside of Tokyo.

Mr. Lehman's efforts to bring the Exhibit to Brooklyn continued through 1998, and plans were finalized in April 1999. Mr. Lehman, starting in 1998, kept the Museum's Board of Trustees informed of his efforts, and of the Exhibit's controversial nature. The Mayor of the City is an *ex officio* member of the Board, but his representative did not attend certain meetings at which the Exhibit was discussed, although minutes of the meetings were sent to him. The Commissioner of the City's Department of Cultural Affairs, Schuyler Chapin, also is an *ex officio* member of the Board of Trustees. His designated representative did attend meetings regularly and receive minutes of Board meetings. On or about March 10, 1999, Mr. Lehman gave Commissioner Chapin a copy of the catalog for the Exhibit and discussed its content. The catalog includes photographs and descriptions of virtually all of the works in the Exhibit, including every work that the City now finds objectionable. For example, it contains a full page color photograph of "The Holy Virgin Mary" and a description of the materials of which it is made, including elephant dung. On or about April 6, 1999, Mr. Lehman sent letters to members of the Board of Trustees, including Commissioner Chapin and other public officials, stating that the Exhibit was controversial, and he set forth the Museum's plans to charge an admission fee for the Exhibit and to require that all children be accompanied by an adult. The letters specifically described the work of the artist Damien Hirst, recognized "for his sections of various animals (sharks, lambs, etc.) individually preserved and presented in sealed, formaldehyde-filled glass containers." The Museum issued a similar press release on about the same date. A *New York Times* article on April 8, 1999, entitled "British Outrage Heads for Brooklyn," described reactions of shock and condemnation, together with protests, that the Exhibit had generated in London, as well as accusations by detractors that the Exhibit promoted the commercial interests of Charles Saatchi, owner of all of the works in the Exhibit. The article described some of the controversial works in the Exhibit, including that of Hirst. ...

The Exhibit was scheduled to open to the public at the Museum on October 2, 1999. City officials first began raising objections to the Exhibit on September 22. On that date, Commissioner Chapin, stating that he was acting on behalf of the Mayor, advised Mr. Lehman by telephone that the City would terminate all funding to the Museum unless it canceled the Exhibit. Commissioner Chapin specifically referred to the fact that the Mayor found objectionable "The Holy Virgin Mary" by Chris Ofili. (All of the five Ofili works in the Exhibit use elephant dung together with other materials. In addition, on the painting entitled "The Holy Virgin Mary," there are small photographs of buttocks and female genitalia scattered on the background.) The Mayor explained his position publicly that day, taking particular exception to "The Holy Virgin Mary." The Mayor stated that this work "offends me" and "is sick," and he explained his decision to terminate City funding as follows:

> You don't have a right to a government subsidy to desecrate someone else's religion. And therefore we will do everything that we can to remove funding from the [Museum] until the director comes to his senses. And realizes that if you are a government subsidized enterprise then you can't do things that desecrate the most personal and deeply held views of the people in society.

The Mayor also referred to a Hirst work of two pigs in formaldehyde as "sick stuff" to be exhibited in an art museum.

The following day, the Mayor accused the Museum of violating the Lease by mounting an exhibit which was inaccessible to schoolchildren and by failing to obtain his permission to restrict access to the Exhibit, which he made clear he would not give because of his view that taxpayer-funded property should not be used to "desecrate religion" or "do things that are disgusting with regard to animals." In a letter from New York City Corporation Counsel Michael D. Hess to Mr. Lehman, dated September 23, 1999, Mr. Hess stated that "the Mayor will not approve a modification of the Contract to allow [the Museum] to restrict admission to the museum. In light of the fact that [the Museum] has already determined that it would be inappropriate for those under 17 years of age to be admitted to the exhibit without adult supervision (a determination with which the City does not disagree), [the Museum] cannot proceed with the exhibit as planned."

The Mayor and other senior City officials continued, and escalated, their attacks on the Exhibit and their threats to the Museum, vowing to cut off all funding, including construction funding, to seek to replace the Board of Trustees, to cancel the Lease, and to assume possession of the Museum building, unless the Exhibit were canceled. The Mayor asserted on September 24 that he would not "have any compunction about trying to put them out of business, meaning the board." On September 28, the Mayor publicly stated that taxpayer dollars should not "be used to support the desecration of important national or religious symbol, of any religion." A City press release that day denounced "an exhibit which besmirches religion and is an insult to the community." The press release announced that, in response to the Museum Board's formal decision that day to proceed with the Exhibit, the City would end its funding of the Museum immediately. In his deposition, Deputy Mayor Joseph Lhota acknowledged that he had earlier told the Chairman of the Museum's Board of Trustees, Robert Rubin, that all City funding to the Museum would be canceled unless the Museum agreed to remove "The Holy Virgin Mary" from the Exhibit.

In response to the City's threats, including explicit statements by senior officials that the City would withhold its monthly payment of $497,554 due on October 1, 1999, the Museum commenced this action against the City and the Mayor on September 28, 1999, pursuant to 42 U.S.C. § 1983, seeking declaratory and injunctive relief, to prevent the defendants from punishing or retaliating against the Museum for displaying the Exhibit, in violation of the Museum's rights under the First and Fourteenth Amendments, including cutting off funding, terminating the lease, seizing the building or attempting to fire the Board of Trustees. The City has in fact withheld the scheduled October payment to the Museum. Plaintiff filed an amended complaint on October 1, 1999, adding claims for damages against the defendants, and claims of violation of the Equal Protection Clause and state and local law. ...

THE FIRST AMENDMENT CLAIM: THE MUSEUM'S MOTION FOR A PRELIMINARY INJUNCTION

A party seeking a preliminary injunction must ordinarily demonstrate (a) irreparable harm and (b) either (1) likelihood of success on the merits or (2) sufficiently serious questions going to the merits to make them a fair ground of litigation and a balance of hardships tipping decidedly in its favor. ... In any event, as will be seen, the Museum easily establishes a likelihood of success on the merits.

The Museum is suffering and will continue to suffer irreparable harm if an injunction is not granted. "The loss of First Amendment freedoms, for even minimal periods of time, unquestionably constitutes irreparable injury." Because of this, it is sometimes said that "when an injunction is sought to protect First Amendment rights, likelihood of success on the merits and irreparable harm merge into a single threshold requirement."

The City and the Mayor argue that there is no irreparable injury because the Museum has not shown that the withholding of funding prevented it from showing the Sensation Exhibit or that the loss of its operating and maintenance subsidy will force the imminent closing of the Museum. Counsel for defendants further stated at oral argument that the City's own ejectment suit cannot be a sound basis for a preliminary injunction motion because the suit has just begun and, "in the event that that particular action gets to a critical stage," the motion can be renewed. These arguments ignore the very reason that interference with First Amendment rights constitutes irreparable injury.

This is not a case involving the mere assertion of an incidental infringement of First Amendment rights insufficient to establish irreparable harm. Nor does the Museum rely on remote or speculative fears of future retaliation. The Museum has already suffered direct and purposeful penalization by the City in response to its exercise of First Amendment rights. First, the City has cut off appropriated funding. Second, the City has sued in state court to evict the Museum from the property which it has occupied for over one hundred years and in which it houses its enormous collections of ancient and modern art. ... [T]he City asks the court to treat its ejectment suit as brought in good faith, that is, as brought with the goal of ejecting the Museum. It cannot on the one hand seek so serious a penalty (it could, after all, have brought only a declaratory judgment action) and on the other hand claim that no harm is imminent. For a museum of the magnitude of the Brooklyn Museum, planning for a move of one and a half million art objects would obviously be a monumental task. Given the finding of a likelihood of success on the merits of the Museum's claim of a First Amendment violation, the Museum should not have to wait until a City sheriff is at the door to seek equitable relief.

In addition, the facts establish an ongoing effort by the Mayor and the City to coerce the Museum into relinquishing its First Amendment rights. On September 24, the Mayor stated that "since they [the Museum Board members] seem to have no compunction about putting their hands in the taxpayers' pockets … and throwing dung on important religious symbols, I'm not going to have any compunction about trying to put them out of business, meaning the board." Then, on September 28, the Mayor went on to state that "the Corporation Counsel told them what we're going to do, the lease tells us what we're required to do, which is to evict them and to stop dealing with them as a board. We'll do that over a period of time. We'll hold back their funds because they are not a properly constituted board at this point and then over a period of time there will be a substitute board put in place."

That the Museum has so far stood up to these efforts does not deprive it of the right to injunctive relief. The prospect of money damages does not cure the irreparable injury of an already existing, purposeful penalization for the exercise of First Amendment rights. Nor must the Museum endure ongoing efforts to coerce the relinquishment of those rights, including the continuing threat of ejectment, because money damages are available at the conclusion of the suit. Irreparable injury has been established. …

In keeping with that principle, the First Amendment bars government officials from censoring works said to be "offensive," *Texas v. Johnson*, 491 U.S. 397 (1989), "sacrilegious," *Joseph Burstyn, Inc. v. Wilson*, 343 U.S. 495 (1952), "morally improper," *Hannegan v. Esquire*, 327 U.S. 146 (1946), or even "dangerous," *Regan v. Taxation with Representation of Washington*, 461 U.S. 540, 548 (1983). "If there is a bedrock principle underlying the First Amendment, it is that the government may not prohibit the expression of an idea simply because society finds the idea itself offensive or disagreeable."

In *Hannegan*, for example, the Supreme Court held that the Postmaster General could not deny second-class postal privileges to a magazine, admittedly not containing material that was obscene and therefore illegal, because it was found by him not to be conducive to the "public good." In *Joseph Burstyn, Inc.*, the Supreme Court found the First Amendment violated by a New York statute authorizing denial of a license to motion pictures found to be "sacrilegious." While noting the "substantial questions" that might be raised under the religion clauses of the First Amendment if a censor had to determine what fell within the standard, the Court said:

> However, from the standpoint of freedom of speech and the press, it is enough to point out that the state has no legitimate interest in protecting any or all religions from views distasteful to them which is sufficient to justify prior restraints upon the expression of those views. It is not the business of government in our nation to suppress real or imagined attacks upon a particular religious doctrine, whether they appear in publications, speeches, or motion pictures.

343 U.S. at 505.

Similarly, in *Spence v. Washington*, 418 U.S. 405 (1974), the Supreme Court struck, on First Amendment grounds, a flag misuse statute as applied to a college student who hung an American flag with a peace symbol on it upside down out of his window. Among the grounds considered and rejected for upholding the judgment against the student, the Court noted: "that the State may have desired to protect the sensibilities of passersby" is not a basis for suppressing ideas, and that "anyone who might have been offended could easily have avoided the display." *Spence*, 418 U.S. at 412. Thus, "under our system of government there is an accommodation for the widest varieties of tastes and ideas. What is good literature, what has educational value, what is refined public information, what is good art, varies with individuals as it does from one generation to another."

The City and the Mayor acknowledge that the art being shown at the Museum and the ideas which they find that art to express are within the protections of the First and Fourteenth Amendments. Contrary to their assertions, however, although they did not physically remove the art objects from the Museum, they are not insulated from a claim that they are violating the overwhelming body of First Amendment law establishing that government cannot suppress ideas indirectly any more than it can do so directly. ...

In many different contexts, then, the Supreme Court has made clear that, although the government is under no obligation to provide various kinds of benefits, it may not deny them if the reason for the denial would require a choice between exercising First Amendment rights and obtaining the benefit. That is, it may not "discriminate invidiously in its subsidies in such a way as to 'aim [] at the suppression of dangerous ideas.'"

The decision to withhold an already appropriated general operating subsidy from an institution which has been supported by the City for over one hundred years, and to eject it from its City-owned building, because of the Mayor's objection to certain works in a current exhibit, is, in its own way, to "discriminate invidiously in its subsidies in such a way as to 'aim [] at the suppression of dangerous ideas.'" "The Government's purpose is the controlling consideration" in determining whether a restriction on speech is viewpoint discriminatory. By its own words, the City here threatened to withhold funding if the Museum continued with its plans to show the Exhibit. When the Museum resisted, the City withheld its funding and filed a suit for ejectment.

In a case remarkably similar to this one, *Cuban Museum of Arts and Culture, Inc. v. City of Miami*, 766 F. Supp. 1121 (S.D. Fla. 1991), the City of Miami was enjoined from refusing to renew an expired lease with the Cuban Museum because the Court held that the City had violated the museum's First Amendment rights, in that the refusal to renew was motivated by the City's opposition to the museum's exhibition of works of Cuban artists who were either living in Cuba or who had not denounced Fidel Castro. These works were highly offensive to a large segment of the Cuban population of Miami. The Court found that the exhibition was fully protected by the First Amendment, that the absence of a "right" to renewal did not defeat the First Amendment claim, and that the claimed lease violations were pretextual. It found that the "City would not have acted to deny the plaintiffs' continued use and possession of the premises but for the plaintiffs' controversial exercise of their First Amendment rights." The same is true here.

The cases establishing the principle that the government cannot avoid the reach of the First Amendment by acting indirectly rather than directly also illustrate the fallacy in the claim of the Mayor and the City that, while the Exhibit can be shown privately, "the taxpayers don't have to pay for it." Federal taxpayers in effect pay for the mailing of periodicals that many of them find objectionable; and they subsidize all manner of views with which they do not agree, indeed, which they may abhor, through tax exemptions and deductions given to other taxpayers. State taxpayers pay the salary for the professor whom the State wants to fire for speaking out against the State college. In sum, where the denial of a benefit, subsidy or contract is motivated by a desire to suppress speech in violation of the First Amendment, that denial will be enjoined. That is all that is involved here.

This of course does not mean that the taxpayers are being required to "support" a particular viewpoint. On the contrary, the Supreme Court has rejected similar justifications for the suppression of ideas. For example, in *F.C.C. v. League of Women Voters*, 468 U.S. 364 (1984), the Supreme Court struck as unconstitutional a statutory provision that forbade noncommercial stations, which receive a grant from the Corporation for Public Broadcasting, to "engage in editorializing." With the following language, the Court rejected the contention that the provision could be defended on the ground that it was "intended to prevent the use of taxpayer moneys to promote private views with which taxpayers may disagree":

> This argument is readily answered by our decision in *Buckley v. Valeo*, 424 U.S. 1, 90-93 (1976) (*per curiam*). As we explained in that case, virtually every congressional appropriation will to some extent involve a use of public money as to which some taxpayers may object. . . . Nevertheless, this does not mean that those taxpayers have a constitutionally protected right to enjoin such expenditures. Nor can this interest be invoked to justify a congressional decision to suppress speech.

468 U.S. at 385 n.16 (citations omitted).

Clarifying what the case at bar is not about will further illustrate the distinction between requiring the taxpayer to support a particular point of view, which is not involved here, and barring government officials from invidiously discriminating against ideas they find offensive, either to themselves or to members of the community.

First, there is no issue presented here about the City's right to itself take positions, even controversial ones. The Museum does not challenge the principle that government may choose, through its funding, to espouse a viewpoint on a matter of public concern without, as a result, being required to give equal time to an opposing view. See *Rust v. Sullivan*, 500 U.S. 173 (1991). Thus, the doctrine of *Rust*, upon which defendants rely, has no relevance here. That is, the Mayor and the City are permitted to foster the values that they claim to be seeking to foster, such as respect for the most dearly held beliefs of others and lack of vulgarity in art. As the Court stated in *Barnette*, however, "national unity as an end which officials may foster by persuasion and example is not in question. The problem is whether under our Constitution compulsion as here employed is a permissible means for its achievement." ...

Second, the City and the Mayor argue that, if they are not allowed to cut off all financial support to the Museum as a result of its display of the Sensation Exhibit, there will be no limit on what the public is required to support in the name of the First Amendment. This is incorrect. The Museum makes no claim in this case that government has an obligation to fund particular forums of expression such as museums. Nor is there an issue in this case as to whether the City could be required to provide funding to support the Sensation Exhibit or any other particular exhibit, if the Museum had sought funding on an exhibit-by-exhibit basis. The City has not in fact provided the funding – some $2 million – to cover the various expenses involved in presenting the Sensation

Exhibit. Thus, the issue is not whether the City could have been required to provide funding for the Sensation Exhibit, but whether the Museum, having been allocated a general operating subsidy, can now be penalized with the loss of that subsidy, and ejectment from a City-owned building, because of the perceived viewpoint of the works in the Exhibit. The answer to that question is no.

The reliance of the City and the Mayor on *National Endowment for the Arts v. Finley*, 524 U.S. 569 (1998), as support for their claim that viewpoint discrimination in arts funding is permissible, is misplaced. In *Finley*, the Supreme Court rejected a facial challenge to a provision adding "general standards of decency and respect for the diverse beliefs and values of the American public" to the "considerations" to be applied by the NEA in the awarding of grants to individual artists and arts organizations. The Court described the provision's legislative history, including Congress's rejection of language that would have prohibited awards of grants that would have the purpose or effect of denigrating particular religions, or of denigrating people on the basis of race, sex, handicap, or national origin. It noted that, ultimately, "the legislation was a bipartisan proposal introduced as a counterweight to amendments aimed at eliminating the NEA's funding or substantially constraining its grant-making authority." The Court also noted that "Congress declined to disallow any particular viewpoints," and it went on to hold the challenged provision facially constitutional upon finding that it "[did] not preclude awards to projects that might be deemed 'indecent' or 'disrespectful' nor place conditions on grants. . ." and, further, because the Court did "not perceive a realistic danger" that it will be used "to effectively preclude or punish the expression of particular views." Thus, even in *Finley*, where the issue was the "considerations" that could apply in the awarding of grants, unlike here, where funding has already been appropriated for general operating expenses, the Supreme Court upheld the "decency" and "respect" considerations only by reading them, on their face, as not permitting viewpoint discrimination.

When questioned on oral argument whether the City could direct a publicly supported library to remove particular books on pain of a loss of financial support, counsel for defendants responded that the visual art in the Exhibit has a greater impact than do books. Counsel for the Museum, in reply, noted that books like *Mein Kampf* have done enormous harm, but are still protected by the First Amendment. The relative power of books and visual art is of course immaterial. The communicative power of visual art is not a basis for restricting it but rather the very reason it is protected by the First Amendment. As recently stated by the Court of Appeals for the Second Circuit, "visual art is as wide ranging in its depiction of ideas, concepts and emotions as any book, treatise, pamphlet or other writing, and is similarly entitled to full First Amendment protection." ...

The City's motion to dismiss is denied. As the Museum has established irreparable harm and a likelihood of success on its First Amendment claim, its motion for a preliminary injunction is granted.

Trebert v. City Of New Orleans

2005 U.S. Dist. LEXIS 1560 (E.D. La. 2005)

Plaintiff, Marc C. Trebert, sued the City of New Orleans pursuant to 42 U.S.C. § 1983, asserting that §§ 110-121 through 110-132 of the City's Municipal Code violate his constitutional rights of free speech under the First Amendment .... Trebert takes digital photographs, prints them and colors them with pastels. The City granted Trebert a "Jackson Square A" permit dated January 6, 2004, which was to expire on December 31, 2004. ... "to paint and sell works of art in that area defined as 'the Jackson Square set-up area'." "Permit A" allows its holder "to manually paint, sketch or draw on plain surfaces only in . . . the Jackson Square artist set-up area." Trebert intends to make and sell art produced by digital technology, i.e., digital photographs that are colored with pastels. ... On January 14, 2004, the Municipal Court temporarily enjoined Trebert "from selling [presumably within the Jackson Square A area only] any paintings, sketches or drawings produced by or with the assistance of a mechanical devices [sic] and with the use of any process used to duplicate an existing image," until February 3, 2004.

The Municipal Code provides that artists may create and sell only "original" art along the Jackson Square fence. "Original means only those works produced and for sale by the artist which have been accomplished essentially by hand and precludes any mechanical or duplicative process in whole or part." The ordinance prohibits plaintiff from selling, at his Jackson Square site [e.g. the French Quarter], digital photographs that have been printed and colored because they are not within the law's definition of "original" art. The City agreed to dismiss the criminal citation against Trebert and to refrain from enforcing the ordinance against him until the instant lawsuit is resolved. ...

Trebert and the City agree that the ordinance at issue is content neutral and that it regulates the time, place and manner of display and sale of the works it defines as art. They also agree that "preserving the distinctive charm, character and tout ensemble of the [French] Quarter" is a significant governmental interest. ...

The City has presented no evidence to sustain its burden to show that the ordinance is narrowly tailored to serve the City's significant interest in preserving the French Quarter's charm and authenticity. The City merely speculates that any less burdensome alternative would result in its interests being achieved less effectively and that "the obvious effect of lifting the restriction would be the prospect that the area surrounding Jackson Square would become one big photography studio, with cardboard images of President Clinton and faux backgrounds of French Quarter scenes."

The City also asserts that the law is narrowly tailored because "it does not prohibit duplicative processes by brush, charcoal, airbrush, finger-paint, etc." Arguably, the ordinance does prohibit such processes, inasmuch as it "precludes any mechanical or duplicative process in whole or part," and an airbrush is clearly a mechanical tool. One could also argue that an artist who churns out repetitive, albeit handmade, paintings or drawings of the same familiar French Quarter scenes for sale to tourists uses "duplicative" processes. These ambiguities in the ordinance undermine the City's argument that it is narrowly tailored to its purpose.

In Bery, the Second Circuit Court of Appeals invalidated the City of New York's licensing requirement for visual artists who wished to sell their works in public spaces. Despite the City's significant interest in keeping its public spaces safe and congestion-free, the court found that the law was not narrowly tailored because it effectively barred artists from selling their work on the streets. The City produced no evidence to justify such a sweeping bar on an entire category of expression. *Bery v. City of New York*, 97 F.3d 689, 697 (2d Cir. 1996). ...

In contrast to these cases, the First Circuit upheld an ordinance that prohibited licensed commercial activity (including plaintiff's business of motion picture exhibition) between the hours of 1:00 a.m. and 6:00 a.m., based on the town's substantial interest in minimizing traffic, noise, litter and security problems in residential areas around the movie theater. *National Amusements, Inc. v. Town of Dedham*, 43 F.3d 731 (1st Cir. 1995). The court found that the town's avowed purposes were strongly supported by an evidentiary showing, including the records of numerous citizen complaints and the records of town meetings that led to passage of the ordinance.

The First Circuit held that the ordinance was narrowly tailored because it promoted the substantial governmental interest in preserving peace and tranquility, which could not be achieved as effectively absent the regulation, and that plaintiff had ample alternative means of reaching its intended movie-going audience during the remaining 19 hours of the day. ...

The City of New Orleans indisputably has a significant interest in preserving the authenticity and charm of the French Quarter. In this case, the City bears the burden to establish that its ordinance is narrowly tailored to achieve its interest. However, ... the City has produced no evidence to support its speculative assertion that any less burdensome alternative than the challenged ordinance would result in its interests being achieved less effectively. "We have never accepted mere conjecture as adequate to carry a First Amendment burden." Display of plaintiff's works does not detract from the ambiance of the French Quarter any more than electric lights do.

In the absence of any evidence submitted by the City, this court cannot find that the ordinance is narrowly tailored to serve a significant government interest. Because the City has failed to carry its burden to show that the ordinance is narrowly tailored to achieve its interest, Trebert is entitled to partial summary judgment in his favor.

Because that ruling forecloses a finding of constitutionality, the court need not address whether the ordinance leaves open to Trebert ample alternative avenues of expression. Nonetheless, for purposes of any further review of this ruling, I will analyze that prong of the constitutional test as well.

It is well established that Trebert is "entitled to a public forum for [his] expressive activities." The City argues that Trebert may sell his work from tables outside of events inside the City's Convention Center, inside the Superdome, inside arenas where concerts are held or at other events or festivals throughout the New Orleans area. Defendant contends that Trebert has failed to show that these alternative venues are inadequate. The City misconceives the evidentiary burden in this regard. It is not Trebert's burden to show that alternatives are inadequate; it is the City's burden to show that they are ample. ...

None of the City's proposed alternative venues for Trebert's work is Jackson Square. The City has not demonstrated that events in the Convention Center, the Superdome, other arenas or festivals are as easily accessible to plaintiff and/or his intended audience as the fence area of Jackson Square, which is a unique venue for the display and sale of works like Trebert produces to passersby.

Sports events, conventions, concerts and festivals are episodic. Many sports events and concerts occur at night, as compared to plaintiff's daily, daytime access to Jackson Square. The City has not shown that Trebert could obtain access to the inside areas of the Convention Center, the Superdome, the New Orleans Arena or Kiefer UNO Lakefront Arena as simply and cheaply as he is able to obtain a one-year permit from the City for a nominal fee. ...

Trebert [also] argues that the ordinance is unconstitutionally overbroad both on its face and as applied to him. In his motion for partial summary judgment, he asks that the court enjoin enforcement of the ordinance against him and any other person.

"[A] statute or ordinance may be considered invalid 'on its face'–either because it is unconstitutional in every conceivable application, or because it seeks to prohibit such a broad range of protected conduct that it is unconstitutionally 'overbroad.'" … In the instant case, Trebert has "failed to identify any significant difference between [his] claim that the ordinance is invalid on overbreadth grounds and [his] claim that it is unconstitutional when applied to [his photographically originated work]." …

I find that the ordinance is unconstitutional only as applied to Trebert and his activities at Jackson Square that are the subject of this lawsuit. There has been no showing that his pastel-colored, digitally initiated photographs, produced on Jackson Square, interfere with or detract from the "distinctive charm, character and tout ensemble of the [French] Quarter" or that a ban on the type of work he produces would advance protection of that interest.

This does not mean, however, that the City might not be able to show in a different case that a different type of operation than plaintiff's might be banned consistently with the First Amendment. For example, the feared prospect of a commercial photography business, featuring life-sized cardboard cutouts of presidents or other celebrities and faux backgrounds of French Quarter scenes (ironically set against the actual historic backdrop of Jackson Square) with which tourists might pose, or other similar ventures not in keeping with the unique character of Jackson Square, should they materialize, could very well be subject to prohibition under the ordinance without offending the First Amendment. In such a case, it is conceivable that the City and its lawyers might rouse themselves to develop and submit to the court evidence sufficient to bear the burden imposed by the law. In Trebert's particular case, however, they have not done so, and the ordinance unconstitutionally applies to him. Accordingly, appropriate declaratory and injunctive relief will be awarded, limited to Trebert's activities that are the subject of this lawsuit.

Notes and Questions

a. The strong support of the New York courts against Mayor Giuliani's religious outrage suggests a rather unbridled control by the curators of government sponsored art exhibits. To what extent is the variation in outcome based on the independence of the museum (or its statute) and the right of the government to select which speech to adopt? Compare *Esperanza Peace and Justice Center v. City of San Antonio*, 316 F. Supp. 2d 433 (W.D. Tex. 2001) with *Piarowski v. Illinois Community College Dist.*, 515, 759 F.2d 625 (7th Cir. 1985) and *Serra v. U.S. General Services Admin.*, 847 F.2d 1045 (2d Cir. 1988).

b. Mayor Giuliani is not the only political figure who may be offended. The Second City, never to be outdone by New York, had its own controversy. When the Chicago Art Institute displayed a student's painting entitled "Mirth and Girth" depicting deceased former Mayor Harold Washington in a bra, g-string, stockings, and garter belt (based on a rumor he had woman's underwear on when admitted to the hospital), local officials attempted to withhold funding and to physically remove the work. See *Nelson v. Streeter*, 16 F.3d 145 (7th Cir. 1994).

c. To what extent can a jurisdiction use the power to speak for itself and to be selective in financing under *Rust v. Sullivan* and *Finley v. NEA* to choose whether or not to provide a lease for a museum? See *Cuban Museum of Arts and Culture, Inc. v. City of Miami*, 766 F. Supp. 1121 (S.D. Fla 1991).

d. Many of the controversies involving public museums also involve works that have a religious or anti-religious theme. To what extent may a governmental museum or government-funded organization present religious art? Is religious and anti-religious art subject to the same standard? See *Lynch v. Donnelly*, 465 U.S. 668 (1984). See also *Santa Fe Indep. Sch. Dist. v. Doe*, 530 U.S. 290 (2000) (student led prayers deemed governmental speech); *O'Connor v. Washburn Univ.*, 416 F.3d 1216 (10th Cir. 2005), *cert. denied*, 2006 U.S. LEXIS 2044 (2006).

Problem XVII-C

As part of Bryce's current project, Bryce has been working with a local city-owned community center to produce an exhibit of 1950's works of art that were created by local artists of the neighborhood. The board of directors for the community center was supportive of the exhibit and approved the event. Bryce also has permission to film the exhibit and possibly release a documentary about finding the works and presenting them.

Bryce now learns that the neighborhood had a much more vibrant and controversial debate during the 1950's that ended with fears from the anti-communist congressional hearings. The works Bryce has collected include both highly religious works that combine U.S. military images with religious iconography and works that depict workers chained to burning crosses. Although the approval for the exhibit had not included any approval rights over the works in the collection, word has spread regarding the works in the collection. The city Mayor has called the community center President and asked that the exhibit be cancelled. The city has also refused to provide Bryce a filming permit or parking permits necessary to park electrical generators for the lighting equipment that had been planned. Bryce calls you for help to stop the city and community center from frustrating the exhibit and the documentary.

D.   Art Fraud & Trafficking in Art & Artifacts

United States v. An Antique Platter of Gold

known as a Gold Phiale Mesomphalos C. 400 B.C.,
184 F.3d 131 (2d Cir. 1999)

Michael H. Steinhardt appeals from Judge Jones's ordering of the forfeiture of a "Phiale," an antique gold platter. The district court held that false statements on the customs entry forms and the Phiale's status as stolen property under Italian law rendered its importation illegal. As such, the Phiale was subject to forfeiture.

Steinhardt contends that: (i) the false statements on the customs forms were not material under 18 U.S.C. § 542, (ii) stolen property under the National Stolen Property Act ("NSPA") does not encompass property presumed to belong to the state under Italian patrimony laws, (iii) both statutes afford him an innocent owner defense, and (iv) the forfeiture violates the Eighth Amendment. We hold that the false statements on the customs forms were material and, therefore, need not reach issue (ii). We further hold that there is no innocent owner defense and that forfeiture of the Phiale does not violate the Eighth Amendment.

At issue is a Phiale of Sicilian origin that dates from the 4th Century B.C. Its provenance since then is largely unknown, other than its possession by Vincenzo Pappalardo, a private antique collector living in Sicily, who traded it in 1980 to Vincenzo Cammarata, a Sicilian coin dealer and art collector, for art works worth about $20,000. Cammarata sold it in 1991 to William Veres, the owner of Stedron, a Zurich art dealership, for objects worth about $90,000.

Veres brought the Phiale to the attention of Robert Haber, an art dealer from New York and owner of Robert Haber & Company. In November 1991, Haber traveled to Sicily to meet with Veres and examine the Phiale. Haber informed Steinhardt, a client with whom he had engaged in 20-30 previous transactions, of the piece. Haber told Steinhardt that the Phiale was a twin to a piece in the Metropolitan Museum of Art in New York City and that a Sicilian coin dealer (presumably Cammarata) was willing to guarantee the piece's authenticity.

On December 4, 1991, Haber, acting for Steinhardt, finalized an agreement to purchase the Phiale for slightly more than $1 million – plus a 15% commission, making the total price paid by Steinhardt approximately $1.2 million. Haber and Veres also agreed to a "Terms of Sale," which stated, inter alia, that "if the object is confiscated or impounded by customs agents or a claim is made by any country or governmental agency whatsoever, full compensation will be made immediately to the purchaser." It further provided that a "letter is to be written by Dr. [Giacomo] Manganaro that he saw the object 15 years ago in Switz." In fact, Dr. Manganaro, a professor of Greek history and Numismatics, had examined the Phiale in 1980 in Sicily and had determined thereafter that it was authentic and of Sicilian origin.

On December 10, 1991, Haber flew from New York to Zurich, Switzerland, and then proceeded to Lugano, near the Italian border, where he took possession of the Phiale on December 12. The transfer was confirmed by a commercial invoice issued by Stedron, describing the object as "ONE GOLD BOWL–CLASSICAL . . . DATE–C. 450 B.C. . . . . VALUE U.S. $250,000." The next day, Haber sent a fax to Jet Air Service, Inc. ("Jet Air"), Haber's customs broker at John F. Kennedy International Airport in New York, which included a copy of the commercial invoice. Jet Air prepared an Entry/Immediate Delivery form (Customs Form 3461) to obtain release of the Phiale prior to formal entry. This form listed the Phiale's country of origin as "CH," the code for Switzerland. In addition, Jet Air prepared an Entry Summary form (Customs Form 7501), which also listed the country of origin as "CH" and stated the Phiale's value at $250,000, as Haber's fax had indicated. Haber was listed as the importer of record.

On December 15, Haber returned to the United States from Zurich with the Phiale and later gave it to Steinhardt. Before completing the purchase, Steinhardt had the piece authenticated through a detailed examination by the Metropolitan Museum of Art. Thereafter, the Phiale was displayed in his home from 1992 until 1995.

Under Article 44 of Italy's law of June 1, 1939, an archaeological item is presumed to belong to the state unless its possessor can show private ownership prior to 1902. On February 16, 1995, the Italian government submitted a Letters Rogatory Request to the United States seeking assistance in investigating the circumstances of the Phiale's exportation and asking our government to confiscate it so that it could be returned to Italy. In November 1995, the Phiale was seized from Steinhardt pursuant to a warrant. Soon thereafter the United States filed the present in rem civil forfeiture action. The government claimed that forfeiture was proper under 18 U.S.C. § 545 because of false statements on the customs forms. It also claimed that forfeiture was proper under 19 U.S.C. § 1595a(c) because the Phiale was stolen property under the NSPA as a result of Article 44 of Italy's patrimony laws.

Steinhardt entered the proceeding as a claimant, and he and the government moved for summary judgment. In granting judgment for the government, the district court held that the misstatement of the country of origin was material, and, alternatively, that the Phiale was stolen property under Italian law. The court also held that an innocent owner defense was not available under either statute, and that the forfeiture did not violate the Excessive Fines Clause. This appeal followed. ...

Section 545 prohibits the importation of merchandise into the United States "contrary to law" and states that material imported in such a manner "shall be forfeited." 18 U.S.C. § 545.[59] The government claims that the importation of the Phiale was illegal because it violated 18 U.S.C. § 542, which prohibits the making of false statements in the course of importing merchandise into the United States. Steinhardt claims, however, that an element of a Section 542 violation is that such a false statement must be material and that the government has failed to show materiality in the instant case, at least for purposes of summary judgment. ...

Section 542 states in pertinent part:

> Whoever enters or introduces . . . into the commerce of the United States any imported merchandise by means of any fraudulent or false invoice, declaration, affidavit, letter, paper, or by means of any false statement, written or verbal, . . . or makes any false statement in any declaration without reasonable cause to believe the truth of such statement, or procures the making of any such false statement as to any matter material thereto without reasonable cause to believe the truth of such statement [shall be guilty of a crime].

8 U.S.C. § 542. There can be no dispute that the designation of Switzerland as the Phiale's country of origin and the listing of its value of $250,000 were false. Haber had examined the Phiale in Sicily about a month before the sale to Steinhardt, and that sale was for $1 million plus 15% commission. ...

The dispute pertinent to this appeal concerns the proper test for materiality. Steinhardt argues for a "but for" test of materiality, i.e., a false statement is material only if a truthful answer on a customs form would have actually prevented the item from entering the United States. The district court, however, employed a "natural tendency" test, asking whether the false statement would have a natural tendency to influence customs officials. The circuits are divided as to the proper test. The Fifth and Ninth Circuits have adopted a but for test, while the First Circuit has come down in favor of the natural tendency test. We adopt the natural tendency test.

The statutory language, caselaw, and the statutory purpose lead us to this conclusion. First, the statute prohibits importations "by means of" a false statement. Although there is overlap, this language is not synonymous with "because of," and ought not be read so narrowly. Instead, the

---

[59] Section 545 reads, in relevant part:

> Whoever fraudulently or knowingly imports or brings into the United States, any merchandise contrary to law, or receives, conceals, buys, sells, or in any manner facilitates the transportation, concealment, or sale of such merchandise after importation, knowing the same to have been imported or brought into the United States contrary to law [shall be subject to criminal penalties.] ... Merchandise introduced into the United States in violation of this section, or the value thereof, to be recovered from any person described in the first or second paragraph of this section, shall be forfeited to the United States.

18 U.S.C. § 545.

ordinary meaning of the statutory language requires only that the false statements be an integral part of the importation process. In this case, the false statements were on custom forms and thus easily meet the by means of requirement.

Second, the Supreme Court has noted that "the most common formulation of [materiality] . . . is that a concealment or misrepresentation is material if it 'has a natural tendency to influence or was capable of influencing, the decision of' the decisionmaking body to which it was addressed." Both the Supreme Court and this circuit have employed such a standard in numerous contexts. ...

Finally, the natural tendency approach is far more consistent with the purpose of the statute – to ensure truthfulness of representations made during importation – than is a but for test. Under a but for test, lying would be more productive because the government would bear the difficult burden of proving what would have happened if a truthful statement had been made. Moreover, under such a test, liability would not attach for misstatements in cases where truthful answers would still have enabled the goods to enter the United States. Importers have incentives to lie for reasons not related to achieving actual entry of the goods – e.g., to reduce the duties payable or to obtain expeditious customs treatment. The statutory purpose would thus be frustrated by the narrow reading suggested by appellant.

We therefore hold that "a false statement is material under Section 542 if it has the potential significantly to affect the integrity or operation of the importation process as a whole, and that neither actual causation nor harm to the government need be demonstrated." For a trier of fact to determine whether a statement can significantly affect the importation process, it need ask only whether a reasonable customs official would consider the statements to be significant to the exercise of his or her official duties. This analysis is analogous to the securities context, where a statement (or omission) is material if there is a "substantial likelihood" that a reasonable investor would view it as "significantly altering the 'total mix' of information made available." Moreover, this test of materiality applies not only to the decision to admit an item but also decisions as to processing, e.g., expediting importation. With this test in mind, we turn to the misstatements on the Phiale's entry form.

Steinhardt contends that even under a natural tendency test, the misstatements are immaterial. He claims that the customs officials lacked statutory authority to seize the Phiale and that it was customs policy not to review information about the country of origin of such an object. He further argues that the statement of the Phiale's value was relevant only to the imposition of the processing fee, which was unaffected by the misstatement. Because the misstatement of the country of origin was material as a matter of law and thus proper grounds for summary judgment, we need not examine the misstatement of value.

Customs Directive No. 5230-15, regarding the detention and seizure of cultural property, fatally undermines Steinhardt's contention that listing Switzerland as the country of origin was irrelevant to the Phiale's importation. The Directive advised customs officials to determine whether property was subject to a claim of foreign ownership and to seize that property. An item's country of origin is clearly relevant to that inquiry. ...

The Directive provides a basis for seizing cultural property under the NSPA in the seizure provisions of 19 U.S.C. § 1595a(c). Seizure of the Phiale would clearly be authorized by this provision under *United States v. McClain*, 545 F.2d 988 (5th Cir. 1977), which held that violations of a nation's patrimony laws are covered by the NSPA. Because Steinhardt asserts that

McClain was improperly decided, he claims that the customs officials lacked a statutory basis to seize the Phiale.

This argument, however, misperceives the test of materiality. Regardless of whether *McClain's* reasoning is ultimately followed as a proper interpretation of the NSPA, a reasonable customs official would certainly consider the fact that *McClain* supports a colorable claim to seize the Phiale as having possibly been exported in violation of Italian patrimony laws. Indeed, the Directive explicitly references the *McClain* decision and informs officials that if they are unsure of the status of a nation's patrimony laws, they should notify the Office of Enforcement. Knowing that the Phiale was from Italy would, therefore, be of critical importance. ...

Eighth Amendment

While Steinhardt raised an Eighth Amendment claim in the district court [that] the forfeiture violates the Excessive Fines Clause of the Eighth Amendment [in violation of *United States v. Bajakajian*, 524 U.S. 321 (1998).] We disagree. [The] instant case ... bears all the "hallmarks of the traditional civil in rem forfeitures." First, the forfeiture here was not part of a criminal prosecution. While Section 545 is part of the criminal code, this fact alone does not render the forfeiture punitive. Although the question whether a proceeding is civil or criminal is certainly relevant, it is not dispositive. Thus, the fact that the present action is a civil in rem proceeding weighs against a finding that it is punitive.

Even more important to the inquiry is the nature of the statute that authorizes forfeiture. As opposed to Section 982(a), the provisions at issue in *Bajakajian*, Section 545 is a customs law, traditionally viewed as non-punitive. The Phiale is thus classic contraband, an item imported into the United States in violation of law. ... It is forfeiture of the former that *Bajakajian* continues to recognize as nonpunitive and outside the scope of the Excessive Fines Clause.

We therefore affirm.

United States v. Austin

54 F.3d 394 (7th Cir. 1995)

FLAUM, *Circuit Judge*. Defendant Donald Austin was convicted and sentenced to 8 1/2 years for knowingly buying and selling counterfeit works of art. Although we uphold his conviction, the denial of his motion for a new trial, and all but one of the trial court's sentencing determinations, we remand for a reconsideration of whether Austin deserved a sentencing enhancement under the Guidelines for being an "organizer or leader."

Donald Austin owned and operated Austin Galleries, a chain of art galleries in Chicago, Detroit, and San Francisco. Austin, whose business grew from one Chicago gallery in the mid-1960s to over thirty galleries in the mid-1980s, was a "hands-on" manager who took an active interest in all facets of his business and in each of his galleries. Austin Galleries specialized in modern and contemporary artists, including Salvador Dali, Joan Miro, Pablo Picasso, and Marc Chagall, and sold mostly lithographic and serigraphic prints of their works. Although the individual galleries had prints on hand, many customers purchased prints on a "to ordered" basis; a customer would see a copy in a gallery, and order the actual print from Austin's headquarters in Palatine, Illinois.

Lithographic and serigraphic prints can be divided into three categories for the purposes of this opinion. Lithographs and serigraphs are most valuable when they are part of an "original" limited edition print, a "category 1." Art industry standards require that an original be prepared under the artist's supervision. The artist signifies his acceptance of the edition by signing and numbering them. The artist may also reserve a small percentage of the edition for his own use or that of the publisher. Called "artist's proofs," such works are identified by the designation H.C., E.A., or A.P., usually in place of the edition number. Less valuable than originals are "afters" or "category 2" prints. Afters are copies of an original work made by others with the artist's permission; these copies have nominal value in the decorative art market. Finally, there are "category 3" prints: unauthorized reproductions of an artist's work (or independent works made to look like something the artist might have created), made without the artist's involvement or approval. These works do not have an established market, and if they carry an artist's signature, they are forgeries.

Austin sold most of his art as signed original limited edition prints. His customers thought they were buying originals. The customers were wrong; most of what Austin sold were forgeries. Several of Austin's employees recalled that they never seemed to run out of any print and that there was never a time when a customer requesting a specific edition number was told that the number had been sold or was otherwise unavailable. Others noticed that a number of works they were selling were obvious forgeries and brought this to Austin's attention, to no avail. Two employees even tried removing what they thought were frauds from the walls of one gallery, but when Austin learned of this he merely became angry and ordered them to place the prints back on display.

Acting on complaints, the Federal Trade Commission ("FTC") brought suit against Austin in May, 1988. A district court placed a temporary restraining order on Austin on May 5, 1988, restricting Austin's sales of Dali, Picasso, and Chagall prints and permitting the FTC to enter Austin's galleries to inspect his prints and documents. The inspection yielded widespread evidence of forgeries among Austin's inventory and prior sales. One expert who examined 490 prints, including 387 in current inventory and 103 sold to customers, did not find a single authentic original. Records also revealed that Austin had been able to acquire prints in suspiciously large quantities, some quantities even exceeding the number in the actual edition of the print. The results of the investigation also raised concerns about the authenticity of Austin's Miro prints, and the court, after the FTC amended its complaint, added Miro's works to the list of those Austin could not sell.

Following the investigation, in April, 1990, Austin entered into a settlement agreement with the FTC. The agreement, as approved by the court, forbade Austin from making misrepresentations in the sale of artwork. Austin also agreed to surrender all of his pencil-signed Miros, Chagalls, and Picassos. Austin was allowed to sell Dalis so long as he did not represent them as authentic works of art. Additionally, the court ordered Austin to pay $625,000 into a consumer redress fund to be administered by the FTC, with the condition that if he did not pay the entire sum by January 1, 1991, or if he declared bankruptcy before that day, the amount would increase to $1.5 million. As a final part of the settlement, Austin signed a stipulation for judgment admitting the allegations of fraud contained in the complaint. The stipulation was to be filed only in the event Austin went into bankruptcy or defaulted on his payments to the FTC.

The FTC settlement failed to deter Austin. Austin did not turn over all of the Chagalls, Miros, and Picassos as required. He also attempted to sell several Chagalls to one of his art suppliers, Michael Zabrin, and to sell to another supplier, Phillip Coffaro, a "package" of Chagalls and Miros, although both men turned him down. Most significant, Austin sold nine

Chagall prints to a customer, Merlin Hanson, for $50,000, with an option to repurchase within six months. Austin originally had requested only a loan from Hanson and had offered the prints as collateral, but Hanson's financial advisor had insisted on the buy-back arrangement to avoid any losses should Austin enter bankruptcy. Austin represented the prints as having a value of $70,000 wholesale and $140,000 retail. Prior to the sale, which was made eleven days after the FTC settlement, an FTC expert had informed Austin's attorney that at least one of the prints sold to Hanson was a fake.

Following these events, the government initiated criminal proceedings against Austin, and a grand jury indicted him on March 11, 1993. Counts I through VII of the indictment alleged violations of the mail and wire fraud statutes, 18 U.S.C. §§ 1341 & 1343, while Count VIII charged Austin with causing money he knew to have been taken by fraud to be transmitted in interstate commerce, 18 U.S.C. § 2314. The first five counts related to transactions prior to the FTC proceeding, while the last three concerned the Hanson sale. In the course of its investigation, the grand jury subpoenaed Austin's records for sales of Chagalls after 1988. In response, Austin did not turn over information regarding the Hanson sale; Austin testified at trial that he thought the sale was a loan and did not have to be reported.

The government, which relied heavily on the information produced by the FTC investigation, introduced at trial extensive evidence of fraud against Austin. A jury returned guilty verdicts against Austin on all counts, and the trial judge sentenced him to 102 months imprisonment to be followed by two years supervised release. The court also ordered Austin to pay into the FTC's compensation fund $505,000, which was the difference between the restitution he had already made, about $120,000, and the original sum stipulated in the FTC settlement, $625,000.

On appeal, Austin raises several challenges to his conviction. He contends that double jeopardy barred his conviction because of the earlier FTC suit and settlement and that the trial court erred in admitting much of the government's evidence. ...

Austin first maintains that the FTC settlement had placed him once in jeopardy for any fraud he might have perpetrated on his customers. Austin does not argue that the $625,000 he was initially required to pay into a "consumer redress fund" constituted a punishment for his actions; he admits that that sum was a remedial payment. Rather, Austin submits that when he defaulted on the $625,000 installment plan and his liability jumped to $1.5 million, the $875,000 increase constituted a punishment above and beyond his agreement to return his customers' money. This civil sanction, he suggests, placed him once in jeopardy, thereby rendering the criminal trial an unconstitutional proceeding.

Austin is correct that "punitive" civil sanctions can constitute punishment for the purposes of the double jeopardy clause. Austin is also correct that even where a civil punishment precedes a criminal trial, jeopardy may attach. Austin's argument falters, however, when he asserts that if $625,000 satisfied the FTC's remedial interests, any payment above that amount is properly categorized as "a deterrent or retribution." The FTC accepted $625,000 initially because it feared that the defendant might go into bankruptcy. The FTC's offer amounted to a discount for prompt and early payment of the total loss Austin had caused, a sum the FTC estimated to be in excess of $3.8 million. When Austin violated the terms of the settlement and the amount he owed increased, the FTC was still only holding Austin liable for an amount less than that it thought his fraud had caused. Thus, the net consequence of the FTC's actions was still remedial. Such circumstances do not implicate the Double Jeopardy Clause.

Second, Austin objects to the trial court's admission of extensive evidence relating to the FTC settlement, including the terms of the consent decree and Austin's stipulation in the settlement admitting to the allegations in the FTC's complaint. He asserts that this evidence was unfairly prejudicial because it likely led the jury to think that "the same issues had already been determined in the civil action." We review the admission of this evidence for abuse of discretion.

Austin's contentions on this point are equally unavailing. Prior to trial, the government informed Austin that it would introduce the consent decree in order to show Austin's criminal intent in subsequently violating its conditions. While Federal Rule of Evidence 408 prohibits the admission of statements made in the course of settlement to prove liability and Rule 404(b) prohibits the admission of other wrongs in order to show action in conformity therewith, both rules allow the admission of such evidence when offered for another purpose. The evidence from the civil suit served a number of alternative purposes. First, it showed that Austin was on notice when he subsequently sold other prints that those prints were forgeries. It also demonstrated Austin knew he could not sell those prints without reporting the sale to the FTC. Moreover, the facts from the FTC case both provided the background for Austin's indictment and laid the evidentiary foundation for many of the governments exhibits in the criminal proceeding. Finally, the stipulation itself constituted a direct judicial admission to the accusation of fraud in the conduct underlying the indictment. These purposes provided sufficient bases to introduce this evidence against Austin.

We also do not think that the evidence, in light of its relevance, was so "unfairly prejudicial" that the trial court should have excluded it under Fed. R. Evid. 403. …

Austin also raises … issues relating to his sentencing. … Austin challenges the district court's imposition of a 2-level enhancement to his sentence for obstruction of justice under U.S.S.G. § 3C1.1. At sentencing, the government argued that three factors made Austin eligible for this enhancement: his violation of the court order from the FTC suit by concealing certain Chagall prints during the settlement of that case, his concealment of certain records relating to the sale of those prints from the grand jury in response to a subpoena, and his false trial testimony. Austin objects to the first two factors on grounds of "double counting." He notes that the district court imposed an enhancement under § 2F1.1(b)(3)(B) for his violation of the FTC injunction by selling the Chagall lithographs to Hanson. Thus, he concludes, the court could not penalize him twice for that same activity by simply giving it a new name. Alternatively, Austin contends that the district court did not make the specific findings required to justify the enhancement, especially with regard to the alleged perjury, and that a remand is warranted.

We disagree with Austin's contention that the first two factors did not justify the obstruction of justice enhancement. Austin is correct that double counting is not permitted under the Guidelines. The Application Notes to § 3C1.1 also specifically forbid an increase for obstruction of justice where the defendant is convicted for a number of related offenses, including perjury, contempt, failure to appear, and misprision of felony. However, the Hanson sale, for which Austin received the § 2F1.1(b)(3)(B) enhancement, is factually distinct from Austin's concealing Chagall and Miro prints from the FTC. Although Austin's concealment of the prints enabled him to make the sale, the concealment and the sale are distinct acts that do not collapse into one another. Austin's failure to turn records of the Hanson sales over to the grand jury despite a subpoena also constitutes obstruction. Again, the failure was only possible because Austin made the improper sale, but it was nonetheless conduct separate from the sale. Furthermore, the court was free to reject Austin's defense to the second factor–that he considered the sale a loan–as it apparently did. ...

Finally, Austin objects to the four-level enhancement for being the organizer or leader of a criminal activity that involved five or more participants or was otherwise extensive. U.S.S.G. § 3B1.1(a). The district court applied the enhancement by finding that there were five people under Austin's control. Austin submits, however, that the government offered no proof that these people knowingly participated in the fraud scheme. While Austin admits that some of these people testified to having had "suspicions" about the prints sold at Austin Galleries, he asserts that the government did not prove by a preponderance of the evidence that any of them were criminally responsible.

On this issue we agree with Austin. The government argued at the sentencing hearing that Austin had led an organization that contained five or more persons. The government relied on evidence that a number of Austin's employees openly joked about the inauthenticity of the prints they were selling and that one employee continued working for Austin even after he had seen Austin change the numbers on a print. Yet of the four employees to whom the government referred at sentencing, none was prosecuted, and three had been assured by Austin that the works were genuine. This evidence does not establish that Austin led "five or more persons sharing criminal responsibility." Indeed, the government itself seems to have abandoned this argument on appeal, focusing instead on whether the evidence showed that Austin's organization was "otherwise extensive."

Although there were insufficient findings that Austin led an organization of five or more persons, this may well be a case where the defendant's organization was "otherwise extensive." Application Note 3 to § 3B1.1 states: "In assessing whether an organization is 'otherwise extensive,' all persons involved during the course of the entire offense are to be considered. Thus, a fraud that involved only three participants but used the unknowing services of many outsiders could be considered extensive." Austin had over thirty galleries and hundreds of employees at his disposal to help him defraud the art-buying public; such facts certainly might lend themselves to an "otherwise extensive" finding.

The question is whether we can affirm on the basis of the "otherwise extensive" prong given the government's and the district court's exclusive focus at sentencing on the "five or more participants" prong. ... [T]he government here "insists that sufficient support for the increase can be found in the record," and asks us to affirm the sentencing enhancement on this alternate ground. But ..."it is not this court's role to make the factual findings necessary to support a sentencing calculation; that is a task for the district court." The government contends that a remand on this issue would be a "useless, formalistic act." We find that contention somewhat inappropriate. Sentencing decisions, like most fact-sensitive inquiries, are best left to the trial court. There is no reason to depart from that general rule in the instant case.

For the foregoing reasons, we affirm Austin's conviction and the district court's sentencing determinations in all but one respect, vacate the district court's enhancement of Austin's sentence under U.S.S.G. § 3B1.1, and remand for resentencing on the § 3B1.1 issue only.

Notes and Questions

a. In *United States v. Schultz*, 333 F.3d 393 (2d Cir. 2003), the Second Circuit formally addressed the application of the National Stolen Property Act (NSPA), 18 U.S.C. § 2315, to antiquities that are not stolen from a private owner but rather excavated in violation of state law. Many countries have laws which provide for state ownership of excavated antiquities. The Court reaffirmed the position that these patrimony laws provide sufficient ownership of the property to allow for enforcement of the NSPA. See also *United States v. McClain*, 545 F.2d 988 (5th Cir. 1977).

b. Other federal statutes provide criminal sanctions, including theft of major artwork, 18 U.S.C. § 668 (to obtain by theft or fraud any object of cultural heritage from a museum); interstate or foreign shipments by carrier; state prosecutions, 18 U.S.C. § 659 (to steal or obtain by fraud anything from a conveyance, depot or terminal, any shipment being transported in interstate or foreign commerce); frauds and swindles, 18 U.S.C. § 1341 (to cause anything to be sent through the U.S. mails in furtherance of a scheme to defraud); fraud by wire, radio, or television, 18 U.S.C. § 1343 (to cause any electronic signal to cross state lines in furtherance of a scheme to defraud); interference with commerce by threats or violence (Hobbs Act), 18 U.S.C. § 1951 (to obstruct interstate commerce by robbery, extortion, threat of violence or actual violence); and illegal trafficking in Native American human remains and cultural items, 18 U.S.C. § 1170 (discussed below).

c. One analogy to the NSPA for intellectual property applies to the transportation and sale of bootleg records. Is there a sufficient ownership in the copyright underlying the bootleg records or the public performance of the artist to give rise to a cause of action? See *Dowling v. United States*, 473 U.S. 207 (1985).

d. The Native American Graves Protection and Repatriation Act. The treatment of Native American sacred sites and gravesites has been one of the many troubling aspects of expropriated art and artifacts. In 1990, Congress enacted The Native American Graves Protection and Repatriation Act, codified at 25 U.S.C. §§ 3001-3013 and 18 U.S.C. § 1170. "Shorn of its excess legal verbiage, what the statute says is that it is a crime (1) to dig up, remove or damage archaeological resources on federal or Indian land; (2) to receive, transport or deal in what has been dug up or removed; or (3) to receive, transport or deal in what has been dug up or removed from private land in violation of State or local law."[60]

The bill summary provides a simple outline of the legislation:

- Clarifies the right of ownership of Indian, Alaska Native, and Native Hawaiian (Native American) human remains and artifacts, including funerary objects, religious artifacts, and objects of cultural patrimony, found on Federal or tribal lands.

- Establishes conditions for the excavation or removal of Native American human remains or cultural artifacts, including the consent of the appropriate tribe or Native American organization.

- Establishes notification requirements for the inadvertent discovery of Native American human remains or cultural artifacts on Federal or tribal lands.

- Establishes criminal penalties for the sale, purchase, or transport of Native American human remains or cultural artifacts without a legal right of

---

[60] Stefan D. Cassella, *Using the Forfeiture Laws to Protect Archaeological Resources*, 41 IDAHO L. REV. 129, 135 (2004).

possession.

- Directs Federal agencies and museums receiving Federal assistance to identify the geographic and tribal origins of human remains or cultural artifacts in their collections, and require the return of the remains or artifacts to the appropriate tribe or Native American organization upon request.

- Establishes a Department of Interior advisory committee to review the identification and repatriation processes for Native American human remains and cultural artifacts held by Federal agencies and federally assisted museums.

- Establishes civil penalties for museums failing to comply with requirements of this act.

e. Another difficult issue in theft and misappropriation of art and cultural artifacts stems from the atrocities of the Nazi regime during its reign through the end of World War II. Limited legal activity continues today, and new evidence provides a better historical record, if not any meaningful measure of legal relief. See *Alperin v. Vatican Bank*, 410 F.3d 532 (9th Cir. 2005) *cert. denied, Order of Friars Minor v. Alperin*, __ U.S. __, 126 S. Ct. 1141, 163 L. Ed. 2d 1000 (2006), *cert. denied, Istituto per le Opere di Religione v. Alperin*, __U.S. __, 126 S. Ct. 1160, 163 L. Ed. 2d 1000 (2006).

A group of twenty-four individuals and four organizations (the "Holocaust Survivors") claim that the Vatican Bank, known by its official title Istituto per le Opere di Religione, the Order of Friars Minor, and the Croatian Liberation Movement (Hrvatski Oslobodilacki Pokret), profited from the genocidal acts of the Croatian Ustasha political regime (the "Ustasha"), which was supported throughout World War II by Nazi forces. That profit allegedly passed through the Vatican Bank in the form of proceeds from looted assets and slave labor. The Holocaust Survivors brought suit in federal court claiming conversion, unjust enrichment, restitution, the right to an accounting, and human rights violations and violations of international law arising out of the defendants' alleged involvement with the Ustasha during and following World War II. ...

The viability of the Holocaust Survivors' claims apart from the issue of the political question doctrine is not before us. Nevertheless, looking ahead, we note that the statutory grounds on which the Holocaust Survivors base their claims have, for the most part, not fared well in recent litigation. Just last term, the Supreme Court limited the [Alien Tort Statute (ATS)] in *Sosa v. Alvarez-Machain*, 542 U.S. 692 (2004) (curtailing the scope of actionable international norms under the ATS but explaining that "the door is still ajar subject to vigilant doorkeeping"); see also *Weiss v. Am. Jewish Comm.*, 335 F. Supp. 2d 469 (S.D.N.Y. 2004) (dismissing claim under the ATS for injunctive relief in connection with the construction of a Holocaust memorial in light of the Court's holding in Sosa).

The contours of the [Foreign Sovereign Immunities Act (FSIA)] have also changed with the Supreme Court's holding in Republic of *Austria v. Altmann*, 541 U.S. 677 (2004), that the FSIA applies retroactively. See also *Abrams v. Societe*

Nationale des Chemins de Fer Francais, 389 F.3d 61, 64-65 (2d Cir. 2004) (dismissing case for lack of subject matter jurisdiction because the French government's acquisition of defendant railroad company immunized it from suit under the FSIA). In *Deutsch v. Turner Corp.*, 324 F.3d 692, 719 (9th Cir. 2003), we held that a California statute on which the Holocaust Survivors' claims are based in part, Cal. Civ. Proc. Code § 354.6, unconstitutionally intruded on the foreign affairs power of the federal government. We leave the district court to determine in the first instance to what extent the Holocaust Survivors have correctly invoked these and other jurisdictional bases.

Is the current trend against enforcement of claims for property stolen by Nazi governments consistent with the NPSA or the Native American Graves Protection and Repatriation Act? Should the provenance of stolen art or cultural artifacts be subject to a statute of limitations? Does it matter whether the work has religious significance, and if so, significance to whom?

f. Can there be an innocent art dealer in the chain of title for stolen art and artifacts? Again, does the answer change if the works are religious in nature or if they were stolen as part of an occupational government or during the commission of human rights violations? See *Autocephalous Greek-Orthodox Church v. Goldberg & Feldman Fine Arts, Inc.*, 917 F.2d 278 (7th Cir. 1990).

Problem XVII-D

As Bryce has worked in the neighborhood on his feature film, art exhibit and documentary (see Problems XVIII-B, XVIII-C), Bryce has gained the trust and respect of many of the more elderly artists in the area. Alice McGreevy, one of the artists, gave Bryce a group of five oil paintings that she had made in 1952. McGreevy explained that she had sold the paintings to a collector in 1952 but then found out that the collector was planning to destroy the work out of fear that the pieces would result in his identification as a Communist sympathizer. (The collector, in fact, had attended Communist political party meetings twice in the 1930's.) McGreevy explained that she "took the artwork back" from the unnamed collector – but kept the payments.

Bryce accepted the gift, but now is worried. The exhibit and the associated publicity have generated a great deal of interest in these works. The children of the collector have contacted Bryce claiming ownership of the five works and demanding their return. McGreevy says that the family has no claim over the works, so she can dispose of them whatever she wants. Bryce requests your advice and guidance.

E.   **Museum Operations as Charitable Entities**

Introduction

Nonprofit organizations are creatures of state law and federal tax law. State law governs the organizational aspects of the nonprofit entity, typically providing that the entity is a corporation organized with no shareholders and with a charitable purpose that meets the applicable state law definition. Depending on the specifics of state law, organizations can also be trusts, governmental entities or limited liability companies. Not all nonprofit organizations are tax exempt for federal tax purposes. For example, mutual benefit organizations such as trade associations are nonprofit organizations but do not provide the members or donors a tax deduction for donations.

Charitable organizations organized and operated exclusively for religious, charitable, scientific, public safety testing, literary, or educational purposes are exempt from federal income taxation under Internal Revenue Code, 26 U.S.C. § 501(c)(3). Donations made to those organizations may be deductible against the donor's tax liability. The organization is further limited by statute so "no part of the net earnings ... inures to the benefit of any private shareholder or individual, no substantial part of the activities ... is carrying on propaganda, or otherwise attempting, to influence legislation (except as otherwise provided in subsection (h)), and ... does not participate in, or intervene in (including the publishing or distributing of statements), any political campaign on behalf of (or in opposition to) any candidate for public office." 26 U.S.C. § 501(c)(3).

Museums and arts organizations generally qualify as tax-exempt as educational organizations. As explained in the tax exemption application, "[a] public charity has a broad base of support, while a private foundation receives its support from a small number of donors."[61] More specifically, tax-exempt organizations are those "that receive substantial support from grants, governmental units, and/or contributions from the general public." The primary test is the one-third support test, under which an organization will be deemed charitable if it "normally receive[s] more than one-third of their support from contributions, membership fees, and gross receipts from activities related to their exempt functions, and not more than one-third of their support from gross investment income and net unrelated business income."[62]

In addition to fulfilling the financial support requirements, the purpose of the organization must be charitable, as such term is generally used. Museums and cultural institutes are generally included as charitable educational institutions, assuming the other obligations are met.

> To be organized exclusively for a charitable purpose, the organization must be a corporation, community chest, fund, or foundation. A charitable trust is a fund or foundation and will qualify. However, an individual will not qualify. The articles of organization must limit the organization's purposes to exempt purposes set forth in section 501(c)(3) and must not expressly empower it to engage, other than as an insubstantial part of its activities, in activities that are not in furtherance of one or more of those purposes. This requirement may be met if the purposes stated in the articles of organization are limited in some way by reference to section 501(c)(3).

> In addition, an organization's assets must be permanently dedicated to an exempt purpose. This means that if an organization dissolves, its assets must be distributed for an exempt purpose, to the federal government, or to a state or local government for a public purpose. To establish that an organization's assets will be permanently dedicated to an exempt purpose, its articles of organization should contain a provision insuring their distribution for an exempt purpose in the event of dissolution. Although reliance may be placed upon state law to establish permanent dedication of assets for exempt purposes, an organization's application

---

[61] Instructions for Form 1023 - Introductory Material, http://www.irs.gov/instructions/i1023/ar01.html.
[62] Id.

can be processed by the IRS more rapidly if its articles of organization include a provision insuring permanent dedication of assets for exempt purposes.[63]

In addition to the charitable purpose, the organization's operation cannot result in the private inurement or financial benefit of private individuals. While reasonable salaries can be paid by the organization, transactions between the charity and its leadership are closely scrutinized and personal benefits are avoided. Similarly, income by the charity which stems from non-tax-exempt activities, such as sales of goods that do not further the organization's charitable purpose, must not grow too large or the organization may lose its tax-exempt status.

As a result, while museums generally fall within the normal range of charitable entities, galleries that sell private works of art have innumerable troubles operating in the nonprofit arena. Organizations that fill both roles also risk problems with private inurement and unrelated business income tax obligations and an income that can threaten the public support requirement of the charity.

The governance of charitable organizations must fit within both the federal obligations embedded in the tax laws and the state nonprofit corporation laws. Among these many duties are the obligation to treat the assets of the charity as a public trust and to meet the duties of care and loyalty to the entity. Similarly, the charities often serve as trustees for donations made in the form of express trusts or gifts that have trust-like fiduciary responsibilities to the donors. These obligations limit how museum boards can manage the assets under their control.

Museum of Fine Arts v. Beland

432 Mass. 540, 735 N.E.2d 1248 (2000)

This is an action brought under G. L. c. 231A by the Museum of Fine Arts (MFA), seeking a declaration that the will of the late Reverend William E. Wolcott (Wolcott) does not allow the defendants to sell any of the seventeen paintings that were bequeathed to a charitable trust. The record establishes the following relevant undisputed facts. Wolcott died in 1911. In his will, executed on June 20, 1907, Wolcott bequeathed seventeen paintings, including paintings by Eugene Boudin, Camille Pissarro, and Claude Monet, to the trustees of The White Fund (trustees), a charitable trust. The provisions of the bequest read as follows:

> "3. Whenever the pictures or any part of them shall come into the actual possession of the said Trustees, they shall offer the same for purposes of exhibition to the Museum of Fine Arts in the City of Boston, unless they shall determine otherwise in accordance with the discretion confirmed on them in the following paragraph:

> "4. If at the time of my decease or at any subsequent time there shall exist within the present limits of the city of Lawrence a public art gallery housed in a fire-proof building and under such management as the Trustees of the White Fund shall approve, the said Trustees may deposit the aforesaid pictures with such art gallery for purposes of exhibition.

---

[63] Exemption Requirements, available at http://www.irs.gov/charities/charitable/article/0,,id=96099,00.html.

"5. The ownership and control of the pictures shall be vested permanently and inalienably in trust nevertheless, as aforesaid, in said Trustees of the White Fund and their successors.

"6. My purpose in making this bequest is to create and gratify a public taste for fine art, particularly among the people of the City of Lawrence. And I give to the said Trustees of the White Fund full and absolute authority in any contingency not fully provided for in the above stipulations to take such action as they judge best fitted to serve the purpose described."

In the years after Wolcott's death, the trustees came into possession of, and offered, the paintings to the MFA for exhibition. Currently, the MFA possesses all seventeen paintings, and regularly exhibits three of them. The remaining fourteen paintings are in storage, and the MFA does not plan to exhibit them in its galleries. The fourteen paintings held in storage are available, in certain circumstances, to be shown to persons interested in viewing them.

After learning that the trustees wanted to sell some or all of the paintings, the MFA brought this action in the Superior Court seeking a declaratory judgment, for purposes relevant here, that the terms of Wolcott's bequest do not permit the trustees to sell any of the paintings. The MFA moved for summary judgment, and the Attorney General, a necessary party to the litigation, filed a cross motion for partial summary judgment. The trustees filed a memorandum in support of the Attorney General's motion. A Superior Court judge allowed the MFA's motion in part, concluding that the provisions of Wolcott's bequest do not permit the trustees to sell the paintings. As to the Attorney General's claim that the primary purpose of the charitable trust created by the bequest was not being satisfied, and that the bequest should therefore be modified under the doctrines of cy pres or reasonable deviation, the judge concluded that (1) as to the three paintings currently exhibited, Wolcott's intent was being carried out; and (2) as to the fourteen paintings not being exhibited, a trial was necessary to decide whether the trustees should be allowed to sell the paintings through cy pres. She therefore denied the Attorney General's motion for partial summary judgment. Pursuant to G. L. c. 231, § 111, and Mass. R. Civ. P. 64 (a), as amended, 423 Mass. 1403 (1996), another judge in the Superior Court entered a judgment and reported the propriety of the orders to the Appeals Court. We allowed the defendants' applications for direct appellate review. We conclude that the MFA is entitled to summary judgment, that the bequest does not permit the trustees to sell any of the paintings, and that, as a consequence, a trial is not necessary. We shall direct that an appropriate declaration be entered in the case.

1. The trustees argue that, under the express terms of Wolcott's bequest, they have the complete power to sell the paintings. They maintain that this power comes into play because Wolcott's intent, "to create and gratify a public taste for fine art, particularly among the people of the City of Lawrence," is not being fulfilled in any meaningful way by the exhibition of only three paintings at the MFA. Consequently, pursuant to the "full and absolute authority" conferred on them under paragraph 6 of the bequest, the trustees conclude that they are authorized to sell the paintings. We disagree. …

Paragraph 5 of the bequest states: "The ownership and control of the pictures shall be vested permanently and inalienably . . . in [the] Trustees." The judge correctly interpreted the meaning of the words in this paragraph by the application of commonly accepted rules. Contrary to the trustees' assertions, the judge did not "overlook" a secondary meaning of the term "inalienable."

The contention that Wolcott must have intended the word "inalienable" to be used in the bequest the same way as the word had been used in the Declaration of Independence is not persuasive. The judge properly concluded that "the phrase 'permanently and inalienably' in the will means exactly what it says – the Trustees are to have *permanent* possession and control of the paintings" (emphasis original). The bequest makes clear that the paintings may not be sold by the trustees.

The trustees read too much into the discretion conferred on them by paragraph 6 of the bequest. While the provision grants to the trustees "full and absolute authority . . . to take such action as they judge best fitted," that authority is expressly limited, and the power becomes operative only in the event "any contingency [is] not fully provided for in the [earlier paragraphs or the bequest]." The record establishes that no such contingency has yet occurred. As provided in paragraph 3, the MFA has accepted the paintings and regularly exhibits three of them. Although fourteen of the paintings are normally kept in storage, the MFA has not refused to make the paintings available for exhibition, and, although not required to do so, the MFA has continued to insure and protect the paintings.

2. We reject the defendants' argument that either the doctrine of cy pres or the doctrine of reasonable deviation[64] should be applied to the bequest because it is impracticable or impossible to carry out its purpose. The defendants maintain that Wolcott's primary purpose was to promote fine art, particularly for the people of Lawrence. They assert this purpose is not being fulfilled because exhibition of only some of the paintings at the MFA does not benefit the people of Lawrence, and because there is little likelihood that an art gallery suitable to exhibit the paintings will be built, or can be acquired, in Lawrence.

Wolcott's expressed general charitable intent was "to create and gratify a public taste for fine art," through the auspices of the MFA, with a preference that the people of Lawrence enjoy the paintings. The inability to exhibit in Lawrence the three paintings currently on display at the MFA provides no support for the defendants' argument. Those paintings are on display in a manner that accords with the provisions of paragraph 3 of the bequest and Wolcott's general intent.

The current inability to exhibit the other fourteen paintings in Lawrence would not justify the application of cy pres or reasonable deviation to sell the paintings. A sale of the fourteen paintings would be the antithesis of Wolcott's intent because the sale could deprive the public of any opportunity to view them. There is information in the record suggesting that it might be possible to display some or all of the fourteen paintings at a gallery in Lawrence or at a fine arts center in nearby Andover. ... The record shows that the trustees have not made reasonable efforts to explore alternative locations for exhibition. Until such efforts are made, and are shown to be futile, there is no need for further proceedings on the issue whether cy pres would apply to allow sale of the fourteen paintings in storage. ... A judgment is to be entered declaring that the doctrines of cy pres and reasonable deviation do not apply, and that none of the paintings held by the trustees that are the subject of the bequest can be sold.

---

[64] Under the doctrine of reasonable deviation, "the court will direct or permit the trustee of a charitable trust to deviate from a term of the trust if it appears to the court that compliance is impossible or illegal, or that owing to circumstances not known to the settlor and not anticipated by him compliance would defeat or substantially impair the accomplishment of the purposes of the trust." Restatement (Second) of Trusts § 381 (1959).

Notes and Questions

a. The donor of a work of art may lose the ability to receive a tax deduction for a charitable gift of a work of art to a museum if limitations imposed on the museum by the donor create a risk of the work's subsequent removal.

> Treas. Reg. § 1.170A-1(e) Transfers subject to a condition or power. If as of the date of a gift a transfer for charitable purposes is dependent upon the performance of some act or the happening of a precedent event in order that it might become effective, no deduction is allowable unless the possibility that the charitable transfer will not become effective is so remote as to be negligible. If an interest in property passes to, or is vested in, charity on the date of the gift and the interest would be defeated by the subsequent performance of some act or the happening of some event, the possibility of occurrence of which appears on the date of the gift to be so remote as to be negligible, the deduction is allowable.

> For example, A transfers land to a city government for as long as the land is used by the city for a public park. If on the date of the gift the city does plan to use the land for a park and the possibility that the city will not use the land for a public park is so remote as to be negligible, A is entitled to a deduction under section 170 for his charitable contribution.

See also Treas. Reg. § 20.2055-2(b); Treas. Reg. § 25.2522(c)-3(b)(1) (same result).

b. Beginning in 1916, the Museum of the American Indian, Heye Foundation, developed a tremendous collection of Native American art, history and artifacts at its initial location at 155th Street and Broadway in Manhattan. In 1989 it used *cy pres* to allow it to enter into an agreement to shift its collection to the Smithsonian as part of the National Museum of the American Indian (20 USC § 80q *et seq.* (2006)). A second *cy pres* action was brought by the Museum of the American Indian claiming that a transfer of its library collection to the Huntington Free Library was no longer appropriate, in part because of the resources it now had pursuant to the legislation and the role of the Smithsonian. In an action by the Museum of the American Indian to recover the library from the Huntington Free Library under *cy pres*, what result? See *Bd. of Trs. of the Am. Indian, Heye Found. v. Bd. of Trs. of the Huntington Free Library and Reading Room*, 610 N.Y.S.2d 488, 493 (1994), *appeal denied*, 86 N.Y.2d 702 (1995).

c. To what extent can *cy pres* be used to accelerate a cash gift or otherwise be used as the charitable museum determines to be the most efficient use of the funds? See *Museum of Fine Arts v. Beland*, 432 Mass. 540, 735 N.E.2d 1248 (2000).

d. To what extent does economic efficiency take priority over the specific intent of the testator? Judge Richard A. Posner has had some thoughts on the subject:

> The dilemma of whether to enforce the testator's intent or to modify the terms of the will in accordance with changed conditions since his death is often a false one. A policy of rigid adherence to the letter of the donative instrument is likely to frustrate both the donor's purposes and the efficient use of resources. ... [E]nforcement would in all likelihood be contrary to the purposes of the donor, who intended by his gift to contribute to the cure of disease, not to perpetuate useless facilities. ... Since no one can foresee the future, a rational donor knows that his intentions might eventually be thwarted by unpredictable circumstances

and may therefore be presumed to accept implicitly a rule permitting modification of the terms of the bequest in the event that an unforeseen change frustrates his original intention.

Richard A. Posner, ECONOMIC ANALYSIS OF LAW 556-557 (5TH ED. 1998). Should the testator be presumed to be frustrated by an inability to foresee the future or by donees that prefer posthumous renegotiation?

e. Beyond the economic efficiency of trusts, there is the very practical matter of drafting the trust documents. A testator's or donor's intent can express a willingness to vary the gift as times change – if the parties draft that understanding into the trust documents. Given the ability of the donor to draft the trust and the ability of the charity to refuse gifts that do not have sufficient flexibility, what relevance do notions of efficiency have regarding the donation?

f. Another significant issue is taxable income at a tax-exempt charity. The IRS website provides a helpful introduction to the topic:

> Unrelated business income tax. Even though an organization is recognized as tax exempt, it still may be liable for tax on its unrelated business income. Unrelated business income is income from a trade or business, regularly carried on, that is not substantially related to the charitable, educational, or other purpose that is the basis of the organization's exemption. For most organizations, an activity is an unrelated business (and subject to unrelated business income tax) if it meets three requirements:
>
> 1. It is a trade or business,
>
> 2. It is regularly carried on, and
>
> 3. It is not substantially related to furthering the exempt purpose of the organization.
>
> There are, however, a number of modifications, exclusions, and exceptions to the general definition of unrelated business income.
>
> To determine if a business activity is *substantially related* requires examining the relationship between the activities that generate income and the accomplishment of the organization's exempt purpose. Trade or business is related to exempt purposes, in the statutory sense, only when the conduct of the business activities has causal relationship to achieving exempt purposes (other than through the production of income). The causal relationship must be substantial. The activities that generate the income must contribute importantly to accomplishing the organization's exempt purposes to be substantially related.

See Publication 598, Tax on Unrelated Business Income of Exempt Organizations (Rev. March 2005) *available at* http://www.irs.gov/pub/irs-pdf/p598.pdf. The publication provides some additional examples:

> **Artists' facilities:** An organization whose exempt purpose is to stimulate and foster public interest in the fine arts by promoting art exhibits, sponsoring cultural events, and furnishing information about fine arts leases studio apartments to artist tenants and operates a dining hall primarily for these tenants. These two

activities do not contribute importantly to accomplishing the organization's exempt purpose. Therefore, they are unrelated trades or businesses.

Museum eating facilities. An exempt art museum operates a dining room, a cafeteria, and a snack bar for use by the museum staff, employees, and visitors. Eating facilities in the museum help to attract visitors and allow them to spend more time viewing the museum's exhibits without having to seek outside restaurants at mealtime. The eating facilities also allow the museum staff and employees to remain in the museum throughout the day. Thus, the museum's operation of the eating facilities contributes importantly to the accomplishment of its exempt purposes and is not unrelated trade or business.

Museum greeting card sales. An art museum that exhibits modern art sells greeting cards that display printed reproductions of selected works from other art collections. Each card is imprinted with the name of the artist, the title or subject matter of the work, the date or period of its creation, if known, and the museum's name. The cards contain appropriate greetings and are personalized on request.

The organization sells the cards in the shop it operates in the museum and sells them at quantity discounts to retail stores. It also sells them by mail order through a catalog that is advertised in magazines and other publications throughout the year. As a result, a large number of cards are sold at a significant profit.

The museum is exempt as an educational organization on the basis of its ownership, maintenance, and exhibition for public viewing of works of art. The sale of greeting cards with printed reproductions of artworks contributes importantly to the achievement of the museum's exempt education purposes by enhancing public awareness, interest, and appreciation of art. The cards may encourage more people to visit the museum itself to share in its educational programs. The fact that the cards are promoted and sold in a commercial manner at a profit and in competition with commercial greeting card publishers does not alter the fact that the activity is related to the museum's exempt purpose. Therefore, these sales activities are not an unrelated trade or business.

Id.

Problem XVII-E

As Bryce has worked in the neighborhood on his feature film, art exhibit and documentary (see Problems XVIII-B, XVIII-C), Bryce has gained the trust and respect of many of the more elderly artists in the area. Many of the artists want to keep their works together as a collection because they believe that the history of their neighborhood and the political pressures that resulted in the collection are important to history. They would like Bryce to use the documentary about the exhibit and the works in the creation of a permanent collection. The artists are willing to donate their works to a museum or nonprofit organization if they can be assured the collection will not be broken up or sold off in parts. Please advise Bryce on the manner in which these concerns can be alleviated. Assuming that a recipient agency can be identified and agreed upon, please draft a donative document that satisfies the concerns of the donors.

F. Bibliography and Links

Phillip J. Zisook, *In This Issue: Suppressing Controversy: Free Speech And The Government's Ability to Regulate Creative Art*, 19 CBA RECORD 36 (2005).

Patty Gerstenblith, *Acquisition and Deacquisition of Museum Collections and the Fiduciary Obligations of Museums to the Public*, 11 CARDOZO J. INT'L & COMP. L. 409 (2003).

Andrea Cunning, *U.S. Policy on the Enforcement of Foreign Export Restrictions on Cultural Property & Destructive Aspects of Retention Schemes*, 26 HOUS. J. INT'L L. 449 (2004).

Stefan D. Cassella, *Using the Forfeiture Laws to Protect Archaeological Resources*, 41 IDAHO L. REV. 129 (2004).

Kurt G. Siehr, *Globalization and National Culture: Recent Trends Toward a Liberal Exchange of Cultural Objects*, 38 VAND. J. TRANSNAT'L L. 1067 (2005).

Websites:

United States Department of State Bureau of Educational and Cultural Affairs, http://exchanges.state.gov/culprop/index.html.

United Nations Educational, Scientific and Cultural Organization, www.unesco.org.

Publication 557 (3/2005), Tax-Exempt Status for Your Organization, http://www.irs.gov/publications/p557/index.html.

Art and Cultural Property Law, http://www.hg.org/art.html.

California Arts Council, http://www.cac.ca.gov.

Federal Bureau of Investigation, Art Theft Program, http://www.fbi.gov/hq/cid/arttheft/arttheft.htm.

APPENDIX

IFPI Overview of International Copyright
Provided by the International Federation of the Phonographic Industry (IFPI)[65]

These materials provide a simple but comprehensive overview of international copyright protection from the perspective of the leading international organization for music and sound recording distribution.

The WIPO Treaties (March 2003)

1. The WIPO Treaties – Introduction[66]

The WIPO Treaties: Bringing Copyright into the New Millennium

What Are The WIPO Treaties?

The 'WIPO Treaties' refer to two new international copyright-related treaties adopted at a Geneva diplomatic conference of the UN's World Intellectual Property Organisation (WIPO) in December 1996. These treaties reflect international consensus on the protections that copyright and related rights owners need at the beginning of the new millennium. These treaties, the WIPO Copyright Treaty (**WCT**) and the WIPO Performances and Phonograms Treaty (**WPPT**):

- **Confirm protection of traditional copyrighted materials and distribution mechanisms;**

- **Clarify how copyright and related rights apply in the electronic environment;**

- **Protect against the hacking of technical protections applied to copyrighted products.**

The **WCT protects authors**, composers and other creators of literature, art, music, films, software and other such creative works.

The **WPPT protects producers of 'phonograms'** including music CDs, cassettes and other recordings produced by entities such as the members of IFPI. It also covers **performers**, such as singers and musicians.

Approximately 50 countries signed the WCT and the WPPT, which needed 30 formal 'ratifications' in order to come into force. The WCT came into force on 6 March 2002, and the WPPT entered into force on 20 May 2002.

Executive Summary

The two new WIPO Treaties, adopted by the international community in 1996, reflect international consensus as to how copyright needs to adapt in the new millennium. Having entered into force in 2002, the treaties typically require only a limited number of changes to any particular national law. These treaties provide needed incentives and protections for creative individuals and companies in every country, both to reward and promote national culture and creativity, and to pave the way for electronic commerce in copyrighted works and products.

---

[65] Copyright International Federation of the Phonographic Industry (IFPI), London, www.ifpi.org. Reprinted with permission. Photographs, captions, and some inset text boxes have been removed.
[66] http://www.ifpi.org/content/library/wipo-treaties-introduction.pdf

Why Are The WIPO Treaties Important?

Like all copyright and related protections, the WIPO Treaties provide important economic incentives to creative individuals and companies. They promote national culture, and discourage counterfeiting and piracy. The treaties also provide a substantial legal basis for healthy electronic commerce.

- **Economic incentive**. The treaties, and copyright law generally, provide creative people 'exclusive rights' to determine whether and how their works are copied and distributed. This ensures that they enjoy the economic rewards of their creativity, which serves as a powerful incentive to produce and distribute their creative products. This incentive is real: Intellectual-property based product sales hit $1 trillion globally in 1998. Sound recording sales were $33.6 billion world-wide in 2001.

- **Cultural protection**. Copyright also encourages local and national expressions of culture. Inadequate protections deprive *local* musicians, producers and other creative people of adequate compensation, and subject them to unfair competition from counterfeit copies of international products.

- **Piracy deterrent**. Counterfeiting and other forms of piracy (unauthorised copying and distribution) have become a major criminal enterprise. The global pirate music market totalled 1.9 billion units in 2001, worth an estimated US $4.3 billion. This not only hurts rights owners, but destroys legitimate jobs and deprives governments of substantial tax revenues. The WIPO Treaties and other copyright laws provide the principal legal tools for fighting piracy.

- **E-commerce engine**. Electronic commerce in copyrighted products requires a healthy trading environment where only legitimate copies of works are transmitted, under the terms permitted by the rights owner. The WIPO Treaties provide rights owners such legal certainty. As the treaties are adopted world-wide, they will ensure consistent protections and prevent 'piracy havens' from developing across the wide reach of the Internet.

What Do The WIPO Treaties Require?

The WIPO Treaties ensure authors, producers and performers a minimum set of rights in the traditional and electronic worlds, and provide legal tools to prevent hacking of technological 'locks' applied to their works. Most countries have found that **only a limited number of copyright-law changes are needed** in order to comply with the WIPO Treaties. This largely depends on how well a country's law already deals with electronic copying and distribution.

In brief, the treaties require copyright laws to provide many protections already afforded by national copyright law to authors, 'phonogram' producers and performers:

- **Protection of literary and artistic works, software, databases, phonograms and nonaudiovisual performances;**

- **Rights to control reproduction, fixation of performances, physical distribution, and rental; and**

- **Authorisation or remuneration for public communication.**

In addition, the treaties require authorisation by the author, phonogram producer and performer before a work can be **'made available' by interactive communication**, such as when the work is to be posted on the Internet. The treaties give non-audiovisual performers the **'moral right'** reasonably to be identified as the performer, and to prevent modifications that damage their reputation.

Finally, the treaties require protection against certain acts of circumvention or removal of **technological protection measures** (including access and copy controls), or **rights-management information** (information about rights ownership or licence terms), that rights owners may apply to their works or recordings.

Frequently Asked Questions (FAQs)

Is membership of any other treaty necessary before joining the WIPO Treaties? No. The WIPO Treaties incorporate Berne Convention obligations by reference, contain Rome-Convention compatible rules for phonograms, and require enforcement procedures that permit WTO TRIPs-standard 'deterrence'.

What provisions typically need to be adopted in implementing the WIPO Treaties? Most countries have had to implement new provisions on technological protections, rights-management information, and the 'making available' right. Some have also had to add moral rights for non-audiovisual performers.

Do the Treaties require treatment of service-provider liability? No. The issue of third-party 'contributory' or 'accessory' liability is not dealt with in the treaties, and will depend on national law. Some countries have dealt with this issue in their implementing legislation (e.g. USA), and some have not (e.g. Japan).

When did the Treaties come into force? The WCT entered into force on 6 March 2002 and the WPPT came into force on 20 May 2002.

Which countries have ratified the treaties? (as of March 2003)

Albania	Guatemala	Nicaragua
Argentina	Guinea	Panama
Belarus	Honduras	Paraguay
Bulgaria	Hungary	Peru
Burkina Faso	Indonesia	Philippines
Chile	Jamaica	Romania
Colombia	Japan	Saint Lucia
Costa Rica	Kyrgyz Republic	Senegal
Croatia	Latvia	Slovakia
Czech Republic	Lithuania	Slovenia
Ecuador	Mali	Togo
El Salvador	Mexico	Ukraine
Gabon	Moldova	United States
Georgia	Mongolia	Yugoslavia

Prompt Ratification Is Needed

The WIPO Treaties guide the way for adapting copyright to the age of electronic commerce. The Treaties are critical for creating a legal environment in which rights owners can protect against infringement in information networks, and develop new, more sophisticated products and licensing options. The Treaties also provide a strong practical support for intellectual property rights by encouraging and protecting the use of technological measures in controlling and administering these rights. Undoubtedly the single most important task for governments that want to make their copyright and related-rights regimes suitable for the age of electronic commerce is prompt ratification and faithful implementation of both WIPO Treaties.

2. Reproduction Right[67]

The WIPO Treaties: Reproduction Right

What Is The Reproduction Right?

The right of authors, performers and 'phonogram producers' to authorise or prohibit copying of their works and other protected material has been a longstanding feature of international instruments in the copyright field before the 1996 WIPO Treaties.

The Berne Convention (1971), Rome Convention (1961), Geneva Phonograms Convention (1971), and the WTO TRIPs Agreement (1994) by incorporation of Berne Convention requirements, all require protection of this important right. A major achievement of the 1996 WIPO Treaties was to clarify and confirm the **broad scope of this reproduction right,** particularly in its application to works and phonograms in the digital environment.

Both the WIPO Copyright Treaty (WCT) and the WIPO Performances and Phonograms Treaty (WPPT) re-state the Berne Convention requirement that the reproduction right must cover reproductions in **'any manner or form'**. Furthermore, the WPPT explicitly protects **'direct and indirect reproductions,'** as provided by the Rome Convention.

The full scope of this right is further clarified in an agreed statement that was adopted unanimously in the treaty negotiations. The agreed statement confirms that the right of reproduction **fully applies in the digital environment,** in particular to the use of phonograms in **digital form**. It is understood that **storage** of a protected phonogram in digital form **in an electronic medium** constitutes a reproduction.'

(WPPT, Articles 7, 11 and 16 and Agreed Statements; WCT, Agreed Statement Concerning Article 1(4).)

Executive Summary

The right to control copying of protected material is a critical feature of 21st century copyright protection. Rights owners depend upon this right in order to fight growing piracy problems on one hand, and to develop business models for on-line commerce on the other.

Accordingly, the WIPO Treaties confirm that authors, performers and phonogram producers retain a broad right of reproduction. The treaties build upon the Berne Convention, and clarify that the rights owners' reproduction right applies fully in the digital environment, irrespective of the technology or medium used, or of the nature or duration of the copying.

---

[67] http:// www.ifpi.org/content/library/wipo-treaties-reproduction-right.pdf.

Why Is This Right Important

For phonogram producers, the right to authorise the making of copies of their phonograms constitutes the basic tool not only to **license legitimate uses** of their phonograms, but also to **fight piracy**—the unauthorised reproduction and dissemination of phonograms.

With the advance of high-volume CD and other optical disc production, as well as digital technologies and interactive networks, controlling permanent and temporary copying has become even more important to rights owners. Phonograms can be reproduced without any loss of quality and with an ease and rapidity that was unforeseeable even a relatively short while ago. The global manufacturing capacity of all CDs, CDROMs and Video-CDs rose an estimated 22% since 1996 to over 23 billion units annually in 2001—nearly four discs per year for every man, woman and child on the face of the planet! Sales of pirate music CDs stood at 500 million units in that year alone.

Music will more and more often be enjoyed not only on the basis of permanent copies such as CDs, but also on the basis of temporary copies that disappear when use of the phonogram ends. Indeed, in many of the most economically valuable on-line uses of works, the most important copyright-cognisable act will be the making of temporary reproductions.

A strong right of reproduction, including temporary reproductions, is therefore essential to ensure that authors' and phonogram producers' and performers' legitimate interests enjoy adequate protection in this changing environment. It is also fundamental for the development of new licensing and business models which will allow consumers to have greater and easier access to music.

How Should This Be Implemented?

Most countries' copyright laws already contain a reproduction right. In implementing the WIPO Treaties, it is necessary to check whether all of the necessary elements of the reproduction right are protected by national statutory or case law. These are as follows:

- **Any manner or form of reproduction, including use and storage in digital form.** This means that the exclusive right should apply irrespective of the technology used in the act of copying or the medium onto which protected material is copied. National law should also ensure that all types of temporary and permanent reproductions that take place in the use and electronic storage of a work in digital form are protected by copyright.

- **Direct and indirect reproduction.** The WPPT grants phonogram producers and performers the exclusive right to authorise indirect as well as direct reproduction. Among other things, this means that the right owner's consent is needed for copying from a tangible phonogram as well as for copying from a broadcast or other type of communication.

- **In whole or in part.** It is clear that protection should cover the use of the whole or parts of a work or phonogram. This is traditionally recognised under most copyright and related-rights laws, and becomes even more important now that technology has made extracting, copying and commercial use of parts of phonograms in advertising, multimedia and sampling so easy.

- **Protection of authors, phonogram producers and performers.** The treaties require that authors (WCT Art. 1(4)), phonogram producers (WPPT Art. 11) and performers of literary or artistic works or expressions of folklore (but not necessarily audiovisual performers) (WPPT Arts. 7, 2(a)) benefit from the exclusive reproduction right.

WIPO Treaty Text

WCT Art. 1(4). *Contracting Parties shall comply with Articles 1 to 21 and the Appendix of the Berne Convention.*

WPPT Art. 7. *Performers shall enjoy the exclusive right of authorising the direct or indirect reproduction of their performances fixed in phonograms, in any manner or form.*

WPPT Art. 11. *Producers of phonograms shall enjoy the exclusive right of authorising the direct or indirect reproduction of their phonograms, in any manner or form.*

WPPT Agreed Statement Concerning Articles 7, 11 and 16: *The reproduction right, as set out in Articles 7 and 11, and the exceptions permitted thereunder through Article 16, fully apply in the digital environment, in particular to the use of performances and phonograms in digital form. It is understood that the storage of a protected performance or phonogram in digital form in an electronic medium constitutes a reproduction within the meaning of these Articles.*

(A corresponding provision for authors and works is contained in Agreed Statement to WCT Article 1(4).)

FREQUENTLY ASKED QUESTIONS (FAQS)

Are exceptions to the reproduction right allowed? Yes. The new treaties allow limitations and exceptions to the reproduction right that comply with the 'three-step test' of Berne Article 9(2). (WCT Art. 10; WPPT Art. 16.) Such exceptions thus must be: (i) confined to certain special cases, which (ii) do not conflict with a normal exploitation of the phonogram and (iii) do not prejudice the legitimate interests of the copyright holder. Note that this approach is more rigorous than the Rome Convention test which vaguely allowed exceptions for 'private use'. The three-step test highlights the appropriate economic and other issues to be considered in determining, for example, whether certain exceptions traditionally permitted in the analogue environment are appropriate for works and phonograms in digital form.

Have countries had to adapt their reproduction right to conform with the treaties? Generally no, although the EU implementation contains an express statement of the reproduction right. Laws that limit the reproduction right to 'tangible,' 'physical' or 'permanent' reproductions may require amendment.

Sample Implementing Legislation

IFPI Model Legislation: *Authors, producers of phonograms and performers shall have the exclusive right to authorise or prohibit the direct or indirect, temporary or permanent reproduction of their respective works, phonograms, or fixations of performances, in any manner or form, in whole or in part.*

Lithuania Copyright Act 1999: *Art. 2(24): Reproduction means the making of a copy of a work or an object of related rights, in whole or in part and in any material form, including their permanent or temporary storage in an electronic form.*

EU Copyright Directive: Art. 2: *'Member States shall provide for the exclusive right to authorise or prohibit direct or indirect, temporary or permanent reproduction by any means and in any form, in whole or in part: (a) for authors, of their works, (b) for performers, of fixations of their performances; (c) for phonogram producers, of their phonograms; (d) for the producers of the first fixations of films, in respect of the original and copies of their films; (e) for broadcasting organisations, of fixations of their broadcasts, whether those broadcasts are transmitted by wire or over the air, including by cable or satellite'. Art. 5(5): 'The exceptions and limitations provided for in paragraphs 1, 2, 3 and 4 shall only be applied in certain special cases which do not conflict with a normal exploitation of the work or other subject-matter and do not unreasonably prejudice the legitimate interests of the rightholder.*

3. "Making Available" or Communication Right[68] - These materials are reprinted at Chapter II, page 5.

4. Technical Measures[69]

The WIPO Treaties: Technological Measures

What Are Technological Measures?

With the introduction of legal protection for technological measures, the WIPO Treaties create a unique new way of protecting Copyrighted products as new digital and internet-based uses emerge. The treaties recognise that authors and other rights owners increasingly rely on technical means—commonly known as technological protection measures or TPMs—such as encryption and other mechanisms to control unauthorised copying, transmission and use of their products.

TPMs take various forms and their features are continually changing, but some major features remain constant. The most basic and most important kind of TPM is access control technology. One common way of controlling access is encrypting or scrambling the content. In such case the user gets the data but must follow an additional procedure to make it usable.

Another form of access control is a procedure that allows access to a source only with proof of authorisation, for example, password protection for a computer server. The other major type of TPM, copy or use controls, enable the rights owner to allow certain permitted activities but to prevent illicit activities by a user who has access to the work.

The WIPO Copyright Treaty (WCT) and the WIPO Performances and Phonograms Treaty (WPPT) require adequate legal protection and effective legal remedies against the circumvention of TPMs applied to protected works and phonograms. (WCT Art. 11; WPPT Art. 18.)

These provisions are formulated in a broad and neutral way, oriented more to the desired result than on how to achieve it. In implementing these treaty provisions, however, governments have recognised that their laws need to cover the **act of circumvention** itself, as well as the manufacture and distribution of a range of **circumvention devices**, in order to provide adequate and effective protection.

Executive Summary

---

[68] http:// www.ifpi.org/content/library/wipo-treaties-making-available-right.pdf.

[69] http:// www.ifpi.org/content/library/wipo-treaties-technical-measures.pdf.

Technological protection measures (TPMs) deter piracy, encourage rights owners to use new media like the internet, and provide consumers a sophisticated new range of ways of enjoying music. The WIPO Treaties require effective legal protection of TPMs. Governments have recognised that this means protecting against 'hacking' and covering a range of circumvention devices and related illicit activities.

Why Is It Important To Protect TPMs?

Technological solutions themselves are not invulnerable. Technical systems can be hacked. Unauthorised passwords and access codes frustrate access-control software. And the making and distribution of circumventing devices pose a serious danger to the integrity of any TPM. As no technological measure can permanently resist deliberate attacks, a TPM is only as good as its legal protection.

Protecting TPMs is important both for rights owners and consumers. Of course, TPMs deter piracy, and encourage rights owners to use new media like the internet. But by allowing a wide range of listening, copying and transmission options, TPMs also permit the development of new marketing, distribution and usage models, which open up a sophisticated new range of ways of enjoying music. Consumers will benefit from these new ways of enjoying music and other copyrighted products, but only if TPMs are meaningfully protected.

TPM protection also benefits telecommunications and equipment providers. Internet services profit from increased traffic and legitimate electronic commerce in copyrighted material. And consumer electronics and computer producers, which spend substantial sums developing new equipment and encryption technologies to play protected material, find their innovation frustrated and their investment rendered worthless if TPMs can be neutralised by hacking.

How Should This Be Implemented?

Most countries are finding that their copyright laws require Some modernising to deal with TPM protection adequately. There are several elements that governments and rights owners have found crucial to effective legal protection for TPMs:

- **Protection of access and copy control technologies**. The treaties require protection of TPMs (1) that are used in connection with the exercise of rights, and (2) that restrict unauthorised acts. This only covers TPMs applied to works protected by copyright or related rights. Clearly this protection should apply to copy and use control TPMs that directly restrict unauthorised reproduction, public communication, or other direct exercises of the rights owner's rights. Protection likewise should apply to access-control technologies, which also meet both tests of the treaties. Rights owners use access control, presently the most popular type of TPM, in connection with the exercise of their rights—whether selling physical copies or disseminating electronic copies to the public. Access controls not only prevent unauthorised use but also discourage unauthorised reproduction, distribution and transmission.

- **Protection against act of circumvention**. The treaties explicitly require legal protection and effective remedies against the act of circumvention of TPMs. Circumvention is sometimes called 'hacking'—manipulating the technological measure in some way so as to limit or eliminate the function it was designed to perform. The US law implementing the treaties defined circumvention as 'avoiding, bypassing, removing, deactivating, or otherwise impairing' a technological measure.

- **Prohibition of circumventing devices**. Adequate legal protection and effective legal remedies cannot stop at prohibiting circumvention itself. In order to control widespread hacking and other circumventing activities, circumvention devices and other means designed to facilitate hacking also must be controlled. This does not require outlawing multi-purpose devices like personal computers as such, simply because they can be used for a range of illicit purposes. Governments have recognised that devices must be controlled, however, if they are **designed or adapted** to circumvent.

This formulation has been refined in EU legislation and elsewhere to include devices that (1) are **primarily designed or produced** for the purpose of circumvention, (2) have only a **limited commercially significant purpose or use** other than to circumvent; or (3) are **marketed, promoted or advertised** for circumvention purposes.

- **Devices, components and other means**. Circumvention devices are not always an isolated 'black box', such as a pirate decoder. They can also be one part of a more complex piece of equipment, or an intangible means such as computer software or access codes, that has the same function as a standalone circumvention device. It is thus important that rules on circumvention devices apply equally to **parts** and **components** of devices, **software, algorithms** and **access information** such as **passwords** and **access codes** that otherwise meet the definition of an illicit device.

- **Manufacture, distribution, offering to the public, communication of devices and services**. A range of activities related to circumvention devices should be covered. In most cases, treaty implementing legislation has extended to all manner of manufacture, marketing, offering to the public and distribution of circumvention devices, as well as services that assist with such circumvention. Not only are the features of TPMs and devices subject to continuous change, but the catalogue of activities that promote circumvention of TPMs also will change over time— requiring a broad definition of the acts covered by legislation dealing with circumvention devices and services.

- **Effective remedies**. The treaties also explicitly call for effective legal remedies. This is of great importance, because action against hacking and other circumvention of TPMs must be sufficiently speedy, efficient and deterrent to counteract the otherwise great incentive hackers and pirates have to break TPMs and steal content. Effective legal remedies should include both **criminal** law sanctions and **civil** law remedies. Criminal penalties should permit fines and prison terms in appropriate cases. To serve as a deterrent, civil law should allow fast and efficient preliminary proceedings, injunctive relief, payment of damages including statutory damages, and the obligation to cooperate in neutralising harm already caused.

To get illicit devices out of circulation, remedies also should allow tracing, seizure, retention and destruction of physical devices and intangible software and information. Criminal penalties and civil remedies should not be any lower than those available for copyright infringement.

WIPO Treaty Text

WCT Art. 11. *Contracting Parties shall provide adequate legal protection and effective legal remedies against the circumvention of effective technological measures that are used by authors in connection with the exercise of their rights under this Treaty or the Berne Convention* *and that restrict acts, in respect of their works, which are not authorised by the authors concerned or permitted by law.*

WPPT Art. 18. *Contracting Parties shall provide adequate legal protection and effective legal remedies against the circumvention of effective technological measures that are used by performers or producers of phonograms in connection with the exercise of their rights under this Treaty and that restrict acts, in respect of their performances or phonograms, which are not authorised by the performers or the producers of phonograms concerned or permitted by law.*

Frequently Asked Questions (FAQs)

How strong must a technology be in order to enjoy protection? A TPM should be protected as long as, in the ordinary course of its operation, it effectively restricts access to or use of the content in any manner. There is no threshold standard of sophistication or security. The fact that a TPM has been circumvented, or the availability of a circumventing device, should not affect whether a device is deemed 'effective'. TPMs that have been subjected to attacks are the ones that need protection most.

Could someone be held liable for unknowingly assisting in the circumvention of a protected TPM? No. The offering and supply of services and assistance in the circumvention of TPMs need only be prohibited if the activity, viewed subjectively or objectively, has this purpose.

Will TPMs lead to excessive restrictions on access to works or even public-domain materials? No. TPMs permit wider and more convenient access. Technology permits rights owners to cater to the demands and tastes of consumers in more refined ways, with more flexible pricing options. Works will remain available in traditional formats as well as protected formats for a long, long time. And legal protections only cover TPMs applied to works protected by copyright or related rights.

What kind of exceptions are appropriate to protection of TPMs? The problem with allowing exceptions to protection of TPMs is similar to allowing someone to break the lock on a safe. Anyone then can get in, for any purpose. Allowing hacking or circumvention devices weakens the overall robustness of the TPM encryption or other technology. Carried too far, this can make use of TPMs pointless and investment in equipment and technologies worthless. Governments therefore have recognised that any exceptions to TPM protection must be carefully limited. US law, for example, provides only a few exceptions, permitting circumvention only for such purposes as encryption testing under carefully limited conditions.

Allowing circumvention in any case where a traditional copyright exception applies is unworkable. Between private copying, educational use, 'fair use', and other typical exceptions, such a rule would effectively allow every citizen of a country to become a hacker. Governments also have recognised that circumvention devices can do even greater harm than individual acts of circumvention. Exceptions to TPM protection generally have allowed only certain acts of circumvention, but not distribution of circumvention devices.

Sample Implementing Legislation

IFPI Model Legislation (Option 1): It shall be unlawful to circumvent any technological protection measure applied to a work or phonogram; or to manufacture, offer to the public, distribute or in any other way traffic in devices, components, services or other means designed, adapted or promoted to circumvent such a measure. The civil and criminal procedures, remedies and sanctions applicable to copyright infringement shall apply to any violation of this provision.

IFPI Model Legislation (Option 2):

(a) It shall be unlawful to circumvent any technological measure that is applied to a work, phonogram or other protected material and that is designed to prevent or restrict, in the normal course of its operation, access to the material or acts that are not authorised by the rights owner. 'Circumvent' shall mean avoid, bypass, remove, deactivate or otherwise impair.

(b) It shall be unlawful to manufacture, import, distribute, sell, rent, possess for commercial purposes, offer to the public, advertise, communicate or otherwise provide any device, part, component, technology, service or other means that—

(1) is primarily designed, produced, adapted or performed for the purpose of circumventing,

(2) has only a limited other commercially significant purpose or use other than to circumvent,   or

(3) is marketed, promoted or advertised for the purpose of circumventing any such technological measure.

(c) The civil and criminal procedures, remedies and sanctions applicable to copyright infringement shall apply to any violation of this section.

Other example: Lithuania Copyright Law, Art. 64(1)(4): The following acts shall constitute infringements of copyright: (4) removal of technological protective measures used by subjects of copyright and related rights for the exercise and protection of the rights provided for in this Law, as well as the manufacture, importation, transportation, keeping for the purpose of distribution and distribution of any technical devices or equipment specifically designed or adapted to circumvent those technological protective measures.

5. Rights Management Information[70]

The WIPO Treaties: Protection of Rights Management Information

What Is Rights Management Information?

Rights management information (RMI) is information that identifies content protected by copyright or related rights, the rights owners in such content and the terms and conditions of use associated with it. RMI often takes the form of an electronic **watermark** placed in protected content. Watermarks can exist on their own simply as a rights owner's 'label'. Watermarks may also interact with devices that receive or play content and determine the conditions of use of such content. They may provide the basis for **additional user services**, such as information accompanying a radio broadcast that gives artist, track and purchase details about particular songs.

---

[70] http://www.ifpi.org/content/library/wipo-treaties-rights-management-information.pdf.

In copyright terms, RMI frequently serves as a means of compliance with the **moral right of attribution,** in that it identifies the author and performer of a work. One of its most important uses is the **digital management of rights.** Automated digital rights management systems provide a fast and easy tool for users to secure licences for the use of particular content, and for rights owners to collect information about such usage.

The WIPO Treaties protect all such RMI: **information about works, phonograms and performances,** as well as the **identification of authors, phonogram producers, performers or other rights owners.**

Protection also extends to information about **terms and conditions of use** of content. This may be either details of a license already granted or information about how and under what conditions a license can be obtained. To enjoy protection, RMI must be attached to or embodied in a copy of the work, phonogram or fixed performance or—for intangible means of use—**appear in connection with the use of the work,** phonogram or performance. It can appear either in the clear in machine-readable form.

Executive Summary

Rights management information (RMI) is the basis for new licensing systems, and can certify the integrity and authenticity of works and phonograms. Combined with other technology, they also prove to be a powerful tool against copyright infringements. The WIPO Treaties require effective legal protection of RMI.

Why Is This Right Important?

Rightholders need RMI to label their works, and to let users identify the works and their conditions of use—particularly in the digital environment where activities move quickly and often leave few residual traces. Works that appear in a digital form can easily be changed, mutilated, misappropriated, reproduced and put into distribution channels without the consent of the rights owner.

The information found on the copy, booklet or cover of a copyrighted product helped rights owners track and prove such illegal activity in the analogue world. RMI fulfils this function in the electronic environment. RMI also benefits consumers. Digital watermarks give consumers confidence in the authenticity of the source of a work or phonogram, and certainty as to the conditions for its use. The manipulation of RMI can lead consumers to draw wrong conclusions about permitted uses, and thus can have an economic effect equivalent to common fraud.

As with technological protection measures generally, the integrity of RMI is vulnerable to attack. It therefore relies on legal protection in order to prevent deliberate manipulation and distortion. In order to enable confidence in the authenticity of works, and the integrity of information about the identity of rights owners and the conditions of use, it is essential to protect RMI itself and to prevent the distribution of copies where such information has been removed or manipulated.

How Should This Be Implemented?

Most countries are finding that their copyright laws require some modernising to deal adequately with the legal protection of RMI. There are several elements that governments and right holders have found crucial to ensure the effective legal protection of RMI:

- **Definition of RMI.** The starting point is the definition of RMI. The treaties themselves provide a clear and useful definition, which may be useful to include in implementing legislation. The definition must include the required categories of protected information (information on works, phonograms or performances; on the identity of the author, the phonogram producer or the performer; or on the terms and conditions of use).

It should also indicate that the information must be attached to a work, a fixation of a performance or a phonogram, or must appear in connection with any intangible type of use including the communication to the public, broadcasting, or 'making available'.

- **Protection against manipulation of RMI.** One of the treaties' main aims of protection is the prohibition of manipulation of RMI. The treaties explicitly mention the **unauthorised removal and alteration** of RMI. Another type of manipulation of RMI having equivalent effect is the **unauthorised addition** of information. This activity can mislead users and businesses as to permitted uses and discourage the use of RMI, just as much as the removal or alteration of RMI does.

- **Protection against dissemination of copies in which RMI has been** manipulated . The second main element of protection is the prohibition of activities relating to copies as to which RMI has been removed or altered without authorisation. To enable rights owners to take such copies out of circulation and prevent further harm, it is important to provide a complete list of prohibited activities including **distribution, export, import for distribution, broadcasting, communication to the public, and the making available to the public of such copies.**

- **Knowledge requirement regarding the impact of the activity on copyright infringement**. Activities relating to RMI need not lead to legal proceedings if they have been performed accidentally and innocently. The knowledge test established by the treaties varies depending on the type of activity. As regards the removal or alteration of RMI without authorisation, the test is whether the person knew, or in the case of civil proceedings had reasonable grounds to know, that such manipulation would induce, enable, facilitate, or conceal infringement of copyright or neighbouring rights.

As regards the dissemination without authorisation of content where RMI has been manipulated or removed, the test is whether the person knew that RMI has been manipulated or removed, as well as whether the person knew, or in the case of civil proceedings had reasonable grounds to know, that the dissemination of content without RMI (or with manipulated RMI) would induce, enable, facilitate, or conceal an infringement.

- **Prohibition of 'watermark washing' devices**. In parallel to the protection of technological measures, meaningful protection against RMI manipulation and removal should extend to **devices designed or adapted to manipulate or remove RMI**. There is a substantial danger that devices that systematically 'wash out' watermarks while leaving the content unchanged will undermine the confidence of rights owners and legitimate users, which is essential to the use of rights management information in the first place.

The protection required by the treaties can be achieved best by also prohibiting the manufacture, importation, distribution, offer to the public, provision or otherwise trafficking in devices designed or adapted to manipulate or remove RMI, and means with equivalent effect.

WIPO Treaty Text - WPPT Art. 19:

(1) Contracting Parties shall provide adequate and effective legal remedies against any person knowingly performing any of the following acts knowing, or with respect to civil remedies having reasonable grounds to know, that it will induce, enable, facilitate or conceal an infringement of any right covered by this Treaty:

(i) to remove or alter any electronic rights management information without authority;

(ii) to distribute, import for distribution, broadcast, communicate or make available to the public, without authority, performances, copies of fixed performances or phonograms knowing that electronic rights management information has been removed or altered without authority.

(2) As used in this Article, 'rights management information' means information which identifies the performer, the performance of the performer, the producer of the phonogram, the phonogram, the owner of any right in the performance or phonogram, or information about the terms and conditions of use of the performance or phonogram, and any numbers or codes that represent such information, when any of these items of information is attached to a copy of a fixed performance or a phonogram or appears in connection with the communication or making available of a fixed performance or a phonogram to the public.

Frequently Asked Questions (FAQs)

Must countries adapt their laws to implement this protection? Yes, virtually all countries have to change their law in order to implement the protection of RMI. Protections already provided under criminal law (computer fraud), moral rights, media law, trademark law, personality right or competition law typically provide only limited aspects of the required protection.

Must this protection be implemented in copyright law? No. This is a new protection regime that could be enacted under other types of legislation.

Sample Implementing Legislation

IFPI Model Legislation:

(1) It shall be unlawful to remove, alter or add rights management information without authority knowing, or with respect to civil remedies having reasonable grounds to know, that this will induce, enable, facilitate or conceal an infringement of copyright or neighbouring rights.

(2) It shall be unlawful to distribute, export, import for distribution, broadcast, communicate or make available to the public without authority copies of works, fixed performances or phonograms knowing that rights management information has been removed, altered or added without authority and knowing, or with respect to civil remedies having reasonable grounds to know, that this will induce, enable, facilitate or conceal an infringement of copyright or neighbouring rights.

(3) It shall be unlawful to manufacture, import, distribute, export, sell, rent, possess for commercial purposes, offer to the public, advertise, communicate or otherwise provide without authority any device, product or component that is designed or adapted to remove, alter or add rights management information.

(4) 'Rights management information' means

(a) information that identifies the work or other protected matter, the author, the performer, the producer of a phonogram or any other rights owner, or

(b) information about the terms and conditions of use of the work, phonogram or performance, and

(c) any number or code that represents such information, when any of these is attached to a copy of a work, phonogram or fixed performance, or appears in connection with the broadcast, communication or making available to the public of the work, phonogram or fixed performance.

Other Sample Legislation: Belarus Copyright Act, Article 39:

5. The following shall also be deemed infringements of copyright or related rights. . .

- the removing or altering of any electronic rights management information without the consent of the holder of copyright or related rights;

- the distribution, importing for the purposes of distribution, broadcasting or communication to the public without the authorisation of the holder of copyright or related rights of works, recorded performances, phonograms or broadcast or cabled programs with respect to which electronic rights management information has been removed or altered without the authorisation of the rightholder.

6. Any copy of a work, a recorded performance, a phonogram or a broadcast or cabled program on which rights management has been removed or altered without the authorisation of the holder of copyright or related rights or which has been manufactured without the authorisation of the holder by means of a device used in an unlawful manner as referred to in the second indent of paragraph 5 of this Article, shall be deemed an infringing copy in accordance with paragraphs 2 and 3 of this Article.

WIPO TREATY TEXT - WCT Art. 12.

(1) Contracting Parties shall provide adequate and effective legal remedies against any person knowingly performing any of the following acts knowing, or with respect to civil remedies having reasonable grounds to know, that it will induce, enable, facilitate or conceal an infringement of any right covered by this Treaty or the Berne Convention:

(i) to remove or alter any electronic rights management information without authority;

(ii) to distribute, import for distribution, broadcast or communicate to the public, without authority, works or copies of works knowing that electronic rights management information has been removed or altered without authority.

(2) As used in this Article, 'rights management information' means information which identifies the work, the author of the work, the owner of any right in the work, or information about the terms and conditions of use of the work, and any numbers or codes that represent such information, when any of these items of information is attached to a copy of a work or appears in connection with the communication of a work to the public.

Summary of Music Rights from Copyright Office Circulars[71]

[The following handout is an edited redaction of material prepared by the U.S. Copyright Office Circulars as supplementary information on the registration of musical compositions (Circular 50), sound recordings (Circulars 56, 56a), and the compulsory license for making sound recordings (Circular 73). Unless otherwise noted, all references are to the United States Copyright Law, 17 U.S.C. § 101 et. seq.

I have edited the information provided to minimize duplication and shorten the document, but I have tried to retain the language of the Copyright Office to the greatest extent possible. I have not, however, marked editorial changes.]

Introduction

A Musical Composition consists of music, including any accompanying words, and is normally registered in Class PA. The author of a musical composition is generally the composer, and the lyricist, if any. A musical composition may be in the form of a notated copy (for example, sheet music) or in the form of a phonorecord (for example, cassette tape, LP, or CD). Sending a musical composition in the form of a phonorecord does not necessarily mean that there is a claim to copyright in the sound recording.

A Sound Recording results from the fixation of a series of musical, spoken, or other sounds and is always registered in Class SR. The author of a sound recording is the performer(s) whose performance is fixed, or the record producer who processes the sounds and fixes them in the final recording, or both. Copyright in a sound recording is not the same as, or a substitute for, copyright in the underlying musical composition.

Musical Works

Copyright law provides for copyright protection in "musical works, including any accompanying words," which are fixed in some tangible medium of expression. Musical works include both original compositions and original arrangements or other new versions of earlier compositions to which new copyrightable authorship has been added.

The owner of copyright in a work has the exclusive right to make copies, to prepare derivative works, to sell or distribute copies, and to perform the work publicly. Anyone else wishing to use the work in these ways must have the permission of the author or someone who has derived rights through the author.

Copyright in a musical work includes the right to make and distribute the first sound recording. Although others are permitted to make subsequent sound recordings, they must compensate the copyright owner of the musical work under the compulsory licensing provision of the law (§ 115).

Sound Recording

Sound recordings are defined in the law as "works that result from the fixation of a series of musical, spoken, or other sounds, but not including the sounds accompanying a motion picture or other audiovisual work." Common examples include recordings of music, drama, or lectures.

---

[71] U.S. Copyright Office Circular 50, 56, 65a, and 73. Available in individual form at http://www.copyright.gov.

Copyright in a sound recording protects the particular series of sounds "fixed" (embodied in a recording) against unauthorized reproduction and revision, unauthorized distribution of phonorecords containing those sounds, and certain unauthorized performances by means of a digital audio transmission. The Digital Performance Right in Sound Recordings Act of 1995, P.L. 104-39, effective February 1, 1996, created a new limited performance right for certain digital transmissions of sound recordings.

Generally, copyright protection extends to two elements in a sound recording: (1) the contribution of the performer(s) whose performance is captured and (2) the contribution of the person or persons responsible for capturing and processing the sounds to make the final recording.

Sound recordings fixed before February 15, 1972, were generally protected by common law or in some cases by statutes enacted in certain states but were not protected by federal copyright law. In 1971 Congress amended the copyright code to provide copyright protection for sound recordings fixed and first published with the statutory copyright notice on or after February 15, 1972. The 1976 Copyright Act, effective January 1, 1978, provides federal copyright protection for unpublished and published sound recordings fixed on or after February 15, 1972. Any rights or remedies under state law for sound recordings fixed before February 15, 1972, are not annulled or limited by the 1976 Copyright Act until February 15, 2047.

Under the Uruguay Round Agreements Act, effective January 1, 1996, copyright was restored for certain unpublished foreign sound recordings fixed before February 15, 1972, and for certain foreign sound recordings originally published without notice. For further information, request Circular 38b, "Highlights of Copyright Amendments Contained in the Uruguay Round Agreements Act (URAA)."

Phonorecords

A sound recording is not the same as a **phonorecord.** A phonorecord is the physical object in which works of authorship are embodied. Throughout this circular the word "phonorecord" includes cassette tapes, CDs, LPs, 45 r.p.m. disks, as well as other formats.

Choosing the Appropriate Copyright Application Form

Copyright registration for a sound recording alone is neither the same as, nor a substitute for, registration for the musical, dramatic, or literary work recorded. The underlying work may be registered in its own right apart from any recording of the performance, or in certain cases, the underlying work may be registered together with the sound recording.

When to Use Form SR

Use Form SR for registration of published or unpublished sound recordings, that is, for registration of the particular sounds or recorded performance. Form SR must also be used if you wish to make one registration for both the sound recording and the underlying work (the musical composition, dramatic, or literary work). You may make a single registration only if the copyright claimant is the same for both the sound recording and the underlying work. In this case, the authorship statement in Space 2 should specify that the claim covers both works. Form SR is also the appropriate form for registration of a multimedia kit that combines two or more kinds of authorship including a sound recording (such as a kit containing a book and an audiocassette).

When to Use Form PA

Form PA is the appropriate form for registration for a musical composition, whether it is accompanied by the deposit of a "copy" (lead sheet or sheet music) or a "phonorecord" (disk or tape). For registration purposes, musical compositions and dramatic works that are recorded on disks or cassettes are works of the performing arts and should be registered on Form PA or Short Form PA. Therefore, if you wish to register only the underlying work that is a musical composition or dramatic work, use Form PA even though you may send a disk or cassette. For information on Short Form PA, request SL-7, "New Short Forms Now Available."

Sounds accompanying a motion picture or other audiovisual work should **not** be registered on Form SR. The copyright law does not define these sounds as "sound recordings" but as an integral part of the motion picture or audiovisual work in which they are incorporated. These sounds are classified as works of the performing arts and should be registered on Form PA.

Appropriate Form for Copyright Registration of Domestic Works				
			What should be deposited	
What is the work being registered	**Form to use**	**How to describe the authorship in Space 2, "Nature of Authorship"**	**Published in the United States**	**Unpublished**
Author creates a song, recorded by independent group; can claim copyright in the song	PA	Music and Words OR Music	1 phonorecord (disk, if published in disk form)	1 complete phonorecord (usually disk or cassette)
Vocalist and band perform and record musical work; can claim copyright in the recorded performance only	SR	Sound Recording	2 complete phonorecords (disks, if published in disk form)	1 complete phonorecord
Author creates music and performs it, recording the performance; can claim copyright both in the music and the recording	SR	Music and Sound Recording OR Music, Words, and Sound Recording	2 complete phonorecords (disks, if published in disk form)	1 complete phonorecord

Author writes a play and records it, but can claim copyright only in the play itself, not in recorded performance	P	Script	1 complete phonorecord (disk, if published in disk form)	1 complete phonorecord
Author writes poem or narrative and records it, can claim copyright both in text and in recorded performance	SR	Text and Sound Recording	2 complete phonorecords (disks, if published in disk form)	1 complete phonorecord
Author creates musical composition in machine-readable copy (computer disk) and can claim copyright in only musical composition	PA	Music OR Music and Words	Transcription of entire work in score or on audio cassette	Transcription of entire work in score or on audio cassette
Author creates musical composition in machine-readable copy (computer or MIDI disk) and can claim copyright in both composition and performance	SR	Music and Sound Recording OR Music, Words, and Sound Recording	Reproduction of entire work on audio cassette	Reproduction of entire work on audio cassette
Author creates musical composition on CD-ROM audio disk and can claim copyright in both music and sound recording	SR	Music and Sound Recording	1 complete CD-ROM package	1 complete CD-ROM package

Application Form

Form SR is for registration of "sound recordings," which are works that result from the fixation of a series of sounds. The author of a sound recording is the performer, or the record producer, or both. Form SR may be used to register both a musical work and a sound recording fixed in a phonorecord, provided that the same person or organization owns the copyrights in both works. If both kinds of work are being registered, Space 2 of Form SR must clearly account for the authorship of both the musical composition (music or words and music) and the sound recording (performance, sound recording, or both).

How to Complete Form the Forms (differences to PA & SR are noted)

Instructions for completing each space of the application accompany the form.

Space 1: Title. Give the title of the work exactly as it appears on the copy or phonorecord.

- A group of **unpublished** works registered as a collection must be given a collection title. The individual titles may be given on a Continuation Sheet.

- For registration of an entire collection of **published** works, give the title of the collection.

- For registration of only some of the individual works in a published collection, give the titles of the individual works, followed by "Contained in (title of collection)."

Space 2: Author

Answer carefully the question "Was this author's contribution to the work a 'work made for hire'?" Check "yes" **only** if that contribution was either (1) prepared by an employee within the scope of his or her employment or (2) specially ordered for a certain use, with an express written agreement signed by both parties that the work shall be considered a work made for hire. Such certain uses include contributions to a collective work, parts of a motion picture or other audiovisual work, or supplementary works, such as new musical arrangements. If the contribution was made for hire, give the name of the **employer,** not the person who actually did the writing, in the "Name of Author" box.

A sound recording is not one of the types of works affected by clause (2) of the 'specially commissioned' definition of "work made for hire" unless it constitutes a supplementary work, collective work, or compilation. Generally speaking, for a new sound recording to be a work made for hire, it must be made by an employee within his or her scope of employment. For more information on works made for hire, request Circular 9, "Works-Made-for Hire Under the 1976 Copyright Act."

Complete the "Nature of Authorship" space to specify what the author created as written or recorded in the copy or phonorecord that accompanies the application. Examples are: "music," "words," "arrangement." Do **not** include elements not present in that copy or phonorecord. Do **not** include elements that are not protected by copyright, such as an idea, concept, name, or title.

Space 3: Year of Creation

The year of creation is the year in which the version of the work to be registered was *first* fixed in writing or recorded in any other tangible form. When a work is written or recorded over a period of time or constitutes a new version of an earlier work, give the completion date of the final work or new version. This year date must always be given.

First Publication

If the version of the work being registered has been published, give the month, day, year, and nation where copies or phonorecords of this version were first published. If publication has not taken place, **leave this part of Space 3 blank.**

Publication

Publication, as defined by the Copyright Act, is the distribution of copies or phonorecords of a work to the public by sale or other transfer of ownership, or by rental, lease, or lending. The offering to distribute copies or phonorecords to a group of persons for purposes of further distribution, public performance, or public display, constitutes publication. A public performance or display of a work does not of itself constitute publication.

"To the public" generally means to persons under no explicit or implicit restrictions with respect to disclosure. The following acts do not constitute publication: performance of the work, preparation of copies or phonorecords, or sending the work to the Copyright Office. The above definition of publication applies **only** to works governed by the copyright law that took effect Jan. 1, 1978.

Space 4: Claimant(s)

The **name** and **address** of the **copyright claimant(s) must be given.** The copyright claimant is either the author or a person or organization to whom the author has transferred **all** the rights in the U.S. copyright. When the claimant named is **not** the author, a brief **transfer** statement is required at Space 4 to show how the claimant acquired the copyright. Examples of generally acceptable statements include: "by written agreement"; "assignment"; "written contract"; and "by will." Do not attach copies of documents of copyright transfer to the application. For information on how to record transfers or other documents pertaining to a copyright, request Circular 12, "Recordation of Transfers and Other Documents."

When the name of the claimant is not the name of the author given at Space 2 but the two names identify one person, the relationship between the names should be explained at Space 4. Examples are: "Doe Publishing Company, solely owned by John Doe" or "John Doe doing business as Doe Publishing Company."

Space 5: Previous Registration

If this work was not previously registered, answer "no" to the first question and **leave the rest of Space 5 blank.** If the work or part of the work was previously registered and a certificate of registration was issued, answer "yes" to the first question and check the appropriate box to show why another registration is sought. Also, give the requested information about the previous registration.

Space 6: Derivative Work or Compilation

Complete this space **only** if the work being registered contains a **substantial** amount of material:

1. that was previously published; or

2. that was previously registered in the United States Copyright Office; or

3. that is in the public domain; or

4. that for any reason is not part of this claim.

- Leave this space blank if the work does not contain a substantial amount of any of these four kinds of material.

- **Space 6a: Preexisting** Material. Briefly describe the preexisting material that has been used.

- **Space 6b: Material Added to this Work**. Complete this space by stating briefly but clearly all the added or revised copyrightable material that forms the basis of the present registration. Examples: "Arrangement for piano and orchestra" or "new lyric."

Derivative Works in Sound Recordings.

A derivative sound recording is one which incorporates some preexisting sounds — sounds which were previously registered, previously published, or which were fixed before February 15, 1972. Registration for a derivative work must be based on the new authorship that has been added. When a work contains preexisting sounds, Space 6 of the application must contain brief, general descriptions of both the preexisting material (Space 6a) and the added material (Space 6b).

For example, Fine Sounds Corporation issues a CD-album containing 16 selections, 2 of which were published last month as singles. On the application for registration of the sounds on the album, the following statement might be given in Space 6a: "sounds for tracks 1 and 3, previously published." The new material might be described in Space 6b as "sounds for 8 tracks" or "sounds for 8 selections."

In cases where the preexisting sounds themselves have been altered or changed in character, Space 6b should be used to describe in more precise terms the engineering techniques involved. For example, Educational Records, Inc., remixes the original tracks of a previously released recording of a Beethoven symphony. Space 6a should identify the preexisting material as "sounds previously published." Space 6b might indicate "remixed from multitrack sound sources" or "remixed sounds." This new material must result from creative new authorship rather than mere mechanical processes; if only a few slight variations or purely mechanical changes (such as declicking or remastering) have been made, registration is not possible.

Compilation of Musical Works

A "compilation" is a work formed by the collecting and assembling of preexisting materials that are selected, coordinated, or arranged in such a way that the resulting work as a whole constitutes an original work of authorship.

When an author contributes a certain minimum amount of authorship in the selection and ordering of **preexisting** musical compositions, the author creates a copyrightable compilation. The copyright in the compilation of the musical compositions is separate and distinct from copyright (if any) in the musical compositions themselves. Protection in the compilation extends only to the selection and ordering of the musical compositions.

For compilations, give a brief, general statement describing both the material that has been compiled **and** the compilation itself. Example: "Compilation of selected 19th century military songs."

Compilation of Sound Recordings

A "compilation" is a work formed by the collecting and assembling of preexisting materials that are selected, coordinated, or arranged in such a way that the resulting work as a whole constitutes an original work of authorship.

When an author contributes a certain minimum amount of authorship in the selection and ordering of **preexisting** sound recordings, the author produces a copyrightable compilation. The copyright in the compilation of recordings is separate and distinct from copyright (if any) in the recordings themselves. It extends **only** to the selection and ordering of the recordings on the disk or tape.

Fill out part b of Space 6. Describe the new material as "compilation of sound recordings." In Space 2, use the same statement to describe the nature of the author's contribution. **For example:** Oldies Record Company has chosen the greatest hits of the big bands recorded in the thirties and forties and published them in a boxed set of disks. The authorship involved in choosing the bands, selecting their "greatest hits," selecting the particular recordings, and ordering them on the disks may be registered as a compilation, even though the recordings themselves are not protected by the federal copyright code because they were fixed prior to February 15, 1972.

Deposit Requirements. The application must be accompanied by a deposit of the work to be registered. The deposit requirement varies according to the type of work for which registration is sought. Deposits cannot be returned.

Unpublished Works. Deposit one complete copy (lead sheet or sheet music) or phonorecord (disk or tape). "Complete" means that the deposit includes everything that is to be covered by the registration. Separate applications for several works may be accompanied by one phonorecord containing all the works. Registration generally covers only the material that is deposited for registration, even though the copyright law automatically gives copyright protection to all copyrightable authorship that is fixed in a copy or phonorecord. Copies of a group of works registered as a collection should be assembled in orderly form and fastened together or placed in a folder. The title of a collection should appear on copies and phonorecords.

Published Works. For a musical work first published in the United States on or after Jan. 1, 1978, the deposit generally is two complete copies of the best edition. Only one deposit is required for musical works that are:

- published only on phonorecords (tapes or disks), unless the claim includes the sound recording, in which case, two phonorecords are required as the deposit;

- published by rental, lease, or lending (Where there is a score and individual parts, only the score is required.);

- published as a single contribution to a collective work, for example, a hymn from a hymnal.

If first published in the United States **before Jan. 1, 1978,** the deposit is two complete copies of the best edition of the work as first published. If first published outside the United States **before March 1, 1989,** the deposit is one complete copy or phonorecord of the work as first published. For a musical work first published outside the United States **on or after March 1, 1989,** the deposit is either one complete copy or phonorecord of the work as first published or the best edition of the work.

Collections of Music

Unpublished Collections. Two or more unpublished songs, song lyrics, or other musical works may be registered with one application and fee, **but only under certain conditions** stated in the Copyright Office regulations. One of those conditions is that the copyright owner or owners must be the same for all the songs. An additional requirement is that there must always be at least one author common to all the songs, even if there has been a transfer of ownership.

When a group of unpublished works is registered as a collection, only the collection title will appear in the catalogs and indexes of the Copyright Office. Individual titles will appear in Copyright Office records only if each work is registered separately or if an application for supplementary registration is submitted to specify the individual titles in a collection. An application for supplementary registration may not be submitted until a certificate of registration has been issued for the collection. For more information on supplementary registration, please request Circular 8, "Supplementary Copyright Registration," and application Form CA.

Published Collections. A published collection of musical compositions may be registered with one application and fee if all the compositions are owned by the same copyright claimant. The entire collection may be registered under the collection title.

THE COMPULSORY LICENSING PROVISIONS

Section 115 of the law provides that, once phonorecords of a musical work have been publicly distributed in the United States with the copyright owner's consent, anyone else may, under certain circumstances and subject to limited conditions, obtain a "compulsory license" to make and distribute phonorecords of the work without express permission from the copyright owner.

The Copyright Office Regulations set out in detail the procedures that must be followed, while the Copyright Arbitration Royalty Panels determine the royalty fee that must be paid by the user under a compulsory license.

Does The Intended User Have To Use a Compulsory License?

No. The person wishing to make and distribute phonorecords of a nondramatic musical work may negotiate directly with the copyright owner or his or her agent. But, if the copyright owner is unwilling to negotiate or if the copyright owner cannot be contacted, the person intending to record the work may use the compulsory licensing provisions of the copyright law.

The statute defines "phonorecords" as "material objects in which sounds, **other than those accompanying a motion picture or other audiovisual work,** are fixed....Since the compulsory license applies only to the making and distributing of **phonorecords,** and soundtracks are not "phonorecords," the compulsory license is not available to one wishing to record on a soundtrack.

When may a Compulsory License be Obtained? A compulsory license is available to anyone as soon as "phonorecords of a nondramatic musical work have been distributed to the public in the United States under the authority of the copyright owner."

Definition of "distributed." For the purpose of computing royalties, a phonorecord is considered "voluntarily distributed" if the compulsory licensee has voluntarily and permanently parted with possession of the phonorecord. The compulsory license is permissible once this has been done to the public.

Under What Conditions May a Compulsory License be Obtained? It may be obtained only if the primary purpose in making the phonorecords is to distribute them to the public for private use. It is not available for phonorecords intended for use in background music systems, jukeboxes, broadcasting, or any other public use.

May a New Arrangement of the Copyrighted Musical Work Be Made For The Recording? Yes. The compulsory license includes the privilege of making a musical arrangement of the work "to the extent necessary to conform it to the style or manner of interpretation of the performance involved." However, section 115 also provides that the arrangement "shall not change the basic melody or fundamental character of the work, and shall not be subject to protection as a derivative work...except with the express consent of the copyright owner."

How Does a Person Obtain a Compulsory License? The first step is to identify the copyright owner of the nondramatic musical work to be recorded. This may be done either by personally searching the records of the Copyright Office or by requesting that the Copyright Office conduct the search.

If the Name and Address of the Copyright Owner Are Found: Before or within 30 days after making, and before distributing any phonorecords of the work, serve a Notice of Intention to Obtain a Compulsory License on the copyright owner by certified or registered mail for each title for which a compulsory license is needed. A copy of this Notice of Intention does not have to be filed in the Copyright Office. Therafter, make royalty payments, accompanied by a Monthly Statement of Account, to the copyright owner on or before the 20th day of each month for every phonorecord made and distributed in accordance with the license, and file with the copyright owner a detailed Annual Statement of Account, certified by a certified public accountant.

If the Name and Address of the Copyright Owner Are Not Found: File a Notice of Intention to Obtain a Compulsory License in the Library of Congress, Copyright Office for each title for which a compulsory license is needed, submit the statutory fee with each Notice of Intention. Upon receipt of such a Notice, the Licensing Division will provide the sender with a written acknowledgment of receipt and filing. Upon request and payment of an additional fee for each Notice of Intention, the Licensing Division will provide a Certificate of Filing. If the copyright owner is later known, then the copyright owner, rather than the Copyright Office, should receive the payments.

Library of Congress • Copyright Office • Licensing Division • 101 Independence Ave., S.E. • Washington, D.C. 20557-6400 • http://www.loc.gov/copyright

Music Licensing Summary Table

The table below provides a rough introduction to the licensing sources and needs:

Usage	Licenses/Rights Needed	License Source
Live Theatrical Musicals and Shows	Grand Performing Rights	Copyright Owner of Composition*
Clubs and Revues – the music may be live or played from radios, TVs or records	Small Performing Rights	Performing Rights Society (PRO)**
Lyric Printing or Sheet Music – whether printed separately or as insert to Album/CD	Reproduction & Distribution Rights under § 106	Copyright Owner (Publisher)
New Recordings of Songs for Albums/CDs	Mechanical License (Reproduction & Distribution Rights under § 106) Compulsory License § 115	Copyright Owner – First Publication Compulsory License § 115 – Subsequent Licensees through Harry Fox Agency, Inc. or Copyright Office
Copying Existing Recordings of Songs for Albums/CDs	Compulsory License § 115 Mechanical License	Harry Fox Agency, Inc. (HFA) or Copyright Office Copyright Owner of Phonorecord. HFA serves as non-exclusive agent.
Music for Film Production (including TV, Video, audiovisual, or industrial production)	Mechanical and Synchronization	Copyright Owner of Composition; Copyright Owner of Phonorecord. HFA serves as non-exclusive agent.
Music for Recording Commercial	Mechanical and Synchronization	Copyright Owner of Composition; Copyright Owner of Phonorecord HFA serves as non-exclusive agent.
Major Television Network Broadcasting (ABC, CBS, NBC, PBS)	Blanket License	PRO
Minor Television Network Broadcasting (Fox, UPN, WB)	Per Program License (or none if license then purchased by local station)	PRO
Local TV or Radio Station Broadcasting	Blanket License or Per-Program License	PRO

Internet Broadcasting or Webcasting	Blanket License or Per-Program License Statutory License for Digital Broadcast	PRO Recording Industry Association of America, digital collective
MP3 Distribution	Mechanical and Synchronization	Copyright Owner of Composition; Copyright Owner of Phonorecord. For most music, HFA has the rights because the National Music Publishers' Association, Inc. (NMPA) and the Recording Industry Association of America (RIAA) jointly agreed to a licensing scheme.
Other Performances/Broadcast – Music-on-Hold, Hotels, Businesses, Muzak®	Small Performance	PRO
Juke Boxes	Juke Box Performance License	Jukebox License Office (a joint venture of ASCAP, BMI and SESAC).

* The copyright initially vests in the author of the work, who may be one or more individuals composers and lyricists, or as a joint work between two or more authors. Often, the exclusive copyrights are assigned to the publisher which administers the copyrights in the songs.

**Any one of a number of "performing rights societies." The three largest are ASCAP, BMI, and SESAC.

Newton N. Minow, Television and the Public Interest[72]

[FCC Chairman's introductory speech delivered to members of the National Association of Broadcasters and other television professionals, May 9, 1961, Washington, D.C.]

Thank you for this opportunity to meet with you today. This is my first public address since I took over my new job. ... It may also come as a surprise to some of you, but I want you to know that you have my admiration and respect. Yours is a most honorable profession. Anyone who is in the broadcasting business has a tough row to hoe. You earn your bread by using public property. When you work in broadcasting you volunteer for public service, public pressure, and public regulation. You must compete with other attractions and other investments, and the only way you can do it is to prove to us every three years that you should have been in business in the first place.

I can think of easier ways to make a living.

But I cannot think of more satisfying ways.

I admire your courage — but that doesn't mean I would make life any easier for you. Your license lets you use the public's airwaves as trustees for 180 million Americans. The public is your beneficiary. If you want to stay on as trustees, you must deliver a decent return to the public — not only to your stockholders. So, as a representative of the public, your health and your product are among my chief concerns.

As to your health: let's talk only of television today. 1960 gross broadcast revenues of the television industry were over $1,268,000,000; profit before taxes was $243,900,000, an average return on revenue of 19.2 per cent. Compared with 1959, gross broadcast revenues were $1,163,900,000, and profit before taxes was $222,300,000, an average return on revenue of 19.1 per cent. So, the percentage increase of total revenues from 1959 to 1960 was 9 per cent, and the percentage increase of profit was 9.7 per cent. This, despite a recession. For your investors, the price has indeed been right.

I have confidence in your health. But not in your product. It is with this and much more in mind that I come before you today.

One editorialist in the trade press wrote that "the FCC of the New Frontier is going to be one of the toughest FCC's in the history of broadcast regulation." If he meant that we intend to enforce the law in the public interest, let me make it perfectly clear that he is right — we do. If he meant that we intend to muzzle or censor broadcasting, he is dead wrong. It would not surprise me if some of you had expected me to come here today and say in effect, "Clean up your own house or the government will do it for you." Well, in a limited sense, you would be right — I've just said it.

But I want to say to you earnestly that it is not in that spirit that I come before you today, nor is it in that spirit that I intend to serve the FCC. I am in Washington to help broadcasting, not to harm it; to strengthen it, not weaken it; to reward it, not punish it; to encourage it, not threaten it;

---

[72] Newton N. Minow, *Speech Before the National Association of Broadcasters* (May 9, 1961), reprinted in *The Vast Wasteland Revisited*, 55 Fed. Comm. L.J. 3 (2003) (symposium issue), available at http://www.law.indiana.edu/fclj/pubs/v55/no3/Speech.pdf.

to stimulate it, not censor it. Above all, I am here to uphold and protect the public interest.

What do we mean by "the public interest?"

Some say the public interest is merely what interests the public. I disagree. So does your distinguished president, Governor Collins. In a recent speech he said,

> *Broadcasting to serve the public interest, must have a soul and a conscience, a burning desire to excel, as well as to sell; the urge to build the character, citizenship and intellectual stature of people, as well as to expand the gross national product. ...By no means do I imply that broadcasters disregard the public interest. ...But a much better job can be done, and should be done.*

I could not agree more.

And I would add that in today's world, with chaos in Laos and the Congo aflame, with Communist tyranny on our Caribbean doorstep and relentless pressure on our Atlantic alliance, with social and economic problems at home of the gravest nature, yes, and with technological knowledge that makes it possible, as our President has said, not only to destroy our world but to destroy poverty around the world — in a time of peril and opportunity, the old complacent, unbalanced fare of action-adventure and situation comedies is simply not good enough.

Your industry possesses the most powerful voice in America. It has an inescapable duty to make that voice ring with intelligence and with leadership. In a few years, this exciting industry has grown from a novelty to an instrument of overwhelming impact on the American people. It should be making ready for the kind of leadership that newspapers and magazines assumed years ago, to make our people aware of their world.

Ours has been called the jet age, the atomic age, the space age. It is also, I submit, the television age. And just as history will decide whether the leaders of today's world employed the atom to destroy the world or rebuild it for mankind's benefit, so will history decide whether today's broadcasters employed their powerful voice to enrich the people or debase them.

If I seem today to address myself chiefly to the problems of television, I don't want any of you radio broadcasters to think we've gone to sleep at your switch — we haven't. We still listen. But in recent years most of the controversies and cross-currents in broadcast programming have swirled around television. And so my subject today is the television industry and the public interest.

Like everybody, I wear more than one hat. I am the chairman of the FCC. I am also a television viewer and the husband and father of other television viewers. I have seen a great many television programs that seemed to me eminently worthwhile and I am not talking about the much bemoaned good old days of "Playhouse 90" and "Studio One."

I am talking about this past season. Some were wonderfully entertaining, such as "The Fabulous Fifties," "The Fred Astaire Show," and "The Bing Crosby Special"; some were dramatic and moving, such as Conrad's "Victory" and "Twilight Zone"; some were marvelously informative, such as "The Nation's Future," "CBS Reports," and "The Valiant Years." I could list many more — programs that I am sure everyone here felt enriched his own life and that of his family.

When television is good, nothing — not the theater, not the magazines or newspapers — nothing is better.

But when television is bad, nothing is worse. I invite you to sit down in front of your television set when your station goes on the air and stay there without a book, magazine, newspaper, profit and loss sheet or rating book to distract you — and keep your eyes glued to that set until the station signs off. I can assure you that you will observe a vast wasteland.

You will see a procession of game shows, violence, audience participation shows, formula comedies about totally unbelievable families, blood and thunder, mayhem, violence, sadism, murder, western bad men, western good men, private eyes, gangsters, more violence, and cartoons. And, endlessly, commercials — many screaming, cajoling, and offending. And most of all, boredom. True, you will see a few things you will enjoy. But they will be very, very few. And if you think I exaggerate, try it.

Is there one person in this room who claims that broadcasting can't do better?

Well, a glance at next season's proposed programming can give us little heart. Of 73 and 1/2 hours of prime evening time, the networks have tentatively scheduled 59 hours to categories of action-adventure, situation comedy, variety, quiz, and movies.

Is there one network president in this room who claims he can't do better?

Well, is there at least one network president who believes that the other networks can't do better?

Gentlemen, your trust accounting with your beneficiaries is overdue.

Never have so few owed so much to so many.

Why is so much of television so bad? I have heard many answers: demands of your advertisers; competition for ever higher ratings; the need always to attract a mass audience; the high cost of television programs; the insatiable appetite for programming material — these are some of them. Unquestionably, these are tough problems not susceptible to easy answers.

But I am not convinced that you have tried hard enough to solve them.

I do not accept the idea that the present over-all programming is aimed accurately at the public taste. The ratings tell us only that some people have their television sets turned on and of that number, so many are tuned to one channel and so many to another. They don't tell us what the public might watch if they were offered half-a-dozen additional choices. A rating, at best, is an indication of how many people saw what you gave them. Unfortunately, it does not reveal the depth of the penetration, or the intensity of reaction, and it never reveals what the acceptance would have been if what you gave them had been better — if all the forces of art and creativity and daring and imagination had been unleashed. I believe in the people's good sense and good taste, and I am not convinced that the people's taste is as low as some of you assume.

My concern with the rating services is not with their accuracy. Perhaps they are accurate. I really don't know. What, then, is wrong with the ratings? It's not been their accuracy — it's been their use.

Certainly, I hope you will agree that ratings should have little influence where children are concerned. The best estimates indicate that during the hours of 5 to 6 P.M. sixty per cent of your audience is composed of children under twelve. And most young children today, believe it or not, spend as much time watching television as they do in the schoolroom. I repeat — let that sink in — most young children today spend as much time watching television as they do in the schoolroom. It used to be said that there were three great influences on a child: home, school, and church. Today, there is a fourth great influence, and you ladies and gentlemen control it.

If parents, teachers, and ministers conducted their responsibilities by following the ratings, children would have a steady diet of ice cream, school holidays, and no Sunday school. What about your responsibilities? Is there no room on television to teach, to inform, to uplift, to stretch, to enlarge the capacities of our children? Is there no room for programs deepening their understanding of children in other lands? Is there no room for a children's news show explaining something about the world to them at their level of understanding? Is there no room for reading the great literature of the past, teaching them the great traditions of freedom? There are some fine children's shows, but they are drowned out in the massive doses of cartoons, violence, and more violence. Must these be your trademarks? Search your consciences and see if you cannot offer more to your young beneficiaries whose future you guide so many hours each and every day.

What about adult programming and ratings? You know, newspaper publishers take popularity ratings too. The answers are pretty clear: it is almost always the comics, followed by the advice to the lovelorn columns. But, ladies and gentlemen, the news is still on the front page of all newspapers; the editorials are not replaced by more comics; the newspapers have not become one long collection of advice to the lovelorn. Yet newspapers do not need a license from the government to be in business — they do not use public property. But in television, where your responsibilities as public trustees are so plain, the moment that the ratings indicate that westerns are popular there are new imitations of westerns on the air faster than the old coaxial cable could take us from Hollywood to New York. Broadcasting cannot continue to live by the numbers. Ratings ought to be the slave of the broadcaster, not his master. And you and I both know that the rating services themselves would agree.

Let me make clear that what I am talking about is balance. I believe that the public interest is made up of many interests. There are many people in this great country and you must serve all of us. You will get no argument from me if you say that, given a choice between a western and a symphony, more people will watch the western. I like westerns and private eyes too, but a steady diet for the whole country is obviously not in the public interest. We all know that people would more often prefer to be entertained than stimulated or informed. But your obligations are not satisfied if you look only to popularity as a test of what to broadcast. You are not only in show business; you are free to communicate ideas as well as relaxation. You must provide a wider range of choices, more diversity, more alternatives. It is not enough to cater to the nation's whims; you must also serve the nation's needs.

And I would add this: that if some of you persist in a relentless search for the highest rating and the lowest common denominator, you may very well lose your audience. Because, to paraphrase a great American who was recently my law partner, the people are wise, wiser than some of the broadcasters — and politicians — think.

As you may have gathered, I would like to see television improved. But how is this to be brought about? By voluntary action by the broadcasters themselves? By direct government intervention? Or how?

Let me address myself now to my role not as a viewer but as chairman of the FCC. I could not if I would, chart for you this afternoon in detail all of the actions I contemplate. Instead, I want to make clear some of the fundamental principles which guide me.

First: the people own the air. They own it as much in prime evening time as they do at six o'clock Sunday morning. For every hour that the people give you — you owe them something. I intend to see that your debt is paid with service.

Second: I think it would be foolish and wasteful for us to continue any worn-out wrangle over the problems of payola, rigged quiz shows, and other mistakes of the past. There are laws on the books which we will enforce. But there is no chip on my shoulder. We live together in perilous, uncertain times; we face together staggering problems; and we must not waste much time now by rehashing the clichés of past controversy.

To quarrel over the past is to lose the future.

Third: I believe in the free enterprise system. I want to see broadcasting improved, and I want you to do the job. I am proud to champion your cause. It is not rare for American businessmen to serve a public trust. Yours is a special trust because it is imposed by law.

Fourth: I will do all I can to help educational television. There are still not enough educational stations, and major centers of the country still lack usable educational channels. If there were a limited number of printing presses in this country, you may be sure that a fair proportion of them would be put to educational use. Educational television has an enormous contribution to make to the future, and I intend to give it a hand along the way. If there is not a nation-wide educational television system in this country, it will not be the fault of the FCC.

Fifth: I am unalterably opposed to governmental censorship. There will be no suppression of programming which does not meet with bureaucratic tastes. Censorship strikes at the tap root of our free society.

Sixth: I did not come to Washington to idly observe the squandering of the public's airwaves. The squandering of our airwaves is no less important than the lavish waste of any precious natural resource. I intend to take the job of chairman of the FCC very seriously. I believe in the gravity of my own particular sector of the New Frontier. There will be times perhaps when you will consider that I take myself or my job *too* seriously. Frankly, I don't care if you do. For I am convinced that either one takes this job seriously — or one can be seriously taken.

Now, how will these principles be applied? Clearly, at the heart of the FCC's authority lies its power to license, to renew or fail to renew, or to revoke a license. As you know, when your license comes up for renewal, your performance is compared with your promises. I understand that many people feel that in the past licenses were often renewed *pro forma*. I say to you now: renewal will not be *pro forma* in the future. There is nothing permanent or sacred about a broadcast license.

But simply matching promises and performance is not enough. I intend to do more. I intend to find out whether the people care. I intend to find out whether the community which each broadcaster serves believes he has been serving the public interest. When a renewal is set down for hearing, I intend — wherever possible — to hold a well-advertised public hearing, right in the community you have promised to serve. I want the people who own the air and the homes that television enters to tell you and the FCC what's been going on. I want the people — if they are truly interested in the service you give them — to make notes, document cases, tell us the facts. For those few of you who really believe that the public interest is merely what interests the public, hope that these hearings will arouse no little interest.

The FCC has a fine reserve of monitors — almost 180 million Americans gathered around 56 million sets. If you want those monitors to be your friends at court, it's up to you.

Some of you may say, "Yes, but I still do not know where the line is between a grant of a renewal and the hearing you just spoke of." My answer is: Why should you want to know how close you can come to the edge of the cliff? What the Commission asks of you is to make a conscientious, good-faith effort to serve the public interest. Everyone of you serves a community in which the people would benefit by educational, religious, instructive or other public service programming. Every one of you serves an area which has local needs — as to local elections, controversial issues, local news, local talent. Make a serious, genuine effort to put on that programming. When you do, you will not be playing brinkmanship with the public interest.

What I've been saying applies to broadcast stations. Now a station break for the networks:

You know your importance in this great industry. Today, more than one half of all hours of television station programming comes from the networks; in prime time, this rises to more than three quarters of the available hours.

You know that the FCC has been studying network operations for some time. I intend to press this to a speedy conclusion with useful results. I can tell you right now, however, that I am deeply concerned with concentration of power in the hands of the networks. As a result, too many local stations have foregone any efforts at local programming, with little use of live talent and local service. Too many local stations operate with one hand on the network switch and the other on a projector loaded with old movies. We want the individual stations to be free to meet their legal responsibilities to serve their communities.

...

But there is more to the problem than network influences on stations or advertiser influences on networks. I know the problems networks face in trying to clear some of their best programs — the informational programs that exemplify public service. They are your finest hours — whether sustaining or commercial, whether regularly scheduled or special — these are the signs that broadcasting knows the way to leadership. They make the public's trust in you a wise choice.

They should be seen. As you know, we are readying for use new forms by which broadcast stations will report their programming to the Commission. You probably also know that special attention will be paid in these reports to public service programming. I believe that stations taking network service should also be required to report the extent of the local clearance of network public service programming, and when they fail to clear them, they should explain why. If it is to put on some outstanding local program, this is one reason. But, if it is simply to carry some old movies, that is an entirely different matter. The Commission should consider such clearance reports carefully when making up its mind about the licensee's over-all programming.

We intend to move — and as you know, indeed the FCC was rapidly moving in other new areas before the new Administration arrived in Washington. And I want to pay my public respects to my very able predecessor, Fred Ford, and my colleagues on the Commission who have welcomed me to the FCC with warmth and cooperation.

We have approved an experiment with pay TV, and in New York we are testing the potential of UHF broadcasting. Either or both of these may revolutionize television. Only a foolish prophet would venture to guess the direction they will take, and their effect. But we intend that they shall be explored fully - for they are part of broadcasting's New Frontier. The questions surrounding pay TV are largely economic. The questions surrounding UHF are largely technological. We are going to give the infant pay TV a chance to prove whether it can offer a useful service; we are going to protect it from those who would strangle it in its crib.

As for UHF, I'm sure you know about our test in the canyons of New York City. We will take every possible positive step to break through the allocations barrier into UHF. We will put this sleeping giant to use and in the years ahead we may have twice as many channels operating in cities where now there are only two or three. We may have a half dozen networks instead of three.

I have told you that I believe in the free enterprise system. I believe that most of television's problems stem from lack of competition. This is the importance of UHF to me: with more channels on the air, we will be able to provide every community with enough stations to offer service to all parts of the public. Programs with a mass market appeal required by mass product advertisers certainly will still be available. But other stations will recognize the need to appeal to more limited markets and to special tastes. In this way, we can all have a much wider range of programs.

Television should thrive on this competition - and the country should benefit from alternative sources of service to the public. And — Governor Collins — I hope the NAB will benefit from many new members.

Another and perhaps the most important frontier: television will rapidly join the parade into space. International television will be with us soon. No one knows how long it will be until a broadcast from a studio in New York will be viewed in India as well as in Indiana, will be seen in the Congo as it is seen in Chicago. But as surely as we are meeting here today, that day will come - and once again our world will shrink.

What will the people of other countries think of us when they see our western badmen and good men punching each other in the jaw in between the shooting? What will the Latin American or African child learn of America from our great communications industry? We cannot permit television in its present form to be our voice overseas.

There is your challenge to leadership. You must reexamine some fundamentals of your industry. You must open your minds and open your hearts to the limitless horizons of tomorrow.

I can suggest some words that should serve to guide you:

> *Television and all who participate in it are jointly accountable to the American public for respect for the special needs of children, for community responsibility, for the advancement of education and culture, for the acceptability of the program materials chosen, for decency and decorum in production, and for*

propriety in advertising. This responsibility cannot be discharged by any given group of programs, but can be discharged only through the highest standards of respect for the American home, applied to every moment of every program presented by television.

Program materials should enlarge the horizons of the viewer, provide him with wholesome entertainment, afford helpful stimulation, and remind him of the responsibilities which the citizen has towards his society.

These words are not mine. They are yours. They are taken literally from your own Television Code. They reflect the leadership and aspirations of your own great industry. I urge you to respect them as I do. And I urge you to respect the intelligent and farsighted leadership of Governor LeRoy Collins, and to make this meeting a creative act. I urge you at this meeting and, after you leave, back home, at your stations and your networks, to strive ceaselessly to improve your product and to better serve your viewers, the American people.

I hope that we at the FCC will not allow ourselves to become so bogged down in the mountain of papers, hearings, memoranda, orders, and the daily routine that we close our eyes to the wider view of the public interest. And I hope that you broadcasters will not permit yourselves to become so absorbed in the chase for ratings, sales, and profits that you lose this wider view. Now more than ever before in broadcasting's history the times demand the best of all of us.

We need imagination in programming, not sterility; creativity, not imitation; experimentation, not conformity; excellence, not mediocrity. Television is filled with creative, imaginative people. You must strive to set them free.

Television in its young life has had many hours of greatness — its "Victory at Sea," its Army-McCarthy hearings, its "Peter Pan," its "Kraft Theaters," its "See It Now," its "Project 20," the World Series, its political conventions and campaigns, the Great Debates — and it has had its endless hours of mediocrity and its moments of public disgrace. There are estimates that today the average viewer spends about 200 minutes daily with television, while the average reader spends 38 minutes with magazines and 40 minutes with newspapers. Television has grown faster than a teenager, and now it is time to grow up.

What you gentlemen broadcast through the people's air affects the people's taste, their knowledge, their opinions, their understanding of themselves and of their world. And their future. The power of instantaneous sight and sound is without precedent in mankind's history. This is an awesome power. It has limitless capabilities for good — and for evil. And it carries with it awesome responsibilities, responsibilities which you and I cannot escape.

In his stirring inaugural address our President said, "And so, my fellow Americans: ask not what your country can do for you; ask what you can do for your country."

Ladies and Gentlemen: Ask not what broadcasting can do for you. Ask what you can do for broadcasting. I urge you to put the people's airwaves to the service of the people and the cause of freedom. You must help prepare a generation for great decisions. You must help a great nation fulfill its future.

Do this, and I pledge you our help.